after all these years

The Hoppers

The Authorized Biography of America's Favorite Family Of Gospel Music

By F. Keith Davis

Foreword By Dr. John Hagee
Introduction By Dr. Charles F. Stanley

CONTENTS

Author Dedication

This book is dedicated to Dianne (Davis) Hampp, my beloved sister and lifelong friend. She moved her residency from Wapakoneta, Ohio, to the portals of Glory in May 2000. She was an avid fan of the Hoppers. Her favorite song, "Shoutin' Time," was played at her funeral.

Hoppers' Dedication

On March 19, 2005, at the time this written account was being prepared, Paul Hopper, Claude's older brother and one of the original members of the Hopper Brothers and Connie, passed away at 3:00 a.m. from a massive stroke. This book is dedicated to his memory.

Likewise, on July 22, 2005, Charles Shelton passed away. Charles was the oldest child in the Shelton family, and was Connie Hopper's brother. This volume is also dedicated to his memory.

Both very special men were loved by family and friends and will be sorely missed, until that great reunion day.

Woodland Gospel
PUBLISHING HOUSE
A Division Of Woodland Press, LLC

ISBN 978-0-9829937-6-7
Published In Beautiful West Virginia by
WOODLAND PRESS, LLC
In collaboration with
THE HOPPER BROTHERS AND CONNIE PUBLISHING
www.thehoppers.com
SAN: 2 5 4 – 9 9 9 9

Foreword

It has been my great privilege to be personally associated with one of America's foremost Southern Gospel groups, known to America and the world as the Hoppers.

The many awards, accolades and achievements of this great family have been born from a passionate commitment to Jesus Christ and the cause of the Gospel presented in song to the nations of the world.

As a minister of the Gospel for 48 years I have had the opportunity to meet many pastors, evangelists and Gospel singing groups. None have a greater commitment to Christ than the Hoppers. Each time they minister to our congregation of 18,000 members the building is filled with a special anointing that comes from a special commitment.

I know you will enjoy reading the story of this musical legacy that began in 1957 when Claude Hopper, who just graduated from high school, and his brothers formed a group called the Hopper Brothers.

Later, Connie Shelton joined the group and it became the Hopper Brothers and Connie. Then Connie and Claude married and the group has continued to this day, crisscrossing America many times over throughout its nearly half century of ministry in song.

Today, they are known around the world as the Hoppers—whose current lineup includes Claude, his wife Connie, sons Mike and Dean, and Dean's wife, Kim Greene Hopper—and they have never sounded better.

Be blessed by this special story of special people with a special anointing to bless the nations with the joyful sound of Southern Gospel music.

Dr. John Hagee
Founder and Senior Pastor
Cornerstone Church in San Antonio, Texas

Introduction

To be called to serve the Lord is the highest calling you can receive. This book tells one family's story of total dedication to telling others of Christ's love through music and song.

In 1957 five Hopper brothers began traveling and singing together. Today Claude and Connie Hopper along with two sons and daughter-in-law travel the United States and many foreign countries appearing night after night to the glory of God.

I believe you will be spiritually inspired as you read the story of their nearly 50 years of faithful service to God.

— Dr. Charles F. Stanley
Pastor of First Baptist Church, Atlanta, Georgia

Preface

You have picked up a book that is first and foremost a story about family and faith. I see the Hopper family as a close-knit unit who continue to sing out of their love for the Savior, each other and the Christian community. This well-known Gospel group is about to celebrate a half-century of ministry at the time of this writing, and they have never sounded better!

When you strip away the Gospel stage, bright lights, video screens and all the so-called glamourous details, the Hoppers are just real people— a wonderful and complex Christian family—who are concerned with living out their faith with poise and integrity. Perhaps you've seen the Hoppers in concert or enjoyed them on the popular Gaither Homecoming videos and television shows. But when you read this biography, you'll discover that America's Favorite Family of Gospel Music had meager beginnings.

Even today, after all these years on the road, the Hoppers carry on with a sense of gratitude and appreciation for this Southern heritage. Despite success in the worldly sense, I will personally vouch for the fact that not one of them acts the least bit haughty. They've not forgotten their rural raising and the eternal purposes behind their music and stage performance.

North Carolina remains home, and Claude and Connie still reside on the same acreage that has been in the Hopper family since the post-Civil War era.

Through the pages of this book, you'll explore the rich family history and development of a popular group, originally known as the Hopper Brothers—later, the Hopper Brothers and Connie—then, just the Hoppers. Discover an American family who have committed their lives to a living Christ and His ministry. Much of their day-to-day existence revolves around living and traveling on a tour bus. But amazingly, the Hoppers are as enthusiastic about their mission today as they were nearly fifty years ago.

It's rather obvious to me when reviewing their schedule, and level of commitment, that these folks haven't taken the Lord's call and His gift of grace for granted. Their faith is mixed with equal portions of hard work, humility and sacrifice.

The prayerful goal of this family [and this author] is that the Heavenly Father will somehow use this volume, and the stories of their lives, to encourage and inspire other families in their own walk of faith.

I hope this project will motivate readers to appreciate his or her own Christian heritage and family. Most importantly, may this book ultimately glorify Christ, for He alone is worthy of all our praise and honor.

— **F. Keith Davis**, *Author*

Chapter 1
The Land Of Rockingham

The land produced vegetation: plants bearing seed according to their kinds and trees bearing fruit with seed in it according to their kinds. And God saw that it was good.

— Genesis 1:12

Rockingham County has been described as a charming place to start a home, where an abundance of green foliage and hearty trees grow freely. Long, thin, leaf-covered branches and gnarled bare limbs reach outward and create charming natural tunnels of green shadowed passageways through which to travel. Native wildflowers, scrub rosebushes, rhubarb patches and large vegetable gardens accentuate property boundaries with little need of fencing. The air is still clean, as God intended it. It's also a land where thick morning fog often carpets the horizon line.

By the end of a day's work, when shadows grow long, a sleepy sunset may cast soft whispers of gold and scarlet on fertile fields of tobacco. Certainly tobacco has long been the bread-and-butter crop for this area and the mainstay of the local economy for as long as homefolks can remember.

It is this picturesque section of North Carolina that covers approximately 566 square miles and is located in the north-central region of the state.

For the most part, the county populace exhibits conservative values and old-fashioned integrity. It's also a special place where the emphasis of the majority seems to be on working hard, raising successful families, remaining faithful stewards of the land, and living out one's faith with fervor and conviction. Manners are encouraged; moral principles are taught, and hospitality is commonplace.

Most of the Hopper family and their ancestors have lived on this portion of the state for the last 150 years, near the small town of

Madison. Centrally located, Madison is a hub of activity and is cradled in a slight valley within thirty miles of Greensboro and Winston-Salem. It is approximately forty minutes across the state line from Danville, Virginia.

Encircled and protected by the rolling Appalachian Mountain range, the area is blessed with a moderate climate. It's part of the rapidly growing Northern Piedmont District. Even so, according to county statistics, there are over seven hundred working farms within the county boundaries at this time.

This region, which boasts a culture rich in agriculture and close-knit community life, is where this story begins.

Chapter 2
William Hopper
Joins Confederacy

What a cruel thing is war: to separate and destroy families and friends, and mar the purest joys and happiness God has granted us in this world; to fill our hearts with hatred instead of love for our neighbors, and to devastate the fair face of this beautiful world.

— General Robert E. Lee

William Archer Hopper

The patriarch of the Hopper family, William Archer Hopper, was born on February 9th, 1843. His parents were William Orren and Henrietta Watkins Hopper. His mother, whom he affectionately called Mammy, died when he was three years old. His father was a roving tobacco trader and was ill-equipped, or just unwilling, to concern himself with William Archer. Instead, because he yearned to travel and had a self-seeking streak, Orren was most concerned with living his own life void of hindrances like children and home responsibilities.

After the loss of his mother, it was William Archer's grandmother, Jane Hooper Watkins, and aunt, Nancy Webster, who chiefly raised him. Nancy, a wealthy and kindly widow with business sense, dwelled on a sprawling plantation in Rockingham County. She owned several slaves who took care of even the most menial of field and home responsibilities. William Archer grew strong and confident in such a privileged environment, and gravitated toward outdoor activities where he could seek out adventures and challenges.

13

By the 1860s, North Carolina was not regarded as a wealthy state, but for the duration of the Civil War it was the state that supplied more men and materials to the Confederate cause than any other.

As William Archer entered young adulthood, he signed on as a Confederate soldier in 1862, at Caswell County, in Reinhart's 41st Regiment of North Carolina troops. He later, in February 1863, became a member of a Confederate outfit called Morgan's Raiders.

Yankee soldiers had nicknames for members of the Confederate Army, including "butternuts" or "greybacks," due to the color of their drab uniforms. More popular names were "Johnny," "Johnny Reb," or "Rebels," since they were considered, by the North, to be in utter rebellion, or insurrection.

Men who joined the Confederate cause from North Carolina were generally known for their exceptional courage and tenacity under fire and for their "natural aptitude for marksmanship."

William Archer was no different from his contemporaries in that he knew how to shoot a muzzle-loader at a very early age. Black-powder muskets, pistols and bowie knives were still common tools for farmers, plantation workers and hunters in rural North Carolina and Virginia during the mid-19th century.

He was taught to be an experienced marksman, trapper and outdoorsman. It was his grandmother and aunt's determination that he learn certain skills and responsibilities to equip him for manhood and self-sufficiency. He readily picked up those abilities by going hunting with plantation workers, cousins and neighbors. Rabbit, opossum, groundhog, squirrel, whitetail deer, wild turkey, pheasant and grouse were typical game William Archer and his companions would bring to the dinner table.

In this time period, farming and plantation life was especially grueling, devoid of steam or gasoline powered tractors or any form of automated farm machinery that was to later spring up as a result of the industrial revolution. Farming, in all its forms, was an up-hill existence that demanded a great deal of hard labor and perseverance by everyone involved. Before his military service, William Archer likely labored alongside slaves in the fields. He was responsible for a variety of strenuous chores. Because of his tendency to get involved in all aspects of farm life, he formed remarkable physical stamina and endurance.

It's also known that, as he entered his teen years, Aunt Nancy decided he should study law. So, he began his studies and did quite well, and may have been an apprentice in a law office for a while.

As a teen, he was an intelligent young man of average height and fair complexion with a muscular build and heavily calloused hands. An expert caretaker of horses and mules on the estate, he became knowledgeable of the inner workings of a tack or blacksmith shop. As an experienced horseman and wing-shot, he later brought a number of these valuable attributes to the battlefield. Like his southern comrades, he was a passionate soldier and was daring in the midst of battle.

William Archer saw action and lost several friends as a member of Morgan's Raiders, a covert gorilla unit of seasoned fighters who were known for their expertise in successfully pulling off raids, burning bridges and performing ambushes against the North. It's known that he participated in important gorilla raids against the South in Tennessee and Georgia.

There is a family story that portrays his courage and tenacity: During one skirmish, in the midst of a battle charge, William Archer's horse was shot out from beneath him. With a loud crack of a Union rifle, the horse was hit and both horse and rider violently tumbled. The dying horse collapsed on William Archer's leg, pinning him to the ground. At that point, although he was in excruciating pain, he was still surrounded by the advancing enemy. As difficult as it was to remain silent, he pretended to be dead so the enemy wouldn't kill him with a bayonet or pistol shot. Lying still certainly saved his life; however, he suffered severe leg damage and the injury bothered him for the remainder of his life.

After successful battles and raids during his early tour of duty, William Archer's life was about to change drastically. In April 1863, he and several members of his unit were relaxing along a remote creek bank. The battle weary soldiers were playing cards when a flash of blue appeared—a swarm of Union soldiers. With rifles cocked and bayonets held steady, the Yanks rushed them from the adjacent woods and encircled them. They demanded their weapons. One Union officer barked that the captives had a choice: "Carry ammunition behind the lines and fight for the glorious North, or be shot on the spot! *Choose your fate, boys!"*

Reluctantly, the men chose to save their own lives that day and followed their captors back to Union camp. For the duration of the war, William Archer and his comrades labored—carrying ammunition, cooking meals, and eventually even fighting—for the 11th Michigan Cavalry.

During that period, William Archer's fears focused more on how Confederate soldiers might react if they identified him, while fighting alongside Yanks, during certain battles. His Southern brothers would never understand his change of allegiance. He knew he'd be hung as a traitor before he could explain himself. Therefore, he temporarily changed his name to "Cuff Watson" for his own protection.

Although he was a prisoner of sorts of the United States Army, as time went on it's believed William Archer, alias Cuff Watson, became fully sympathetic to the Union cause. Although some Hopper family members still believe he was coerced into fighting for the North, others suspect he was eventually willing, even volunteering to fight in certain key battles. William Archer may have even seen more action with the Michigan Cavalry than as a Greyback.

As the war raged on, the fighting proved to be disastrous for the South, and especially North Carolina. History documents that the state of North Carolina suffered the most casualties during the Civil War. The economy was in shambles and the Confederate Army was literally starving to death, for food and supplies were scarce, because supply-lines had been severely compromised by the North.

By war's end, William Archer (still known as Cuff) attempted to make Michigan his new home. Yet, less than a year after General Robert E. Lee surrendered at the Wilmer and Virginia McLean home in the village of Appomattox Court House, he became homesick and chose to return home to Rockingham County. With the move, he also took back his birth name.

> We have shared the incommunicable experience of war. We felt, we still feel, the passion of life to its top. In our

youths, our hearts were touched by fire.

—*Oliver Wendell Holmes*

The first years after the war were difficult for William Archer, as it was for many veterans. He was profoundly affected by the war and his involvement on both sides of the conflict. There's little doubt he regretted some of his decisions during wartime.

Once he returned to North Carolina soil, he had a deep resolve to find tranquility and resume some semblance of a normal life. He moved into a simple frame home in the community of Madison and eventually courted and married a local girl, Elizabeth Thompson Joyce, in 1868.

A year later, Elizabeth and William Archer purchased a tobacco farm outside of Madison, paying for the farm through future crop earnings. They also started their family. William Archer eventually fathered a dozen children, raising ten of them to adulthood (two died as children).

The following years were both challenging and fulfilling as the Hoppers set out to carve a meager existence from the soil, during the difficult time of Southern Reconstruction. They worked hard and long on the farm.

Near the turn of the century, William Archer applied for and, through his perseverance and law background, eventually received two separate monthly pensions: one, a small annuity for service to the Confederacy; the other, a sum of twenty-five dollars a month from the United States of America, for contributions to the Union Army.

In his old age, William Archer sported a long, flowing white beard. He still had a distinctive limp from his long ago battle injury. He retired from heavy farm labor and lived off the pensions. He retained his love for adventure and intrigue and expressed this part of his character through colorful storytelling. He took great pleasure in sharing war remembrances with his grandchildren, often physically acting out certain aspects of the stories.

Even well into his nineties, he was proud and quite vocal about his time as a soldier for the Confederate States of America, but also admitted his unlikely involvements as a Yankee Bluecoat.

Today, it is the direct descendants of William Archer and Henrietta Hopper who still occupy most of these same tracts of farmland in Rockingham County, through inheritance. And it is they, the Hoppers, who still carry on the proud Southern heritage and bloodline of this family.

Chapter 3
James Archer And Dossie Meet

Marriage is not a ritual or an end. It is a long, intricate, intimate dance together and nothing matters more than your own sense of balance and your choice of partner.

— Amy Bloom

It wasn't long after William Archer's return to North Carolina that his family began. The firstborn of William Archer and Henrietta was

James Archer and Dossie

James Franklin Hopper. He was small framed, sharp-witted and carefree in character, with an inexhaustible degree of energy.

As a young boy, after all his chores were complete, James Franklin loved to sit Indian-style on the dusty living room floor next to his dad. It was at these times, usually late at night, when William Archer gathered his offspring around the fireplace. He shared bone-chilling narratives, mostly pertaining to his recollections of the War Between the States.

The flames from the hearth cast dancing shadows around the living room as William demonstrated his special gift for telling tales. Of all the children, James Franklin, who had a naturally active imagination anyway, was especially held spellbound by his father's accounts. James sat frozen as his father recalled long-ago skirmishes where North Carolinians were always triumphant.

Throughout his adolescence, James Franklin tried to please his mother and father and was depicted by the rest of the family as especially trustworthy and dependable. Because of the never-ending

19

responsibilities on the farm, he grew up quickly as a hardworking farmer.

As a young adult, he met and eventually took a wife, Gillie Ann Gentry, who would later be described as a business-minded woman who was "ahead of her time."

James Franklin and Gillie Ann took up housekeeping on a portion of Hopper acreage, building themselves a four-room log cabin. They soon began their own family. James Franklin and Gillie Ann named their firstborn James Archer Hopper (nearly everyone called him Archer).

Dossie and Archer

Archer was actually the oldest of seven. He was extremely close to both parents and depended on them greatly. Yet, he grew up to be hardworking and fiercely independent—even described as bull-headed by some in later life. Since he worked on his parent's farm from the time he could walk and talk, and because he was the firstborn, farm work was expected to be his lifelong vocation.

Archer eventually met a lovely local girl, Dossie Purtle. Through a series of opportune circumstances, the couple courted, then married and had their own large family. From the union of Archer and Dossie Hopper, eleven children were eventually born. In birth-order, they were: Virginia, Monroe, Octola, Catharine, Paul, Will, Claude, Wayne, Richard, Steve, and the baby of the family, Dewey.

The names of these siblings will be especially significant for the remainder of this literary account, for it was this generation of the Hopper family who made a powerful impact upon the Southern Gospel music industry.

Focusing On A Generation

Virginia Hopper Steele, eldest child of Archer and Dossie, retains fond memories of her parents and grandparents. Eighty years old at the time of this writing, she shares many of her recollections for this volume.

As she recalls, Archer and Dossie met at a local square dance: "Mama's daddy, Grandpa Purtle, played several musical instruments, including the five-string banjo. Mama came from a big family with ten children, and most of her family were musically inclined in one way or another."

From an early age, Dossie had an astonishing sense of rhythm and an insatiable love for music. She effortlessly danced with synchronized outward heel kicks and up-and-down body movements—

Dossie, Archer in the field

bending and straightening her knees—in perfect time with the fast-paced rhythm of mountain music. It was said to be a sight to behold!

With her natural sense of tempo, Dossie was often considered the best on the dance floor. Archer and Dossie's middle-son, Claude, remembers his mother's talent: "Some today might call it clogging. Mama was the best I've ever seen! In addition to dancing, Mama liked to sing and play the auto-harp."

Most of the Hopper children remember hearing their father reminisce about the night he first laid eyes on Dossie. She was in the center of a dance floor one evening. Archer was there, and after a few minutes of watching her clog, he thought, "That has got to be the prettiest woman I've ever seen!"

It was then he began thinking about how he could gain her attention and favor. He worked up enough courage to visit her at her parent's home. Then he eventually started courting the young beauty. Conveniently, Dossie, who was just a teenager at the time, lived on a small tobacco farm adjacent to the Hopper property. The couple soon devised a unique way to communicate their growing affection: they chose a medium-sized rock at the approximate halfway point between the two farms. Under this rock they took turns hiding love letters for one another.

Early in the morning, Archer, who was in his mid-twenties,

scribbled short messages for his sweetheart. Sealing the letter in a makeshift envelope, he darted across the pasture to the edge of the Hopper farm; he placed his letter under the rock, and ran back to his daily farm duties. By dusk he'd return to the stone and claim a neatly-penned response.

With a grin, he read and reread the words from Dossie before returning home and eventually falling asleep. This routine continued for quite a long time. Secret letters, and occasional chance encounters, sparked a relationship that began to glow brightly over the months. Both found it easy to talk and loved being in each other's company.

Archer knew early on that this was the person with whom he wanted to spend his life, so he started saving for an engagement ring right away. Tucking away extra money he earned by working on the farm or peddling produce in Madison, he eventually accumulated enough to buy an inexpensive ring from a jewelry store in town.

On a warm evening when Archer could wait no longer, he wrapped the store-bought ring, slipped it into his pants pocket and walked over to Dossie's parents' farmhouse.

Although he practiced the exact words he wanted to say many times before, that night he stumbled and stammered as he attempted to propose. Once he finally blurted out the "big question," Dossie beamed as she accepted. It was then, as they sat on the piano bench, that it happened: Archer leaned over and gently kissed her, consummating the engagement.

"I remember how we used to tease Mama about that story when we were children," Virginia mused, "but she always maintained that that was their first kiss—on the piano bench!"

"Long after they married, Daddy still kept that rock in a large trunk he kept locked up in their bedroom," Virginia remembered, noting how sentimental her father could be when it came to his courtship. "Sometimes he'd show it to us, along with some of the love letters he kept tied together with a string."

It was that precious stone, under which two young lovers once passed messages of love and admiration, that became a lifelong keepsake—the symbolic cornerstone of the love that existed between Archer and Dossie Hopper.

Chapter 4
The Hopper Homestead

A house is not a home unless it contains food and fire for the mind as well as the body.

— Benjamin Franklin

Many years earlier, Gillie Ann Hopper told her young son, Archer, that a great deal of her land would one day belong to him, since he was oldest of her children. He couldn't have imagined when he was small that he would live the life of a sharecropper, residing on the family farm and tilling the soil.

The homplace

Indeed that time eventually came: the main farm was passed down to Archer shortly after he married. The senior Hoppers moved into another house on an adjacent piece of property.

As a sharecropper, or tenant farmer, Archer was in a verbal-partnership agreement with his parents. Because he purchased his own livestock and farm equipment, the arrangement was that he'd keep three-fourths of the profits from the farm, while one quarter went to the landowners — his parents. Archer raised mostly tobacco and corn on the spread and the pact proved beneficial for all.

The homeplace was a small log cabin with rough clapboard siding, a barn and several meager outbuildings. Although it wasn't elaborate by most people's standards, it was a wonderful beginning for a young couple with high hopes and infinite dreams.

When the house was originally built, the kitchen was completely separate from the main house, presumably to keep the heat generated from cooking away from the living quarters during the summertime.

The kitchen area consisted of a large cast-iron woodstove, a stout oak kitchen table, several sturdy chairs, a tall cabinet and some rough pine board shelving for storage. The stove hugged the wall, with a stovepipe extending upward and exiting near the roof.

Archer and Dossie eventually closed in the space between the kitchen and the main house, connecting the kitchen with the rest of the cabin. After the remodeling, family and guests had to step down into the dining room to enter the living quarters and back up when entering the kitchen, for the two buildings didn't align perfectly. The ceiling in the kitchen wasn't very high either. According to Claude's recollections, anyone with any height at all had to bow his or her head upon entering into the room.

There was a small loft above a staircase where Dossie kept canning jars, various cast-iron skillets and pots and pans. As for the main cabin, there were two rooms downstairs, with a hallway in the middle. The home had two large rooms upstairs, where all the boys slept in one room and the girls in the other.

Dossie had all of her babies at home. Typically, Grandma Gillie Ann arrived at the house along with the doctor to assist in the delivery when it was time for each baby to come. The other children had to go to Grandma's house and stay there while awaiting the childbirth.

"My mother gave birth to all eleven children, and one stillbirth, in the same bed, in the same room of the same house," Wayne Hopper said.

The cabin's front sitting room with its small fireplace was where Archer and Dossie's bed was located. Later they added a woodstove, sometimes known as a parlor stove, into the room. It consisted of a cylinder-shaped firebox with a hinged airtight iron door, where firewood was loaded through an iron flap. Ashes collected from the stove's bottom grate were dumped outside.

If this iron door wasn't tightly sealed, air leaked inside and the flame roared until the wood was completely consumed. The sounds of snapping and crackling from smoldering wood in the fireplace became everyday background noise in the Hopper abode. The pleasantly familiar scent filled the house and the air outside the cabin, particularly in the fall and winter months.

There was a certain amount of satisfaction for the children in the realization that they had participated in the process of heating the home by gathering firewood and twigs from the nearby woods. The task of chopping and stacking wood was usually delegated to the older boys.

The Hopper offspring had a natural sense of belonging; perhaps it was because they all worked toward accomplishing an important objective: maintaining the family farm. They seemed to find unity and a sense of purpose in carrying out their farm duties.

On many winter nights, the upstairs of the house could get extremely chilly, since the cabin, like most built in that era, wasn't insulated well. In fact, in the evening the structure was especially drafty, as dropping outdoor temperatures mingled and wrestled with the inside warmth generated from the burning logs. Usually the cold won the all-night dispute for dominance.

"Several of us boys slept together in one big bed with a straw mattress, called a 'tick.' I had one brother that tried to create the first

Dad made sure his sons had plenty of chores on the tobacco farm to keep them busy. The work seemed endless at the time.

waterbed over forty years ago, if you know what I mean," Wayne said and laughed.

On some nights, the children could even see their breath when they ventured out from beneath the layers of covers. By daybreak, when the brood woke up to prepare for another day at grammar school, they raced downstairs. It was common that the kids tried to gather around the fireside, playfully pushing and shoving one another out of the way, in vain attempts to get closer to the roaring fire to warm up before breakfast.

The Hopper farm was positioned on one hundred and twenty acres of prime Rockingham County real estate. On the farmstead was a spring bubbling up from a fast-moving branch. It was located roughly one hundred yards from the house. The crystal-clear water was animated with small minnows, frogs, crawdads and other forms of creek-life. Since there was no inside plumbing at the time, this same clear water was carried from the spring into the kitchen as needed. As soon as the kids were big enough, each carried tin pails of spring water to the cabin throughout the course of a day. The cool running spring also served as a makeshift refrigeration system for storing certain foods that would otherwise spoil. Claude still remembers carrying fresh cow's milk and other perishable items to the spring: "We set the items in a the spring to keep them from spoiling so fast."

Later Archer purchased one of the first aluminum coolers in the area, which kept milk, buttermilk and perishables even colder. Virginia described the cooler as "kind of tall and slender with a ledge inside it." It was positioned in the creek bed where they had to weigh it down to keep it from floating away altogether.

Eventually, they acquired a large icebox. Archer placed hundred-pound blocks of ice, delivered to the farm by buckboard or truck routinely, inside the box to keep items cold. The ice was covered with heavy muslin material when delivered to protect it from the sun's rays, and slabs were unloaded with ice picks shaped like large iron tongs. The icebox was kept beneath a shady walnut tree behind the cabin.

The Hoppers made butter on the farm, and the children took turns with the laborious churning process. The butter churn was a tall, narrow wooden barrel, fitted with a wooden cover. Thick cream was poured inside the cylinder and the children vigorously agitated the contents by hand, using a stout wooden plunger.

A back porch was attached to the cabin. Right across from the porch were two handsome locust trees. There were old mulberry trees near the barn and when the children ran barefoot beneath the trees, their feet were stained dark purple from the berries that had dropped on the ground. There was a rough-cut corncrib near the barn, built from large hand-hewn oak logs, and a henhouse positioned on the hillside.

For many in and around Rockingham County, when autumn came it was time to make lye soap. Typically a large cast-iron kettle was suspended from a makeshift tripod or pole. With a raging fire built beneath the pot, lye was slowly poured into the kettle along with liquid lard—perhaps two or three pounds of lard for every gallon of lye. The foul-smelling concoction bubbled and boiled as it was stirred with a long wooden paddle.

Eventually from this mixture, liquid lye soap was poured into homemade molds. Once the soap cooled and hardened in tin castings, it was cut up into smaller chunks. These squares of soap were then cured for up to two weeks.

Lye soap was used for many purposes on the farm, especially heavy-duty laundry, since it was especially useful to combat grease or black-gum stains. However, as Virginia recalled, lye soap was too harsh to use for bathing. She said the soap would "take the skin off if used during a bath."

Other types of handmade soft soap or gentler concoctions were also made from natural ingredients such as vegetable oils, rose petals, herbs and spices.

A task the Hopper children were familiar with from life on the farm was butchering hogs and curing the meat in salt. Each one of them had a part in the process. "My brother Monroe and I, early on, learned to grind sausage," Virginia said. "One of us would feed the sausage into the mill while the other turned the crank."

The children remember their mother, Dossie, "drying up" lard in a cast-iron pot over the kitchen fireplace by putting the pork fat in a pot and stirring it slowly until it ultimately melted into lard.

There was a stout workhorse on the farm named Lady, and a cantankerous mule, Red Lou, that pulled the plow. Sometimes Red Lou behaved most stubbornly during his plowing detail. Memories of Archer jerking hard on the reins and yelling commands—and a few choice names—still cause the siblings to chuckle.

The Hopper farm was isolated—located one mile away from the main highway—and the power company in the early days wouldn't run poles and power lines just for a single household. Claude, the seventh child, born October 8, 1937, recalls that it wasn't until he was around fourteen when the farm finally got electricity. Up until that time, oil lamps and candles were mainstays. It was much later before they saw indoor plumbing and other modern conveniences.

The Boys:—Monroe, Paul, Will, Claude, Wayne, Richard, Steve and Dewey Hopper

Chapter 5
The Great Depression

American families have always shown remarkable resiliency, or flexible adjustment to natural, economic, and social challenges. Their strengths resemble the elasticity of a spider web, a gull's skillful flow with the wind, the regenerating power of perennial grasses, the cooperation of an ant colony, and the persistence of a stream carving canyon rocks.

— Ben Silliman

When most of the Hopper children were small, the Great Depression was still in full swing. The Depression has been considered the most devastating economic crisis in the history of the modern world, lasting from the Stock Market collapse of 1929 until the monetary upswing of the mid-1940s.

North Carolina, along with the rest of the nation, experienced a dramatic decrease in business opportunity, industrial production and availability of common goods and services. The results were incredibly damaging to the economic climate. Many who were financially affluent were reduced to extreme poverty overnight.

Businesses and banking institutions closed and "victory gardens" became necessary for those fortunate enough to still own farmable land. Other folks skinned the hillsides or cleared off mountain flats just to plant enough corn and other vegetables to survive. Millions of

Stairsteps, from left, Dewey, Steve, Richard, Wayne, Claude and Will Hopper

skilled laborers lost their jobs, homes, transportation and life savings through these challenging years.

The Hopper family, like everyone else, was affected by the Great Depression. Each child was responsible for an even longer list of duties, including working in the fields, keeping farm machinery up-and-running, milking cows and caring for the various livestock. Because of lean times, everyone worked harder and longer, including the youngest of the children. It was imperative that the farm remain productive and self-sufficient. Money and opportunity were in short supply.

"When we were growing up, we had a lot more materially than a lot of folks had, even though some of the family now says we were dirt-poor. Yes, we may have been poor by today's standards, but we girls always had new dresses when school began and the boys had new overalls and lumber jackets," Virginia recalled.

"I have asked every one of my brothers at one time or another, 'Did you ever have the feeling you'd go to the table and not have food to eat?'

"Each of them have answered, 'No!'"

In the first years that Virginia could remember, before the Great Depression, her mother and father did very well: "Mama even had a coat with fur on it. Then I remember the day the banks locked their doors. Daddy came home, leaned against the mantle and wept."

Children from neighboring farms or from downtown Madison, for the most part in those days, were poorly clothed. The Hopper children remember that some of their friends came to school with coats or other garments pinned together with large safety pins or being covered with patches. Many had holes in their shoes and ragged socks and undergarments.

It was around this time that Dossie started working at Washington Mills, located in the neighboring town of Mayodan, a massive operation established in 1895. It was one of the largest employers in the county. Meanwhile, Archer and the children kept the farm running.

Dossie worked twelve hours a day, five days a week on the hoot-owl shift, from 6:00 p.m. to 6:00 a.m. No one worked on Sundays. "In spite of the hours she invested, she never made much of a payday while working," Claude said, "Even so, every little bit helped."

Before she started working, Dossie told Virginia, "Now you take care of little Catharine. She's your baby now!" Virginia was only eight at the time.

Even though Dossie worked outside the home, somehow she and Archer found enjoyable distractions. For example, Dossie still loved to dance, even learning how to do the popular "Charleston."

The couple had one possession they especially cherished. They called it a "graphite"—a windup Victor-Victrola phonograph. From earliest memories, even in the darkest days of the Depression, the Hopper home was full of lively music and neighborhood visitors.

The people around Madison formed a close-knit community. Kinfolk and neighbors visited one another often, especially on weekends. Music and food seemed to be the focus of such get-togethers.

Even after working grueling long shifts at the mill, Dossie still found time to work at home, including making clothing for her children and performing most of the normal duties of a housewife. She even cut the children's hair and shaved her husband every week.

On one occasion Dossie made suits for her sons. The outfits had short pants that buttoned onto jackets along the waistline and jackets with flat collars and short sleeves. When the boys dressed up, they bore strong resemblances to Little Lord Fauntleroy. Each child was proud of such stylish attire and wore the suits to Sunday school, camp meetings, revivals and other public functions.

Monroe Hopper, second-born child, reminisced about growing up in the Depression: "We didn't think about not having money, mainly because nobody else had any either! At school, I used to exchange my homemade sausage biscuits for peanut butter and crackers or peanut-butter-and-banana sandwiches. This was because we didn't have store-bought bread or crackers. Store bought items were a treat for us.

"Mama canned. Boy, that was really a big thing back then! We had blackberry jam, apples, beans, corn and everything you could imagine! We also sold home-canned vegetables, fruit and pork when we went to town. Believe it or not, I didn't even know ham grew on the legs of a hog until I left home, because Dad sold all of that. That was the high dollar stuff! We only ate the belly."

When Monroe grew a little older, he learned to be quite good at catching opossums to earn spending money. "My uncle and I went hunting, and I had a good dog. People who ran the tobacco warehouses, where tobacco was sold to the harvesters, held 'possum suppers," Monroe said. "So, I caught 'possums alive and caged them till they were fattened up."

Monroe pointed out that opossums had a tendency to eat things that were "not particularly desirable," but he fed them leftover cornbread, buttermilk and persimmons.

Dossie

"Once they were fattened, I skinned and dressed them and sold them for a quarter or fifty cents each," he said. "If I shot a rabbit, the fellows at the warehouse gave me a dime. If I trapped the rabbit, they'd give me fifteen cents!"

Laundry Day

Due to the size of the Hopper family, laundry was an all-day proposition, and because of all the other responsibilities that needed to be met, it was only done once a week. "We boiled clothing in a large black pot," Virginia remembered, explaining that they used a long punching stick, a scrub board, several tubs of water and bleach to make things white.

Later on, Archer and Dossie purchased a washing machine with a gasoline motor. It was one of the first washing machines in the region, which naturally created a sensation among the neighbors. The motorized contraption made washday a bit easier on everyone involved, even though it still took a full day to complete laundry detail. Once the single-cylinder gas engine fired up, the loud motor chugged and puffed as it gained operational momentum. The appliance, mobile with small rubber casters, was used on the outside porch because the machine tended to expel wisps of gasoline fumes and carbon dioxide as the tub spun.

Boredom, Hunting And Self-reliance

Boredom never became an issue for such a large family. Living in cramped conditions and staying busy with daily farm tasks kept everyone alert, active and occupied.

"We worked hard on the farm, but no one worked harder than Mama! She was right alongside all of us in the fields, hoeing tobacco and chopping corn," Claude reminisced.

Somehow for the children, in spite of the great number of chores, there was still time for play and relaxation. In the summertime, right after lunch, Claude and his brothers often went fishing or swimming while Archer took his daily nap. Off they ran to their favorite dammed-up swimming hole where the cool spring water felt especially refreshing.

Monroe today

"In the fall, after the first frost, we headed for the woods to squirrel hunt," Claude said. When a hunting trip was planned, the boys woke up before daylight and hiked across the field into the nearby woods; because of frost, the grass crunched beneath their feet as they looked for any sign of a squirrel near hickory trees, or a rabbit darting from a fence line or brush pile.

The Hopper farm was nearly self-reliant, but there were still items the family needed from the general store. Every few weeks Archer bought five-gallon containers of molasses and one-hundred-pound bags of flour and pinto beans.

"By the time World War II was in progress, everyone needed rationing stamps for shoes and other leather goods, tires, gasoline, sugar and eventually, even coffee," Claude remembered. "It seemed like everything was in short supply. There were ration stamps allocated based upon the size of one's family. So we learned to be extremely frugal and good stewards of everything we had."

Claude now believes in hindsight that this long-ago era was a proving ground of sorts, where the Lord taught each of them hard work, responsibility, practicality and conservation. These life lessons proved even more valuable for the Hopper children as the years rolled by.

Chapter 6
Remembering Grandma
And Grandpa Hopper

For some life lasts a short while, but the memories it
holds last forever.

— Laura Swenson

Most of the Hopper children have distinct recollections of their
grandmother, Gillie Ann, and grandfather, James Franklin Hopper.

On occasion, Gillie Ann shared vivid recollections of her family
history with the grandchildren, and Virginia especially listened
intently.

Gillie Ann once told how her father played a fiddle, and on
many occasions, she went with him to square dances. When they
arrived at the location, usually being held at someone's home, the
furniture was shoved back into corners or into the next room.

There were times when Gillie Ann danced all night long, while
her father played song after song on his violin, including favorites
like "Turkey In the Straw." By early the next morning, worn out from
a night of fun, father and daughter mosied back home on horseback.

Although he was a hardworking man whose word was his
bond, for some reason James Franklin didn't particularly want any
property to be put in his name. When business decisions invariably
came up, he pointed to his wife and said, "Go see her!" So, Gillie Ann
negotiated with bankers and other business people when necessary
and controlled the financial responsibilities concerning the farm and
property ventures. She was an astute businesswoman as well as a
smart dresser, according to Virginia: "I remember she always wore
brooches, which we called breast-pins, and I thought they were so
pretty. She wore silk or crepe dresses when she dressed up."

If Gillie Ann needed to go to town, she'd ask Virginia or someone else to go with her. ?They started out on foot.

"It seemed like somebody always stopped and picked us up,"

Virginia said. "Grandma was well-known among citizens in the community. Nothing hindered her!"

On many of these occasions Virginia and Grandma Hopper walked down the road to Meadows Grocery Store where Gillie Ann bought them cheese and crackers for lunch.

Wild And Uninhibited

Wayne recalls: "As we got older, Grandma Hopper would head us off at the pass as we walked up the road to her house. She'd holler, 'Hold it! Hold it!' because she knew we were apt to break the limbs off her apple trees just for the fun of it. We were rough boys—wild and uninhibited!

"Grandma was altogether serious—all business! Grandpa, on the other hand, was a jokester and fun-loving," Wayne said. "Together, they formed a good partnership, just as Mama and Daddy had a partnership. They never crossed one another. What one said, the other backed up."

Though James Franklin and Gillie Ann lived in a dwelling near Archer and Dossie's cabin and farm, they eventually purchased another home and moved several miles away, which allowed Archer, Dossie and the youngest of their children to move into James Franklin and Gillie Ann's former residence. This house was a simple frame house, but far more modern in comparison to the cabin.

Certainly Archer, Dossie and the kids looked at the move as a positive thing. However, it seemed peculiar for everyone to just pull up stakes and move out of a cabin that had always been home. Since the family had such sentimental feelings for the old homeplace, Archer eventually paid twelve hundred dollars to have professional home-movers relocate the cabin to an adjacent open field, within eyeshot of the newer location. The log cabin remains in that field to this day.

Chapter 7
Mama, Daddy
And Uncle Banner

There is no doubt that it is around the family and the home that all the greatest virtues, the most dominating virtues of human society, are created, strengthened and maintained.

— Winston Churchill

James Archer introduced himself to others and signed his name "J. A. Hopper." Yet, as mentioned previously, friends and acquaintances around Rockingham County knew him as Archer.

He, like so many men of his era, was considered a stern father. It was difficult—nearly impossible—for him to adequately exhibit his deepest feelings or emotions in front of family, unless, of course, he was angry. For most of Claude's childhood and into early adulthood, he secretly longed to hear his father say words of love and appreciation. It seemed that Claude and his siblings never experienced outward signs of affection from Archer until much later in life.

"I don't think we ever doubted Dad loved us, even though he was incapable of verbalizing it," Claude said. "I don't think he ever told me he loved me until I was an adult. By the time he did, he was well into his eighties. Even then, I guess I coerced him into it. I told him I loved him and then asked him if he loved me. I then paused and waited for a response. He had to answer me."

Although it was extremely awkward for both of them, Archer stiffened and stumbled over the words: "Well ... sure, Son. I ... uh ... love you, too."

Being that Archer was the primary disciplinarian in their home, the Hopper children had a healthy fear of Dad. "Daddy said what he meant and meant what he said. Period. He really disciplined us when the need arose. He had daily chores lined up for us, and we had to do them! There was no room for compromise or discussion under his leadership. You had to do whatever he expected—no questions asked!" Claude said.

Monroe added: "At home, Daddy was a very serious man, especially when it came to us—sort of like Stonewall Jackson. If you were in trouble and he got ahold of you, it just wasn't fun!"

Claude

"Daddy was one of the few parents I knew that would send you to cut your own switches," Wayne recalled, "and then he carefully inspected them for strength and durability. If the switch didn't pass Daddy's test, you had to get another. Then, and only then, did he whip you!"

"With Mom, you could get away with a lot of things—but not with Daddy. He hurt! He went for blood!" Monroe chuckled. "When Mama said, 'I'm going to tell your daddy,' boy, we straightened right up!"

Archer, The Businessman

Among other things, Archer was a rather ingenious and successful entrepreneur. Besides farming, he was a persuasive peddler. He sold a variety of goods to people around the county. For instance, he took from fifty to one hundred gallons of blackberries to town every week when they were in season. On other occasions eggs and extra produce were packed away on his truck. Interestingly, he never went to town unless he had something in the back of his truck to sell.

It was his notion that if he needed something from a local grocery store or hardware, he packed up enough raw goods to take along to make up for his expected expenditures. He was always determined to earn as much as he planned to spend on any particular day—and he typically exceeded his goals.

With this strategy, he was able to ensure a positive cash flow that encompassed the family's necessities. Likewise, he expected his children to apply the same principle. So, the Hopper boys peddled farm goods when they went to town as well.

Virginia explained that when Archer wasn't peddling, he continuously worked the farm, and there were many times when sweat "poured from his brow and out from beneath his old straw hat" as he

It's cold outside. The Hopper boys pose for a snapshot right after Christmas.

labored.

One of the fonder memories the children have of their father is of his whistling. On most early mornings, he began by feeding Lady, the workhorse. The kids would hear him whistling a melody all the way to the barn. He continued with the same tune as he moved from task to task, seemingly oblivious to anything or anyone else around him. "He sort of whistled his way through life," Virginia said grinning.

The children say that, besides being a whistler, he was a "big talker," who never met a stranger. He frequently told jokes and funny anecdotes to neighbors, friends and customers in town.

"Mom sang while we'd all work together in the field. With the exception of being able to whistle, Dad, on the other hand, wasn't musically talented; he could hardly play a radio!" Wayne said.

Archer was the type of guy who didn't care whether anyone else thought something he said was funny or not; as soon as he told a joke or made a wisecrack, he laughed loudly afterwards and clapped his hands together in glee. Then sometimes, he'd slap someone else nearby on the back.

Wayne commented: "He had a ball with himself! Most often, everybody else was laughing right along with him, too."

Claude recalled special moments: "Sometimes, when we were very young, Dad would sit down in his favorite chair and put one or sometimes two of us on his lap. With three or four days' beard growth on his face, he'd cuddle and kiss on us, tickling us from our ears down to our necks and shoulders, while we giggled and pre-

38

tended to beg him to stop."

"Mama used to say that Daddy wasn't particularly good-looking, but he sure was handsome! To her there was a vast difference," Virginia recalled. Archer and Dossie didn't attempt to hide their affection for each other. There were times when they were openly playful and loving toward one another in front of the children.

"We had a low kitchen window at the house. I remember once it snowed up to that windowsill. Mama stood Monroe and me up in front of the window so we could look out. Mama and Daddy went outside and played in the snow where we could watch."

Virginia recalls other occasions when Archer came in at night, after a hard day of work, and Dossie was cooking at the stove. "Daddy would sneak up behind her and hug and kiss on her. It makes me feel so good to remember things like that. I know they had a really wonderful relationship."

Uncle Banner's Second Marriage

Archer was especially close to a relative, Uncle Banner, who was nearly his age. Uncle Banner was about twenty-five when he first married, and he married twice in his lifetime. It just so happened that Archer took Uncle Banner to get married on both occasions.

Uncle Banner's first wife died prematurely around the age of thirty-six, when Uncle Banner was in his early forties. They had twelve children together.

After her death, most of the family assumed Uncle Banner would stay home and raise his children. Instead, Uncle Banner immediately started seeking a new mate. He eventually found another sweetheart. Her name was Grace, and she was only seventeen (he was forty-four). Archer drove the couple to Martinsville, Virginia, in his Ford Model A pickup to get married.

By that time laws were changing and some states required couples to have blood tests, but not in Virginia. Before they got to the Martinsville church, they went to the courthouse to get a marriage license.

After getting their names, the county clerk asked Grace her age. Grace shyly mumbled,

Dossie and Archer

39

"I'm seventeen." The clerk then explained that they couldn't apply for a license until she was of legal age — eighteen.

Uncle Banner turned toward Grace and mumbled, "Hey, I thought you were eighteen!"

"No, I'm just seventeen," she whispered, as she looked bashfully toward the floor. He leaned toward her and said, "Just tell him you're eighteen!"

"No, I won't tell a lie," she answered sternly. Archer gritted his teeth to keep from grinning and stood motionless until Banner motioned to leave.

After they exited the courthouse, Uncle Banner, being aggravated over the episode, decided they should travel to the next county seat at Rocky Mount. Archer, Banner and Grace jumped into the truck, and Banner said matter-of-factly, "Now Grace, you're going to have a birthday between here and Rocky Mount!"

As the family account goes, before they reached Rocky Mount courthouse, Banner had Grace scribble the number "18" on a piece of paper and stick it inside one of her shoes. When the clerk asked Grace if she was over eighteen, she answered, "Ah … yes, yes, I am over eighteen!"

They were married in Rocky Mount.

Uncle Banner and Grace had even more children, making a total of twenty-two in all, including two sets of twins.

Chapter 8
In Their Spare Time

And in the end it's not the years in your life that count.
It's the life in your years.

— Abraham Lincoln

Dossie was always one to try the latest things on the market. For example, she was first to purchase an electric mixer and first to own a Singer sewing machine in the Rockingham County area. Occasionally she made homemade ice cream for the entire family, beating the ingredients together with her mixer and freezing the concoction in the new icebox.

"Mama also loved to try any type of craft, but she never read directions fully, so she didn't always get the full benefit of a project," Virginia recalled, laughing.

"Mama was also a beautiful woman. When I was a child, I remember people always talked about how pretty she was."

Dossie loved life and living. She had an upbeat attitude toward everything and everybody. To her, life was a giant adventure to be experienced. She was happiest when she was experiencing something new, unique or creative with her family.

When Dossie was a youngster, her father, Grandpa Purtle, went to Madison and bought her a piano, a used upright model. In due course, she taught herself to play limitedly. She loved music and continued to play throughout the years.

Being ahead of her time in so many ways, there were other things she tried. She was one of the first in the area to wear store-bought makeup. Dossie kept a small jar of rouge and wore just a hint whenever she went to town.

Always trying new fashion trends, on one occasion she cut her hair exceptionally short. Women at the time typically wore dust caps at night, usually made of white linen. There was a thin flap turned back around the top and Dossie's cap happened to be embroidered. "She had her dust cap on during the middle of the day. Daddy, being suspicious, asked her why she was wearing it in broad daylight. He then asked, 'Dossie, what have you done—didya' cut your hair?' And she had! They called it 'bobbing' back then," Virginia said.

When he saw the new short hairdo, he was surprised at first, but finally chuckled and wondered why she tried so hard to hide it, since she actually looked pretty.

Dossie was also the more spiritual in the Hopper home. "She really tried her best to raise us right. Mama is the one who made sure the boys walked to church. Dad didn't go to church when we were kids," Claude remembered. "We walked with on a farm road, through the woods, to Sunday School. We went to a little Methodist church and I also remember going to Sunday school at Ellisboro Baptist church."

After the morning church service, considerate neighbors often drove the family to the main road to shorten their walking distance back home.

Virginia recalled. "Daddy even went to Sunday School with us at Ellisboro Baptist in his later years."

"From an early age, all of us knew the basics: we were not to lie or steal. We knew the Golden Rule and other things like that," Monroe explained. "But there were still many times when Mama had to correct us."

Once when the children were young, Monroe and Virginia were playing outside at the chimney corner of the cabin. Monroe did something to tease and annoy Virginia and she called him a fool. "Mama overheard me. Boy, oh boy, she came outside and whipped me, and said, 'I don't want to ever hear you call anyone a fool again!'

"She was enraged, for she knew a Scripture passage, in Matthew 5:22, where it says, 'Whosoever shall say, thou fool, shall be in danger of hell fire.'"

Dossie had a close relationship with the Lord and loved regular church services and revival meetings. She enjoyed singing in the church choir until she passed away.

Dossie had a wonderful testimony about when she was first saved. As she told many times, the greatest moment in her life happened during a revival at Palestine Methodist Church, on Ellisboro Road. Dossie went to the service one night with a neighbor; that evening she gave her life to Christ. James Franklin Hopper was also saved during the same revival, in his old age.

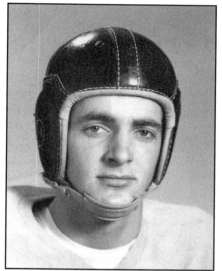

Claude is ready for the game

"Mama was living proof that a person can learn even when older. In her later years, she memorized entire passages of the Bible. This was after she was seventy years old. That was such a blessing," Virginia said. After the Hopper Brothers started singing together at different venues as a group, Dossie was supportive of them, traveling with them as often as she could.

Daddy, Sports and Chores

Claude recalled that at one point there were four Hopper brothers in school at the same time, and all played on the high school football team. Archer took his boys to practice, but they typically had to find their own ride home. The boys participated in other sports as well. During the various ballgames, you could hear Archer's voice above anyone else, as he cheered for his sons. Perhaps that was one of the few outward ways he signified his great delight in his children.

However, Archer placed certain restrictions on the boys when it came to school athletic programs, allowing them to participate in only two sports during a school year, whether it was baseball, football or basketball. The limitations were likely associated with the help he needed on the farm.

"He worked us from the time we got up until we went to school," Claude said. "Then, we worked from the time we got home from school until bedtime. In a way, football practice was much easier than home."

The Hopper boys and their father, Archer, usually had several good hunting dogs on the farm.

43

Chapter 9
The Shelton Family

Family life is full of major and minor crises—the ups
and downs of health, success and failure. It is tied to
places and events and histories. With all of these felt
details, life etches itself into memory and personality.
It's difficult to imagine anything more nourishing to
the soul.

— Thomas Moore

In another region of Rockingham County, Henry Evan Shelton and
Mary Lou Flynn Shelton owned a tobacco farm outside Stokesdale,
North Carolina, across a lazy and narrow stream from the communi-
ty of Little Egypt.

Stokesdale has always been a small community with a line of
stores positioned on one side of the street, with train tracks and a
depot on the opposite side. Trains ran on a regular schedule.

In the late 1940s and into the early 1950s, it was a quaint village
with a post office and a bank. Local resident Willie Powell owned a
drugstore, and Dr. Dalton's office was located in the back. There was
Vaughn's Grocery Store and a funeral home. Penn Lemmons owned
a small dry goods store. Nolan Jones ran a well-stocked hardware.
Five Oaks Dancehall was located in town, too.

It was a bustling little farming community and, for the Sheltons,
the closest place where they could buy groceries and other necessities. The Shelton farm was located about five miles from Stokesdale
and fifteen miles from Madison.

An Earlier Period

Mary Lou Flynn was born in 1900 and grew up to be an attractive woman with unusually strong faith. Those who knew her said
she was a kind and generous person who was strong in her principles, as well as disciplined and deliberate in her actions, since she
was level headed and always focused. Mary Lou also had a keen and
unusual sense of humor.

Henry and Mary Lou

Her father was born in 1865, near the close of the Civil War and lived until 1930. In contrast, Henry Evan Shelton was born in 1899 of Scotch Irish decent. His mother passed away when he was five years old. Later, Henry's father, Papa Jim, remarried, marrying his mother's sister, his aunt. Papa Jim Shelton lived to be 97 years old.

In spite of losing his mama at an early age, Henry remained a good-natured and well-mannered boy. He grew into a kind and friendly personality with a positive mind-set and a strong nose-to-the-grindstone work ethic.

Eventually Henry and Mary Lou met and started dating. After a prolonged courtship, and not long after marrying, they purchased a sixty-five-acre farm. Their down payment for the tract of land came from Mary Lou's kinfolks. Soon afterwards, the couple began their own family.

Henry and Mary Lou raised seven children in all. Among their children was Cornelia Elizabeth Shelton [named after her Grandmother Flynn]. She was the youngest, born July 16, 1940. Almost immediately Henry started calling the child "Connie." From that point forward, the name stuck. The family has used "Connie" ever since.

Her older brothers and sisters included Charles, Henry, Mary Hilda, William "Billy" Hutchison, Jack Marshall, James Donald, and Wilma Genessee Shelton.

Connie Shelton

Five of the offspring were raised in the midst of the Great Depression, while Wilma and Connie came along near the end of those lean years.

"I was born in the country, and our mail came to Route 1, Stokesdale," Connie said. "A lot of Sheltons live in Stokesdale. Our farm was actually situated between the towns of Stokesdale and Pine Hall, North Carolina."

Connie remembers the region with fondness. The people of the area made up a close-knit community. If per chance someone in the neighborhood was sick, temporarily disabled or passed away, neighbors gathered to get the crops in at harvest time, or accomplish immediate chores until the sickness or situation passed.

Citizens of the area planned occasional picnics together, where ladies brought wonderful dishes like potato salad, deviled eggs, coleslaw, fried chicken, ham, biscuits, cornbread, and all the fixings. There were cakes, pies, and cookies to satisfy every sweettooth. While the women were busy organizing the affair, the men played horseshoes and enjoyed the camaraderie and competition. Some of the fellows brought musical instruments and played and sang during the afternoon.

"The neighbors cleared out a convenient piece of ground for such events," Connie recalled. "During the summer, when we were curing tobacco in the tobacco barns, people also gathered at a barn on Saturday nights for wiener roasts. Cutting small branches from trees, we trimmed them and sharpened the end for the hotdog. The weiners were roasted over the fire in the barn furnace."

Connie with her brothers

Everyone knew each other and seemingly enjoyed each other's company. "At the end of summer, before all the fresh garden vegetables were gone, much of the community would gather and undertake the all day job of cooking a 15-gallon pot of Brunswick Stew. It was wonderful," Connie said, explaining that the recipe was a conglomeration of fresh ingredients.

In those early days, Connie's father,

Henry, was one of the men who brought an instrument to community events. He had a great deal of musical talent and especially enjoyed picking on a five-string banjo. His banjo was homemade, handcrafted from materials found on the farm.

"Before I was born, he and others in the area got together to make music, as they often called it back then. They met somewhere, usually at a friend's house, to play and sing," Connie reminisced. Henry was forty-one when Connie was born. By the time she came along, he didn't play the banjo as much as he used to.

My Daddy Was A Banjo Pickin' Man
By Jack Shelton and Connie Hopper

My daddy was a banjo pickin' man.
Daddy never had a gospel band.
But when we'd start to sing,
he'd make his banjo ring.
His pickin' was the best in the land.

My daddy was a banjo pickin' man.
He loved the Lord and helped his preacher man.
When we were all at home, he'd play and sing a song
About our little church in the bend.

My daddy was a banjo pickin' man.
He'd pick and sing with the harvest hands.
They'd reap his fields of white and listen to his pickin' at night.
His music told the story of their lives.

And now my Daddy's gone to be on high.
He joined that royal band up in the sky.
And if you'll listen close, you'll clearly hear the notes
Of a golden five-string coming thru the night.

The Shelton family attended Eden Methodist Church. Henry was a member of a local Gospel singing group as far back as anyone remembers. One group he belonged to had a local radio program, which was broadcast in the county for many years. The fellows sang

Sisters: Wilma and Connie

at various church services and funerals in the area.

Henry loved singing and always sang from the heart. Although he never journeyed outside the area to perform and never stayed overnight to sing, he was well known in the local area. He also led the singing at the Shelton family home church. He sang baritone.

"I remember when Dad told us stories. He sometimes even sang us to sleep at night while he played banjo, too," Connie's sister, Wilma Shelton Fontain, remembered. "By the time I got old enough to really appreciate it, Dad said his fingers were too stiff and didn't play much anymore.

"At one time he could play anything fast! I remember one song he played—'Going Up Cripple Creek'—I remember the good feelings we all had when Daddy got out his banjo," she said.

Wilma said that when she was around twelve, her Uncle Ed passed away and her father was asked to sing "The Old Rugged Cross" at the funeral. He sang without musical accompaniment. She still recalls how proud she was when she overheard an adult behind her whisper, "He's as good as Red Foley!"

"Besides music, I also remember how Daddy cut hair for my brothers," Connie said. He also cut hair for neighbors. When they were too busy to get to the barber shop, they popped in at the Shelton household and asked, 'Henry, got time to cut my hair?'

"My cousin's husband once gave Daddy some nice white Arrow dress

One of Connie's school photos

48

shirts for Christmas because he had cut his hair for him throughout the year. He was pretty good at it, too."

At harvest time, Mary Lou often sat on the porch with washtubs full of ripe tomatoes or other fruits or vegetables, preparing them to be "put up." Canning and preserving foods were necessaries on the Shelton farm. She worked tirelessly and her daughters usually joined in and helped with the canning process. Connie remembers that amid working in the field, her mother canned hundreds of half-gallon, quart, and pint jars of fruit from the farm orchards and vegetables from the garden.

"Mama had the reputation of being one of the best cooks in the county. Her fried chicken was unmatched," Connie remembered. "She could also whip up a Lazy Apple Pie in no time that was to die for!"

Connie

Mary Lou crocheted intricate doilies, which adorned the end tables and dressers in the farmhouse. She also made clothes for all the family. "I remember once when I was in seventh grade our school class was going on a picnic. Because it was so hot, we were all allowed to wear shorts—moderate of course. However, I didn't own any! The night before the picnic, Mama sorted through her cloth remnants and found enough material to make a pair of shorts and a shirt. I was so proud!"

Connie also recalled that her mother often made her sister, Wilma, and her dresses out of XX Daisy feedsacks. The sacks, usually made of tight percale woven cotton, were printed with floral designs, which seemed perfect for dresses and other clothing. Some of the sack designs had delicate lavender daisies or large violet peonies. Others displayed white daisies on light pink backgrounds. Actually, there were countless color combinations and designs available on the sacks.

Since farm life demanded a great deal of effort, every member of the family was expected to toil in the field and hoe tobacco—even the

Connie

youngest of the family, Wilma and Connie.

The Shelton girls never worked quite as hard as their brothers. Connie and Wilma, being closest in age, were likely spared from the hardest work, for times had changed and the economy was steadily improving by the time they were old enough to assist.

"However, when summertime came, everybody worked! You labored hard from the time you got up in the morning until bedtime. I remember going to the house from the tobacco barns at ten o'clock at night, knowing I had to be right back there first thing in the morning," Wilma said.

After a day in the hot field, sleep came especially easy for everyone. After their brothers grew up and moved out, Connie and Wilma spent even more time in the fields.

For relaxation on the farm, Connie often rode her bicycle up and down the lane. "As young girls, my sisters and I went down to the creek and had a lot of fun. We'd sneak off after the chores were done. It was at the creek that we could cool off," Connie said. "We also enjoyed making playhouses, too. We spent hours getting our playhouse ready. Wilma and I had elaborate tea parties."

When Connie was a bit older, her father put up a basketball goal and suspended it from the peak of the barn. "I played basketball all the time," Connie reminisced, explaining that this was the one sport she really enjoyed all through junior high and high school. It made perfect sense since Connie was tall and had a natural aptitude for the game.

Wilma told about a time when she was in college and she traveled

Connie works on the farm

home one weekend. Her father, Henry, was laughing about an experience that had just happened. Connie had not been feeling well that morning and stayed home from school. Around lunchtime, when Connie was beginning to feel better, the principal called and asked her to come back to school for at least one hour. Because of school rules, the basketball team couldn't technically let Connie play during that evening's game unless she attended school that day. They obviously needed her!

Connie was one of the star basketball players for the school.

Connie's older sister, Hilda, was also a star basketball player and later the valedictorian of her graduating class.

Mary Lou could chord a little on the piano and enjoyed picking out tunes and playing church hymns. She also played several other instruments when she was young, including guitar and auto harp.

She sang alto, but the only time any of the children ever heard her sing was at church. Perhaps she got her love for music from her parents, for she had the fiddle and auto harp her father had once played.

Although she always loved music, there was little time to practice, for she worked constantly. Tobacco farming was an all-consuming proposition during its season.

Also, Mary Lou kept a dahlia bed and tended a lovely flower garden. As far back as her children can recall, she raised a wide variety of plants, but it was caring for the dahlia bed that she enjoyed the most. She dug them up at wintertime and re-planted in spring. She also planted rose bushes and generally had a green thumb when it came to beautifying the yard around the farmhouse.

Billy Shelton, a WWII veteran who once helped liberate the concentration camps in Germany, spoke of his mother: "Mama never had any washing machines or electric dryers. She had an old washtub and washboard. She carried her own water from the spring (there was no inside plumbing), and she hung all our clothes on a clothesline to dry. She ironed everything once the clothes were taken down from the line.

"Looking back, I wonder how in the world she managed to do all that and, at the same time, go out into the field every day!"

Connie remembered an unusual conversation with her mother:

"Mama once told me that when she first started having children, she promised herself she would never let her children get as close to her as she had been to her own mother. The reason why was that when Mama's mother passed away, she grieved so long. She almost never got over her mother's death.

"However, she couldn't help herself, apparently, because she loved us deeply and was extremely close to each of us. In fact, a friend of our family once said that had she met any of us individually, she would have thought of us as an only child."

Mary Lou was a caring mother and had the ability to make each child feel as if he or she was special and adored.

"Mama always did what was right and taught us the same principles," Connie added.

Sparkling Water Swirled

Mary Lou and Henry called the fast-moving stream behind their home Pretty Creek. The creek, actually an extension of Belews Creek, was the boundary near the rear property line. Their acreage was an attractive wooded area where large stones bordered a creek all along its breadth and fresh sparkling water swirled and bubbled over the rocks.

Years later, as an adult, Connie wrote a touching song about the creek, with her brother, Jack.

Pretty Creek
By Connie Hopper and Jack Shelton

Chorus

Mama, she named it the Pretty Creek
Because she knew that it was in God's plan
To show her children of His handiwork
A beauty not made by mortal man.

Verse 1

In the summertime we'd romp o'er the rile rocks
Laughing and splashing, as we'd go
Watching the rainbows through the misty skies

A promise and a sign of long ago.

Verse 2

From our house we could see the Blue Ridge Mountains.
As the glowing sunset framed the mountain peak,
Our tender hearts were stirred by God's beauty
And His special gift to us the Pretty Creek

Verse 3

One early morn a big long car came our way.
The man told Daddy, "Sir, you'll have to leave,
Because the double creeks that flow in back of your house—
That's the kind of place the power company needs."

Verse 4

Now time has passed and the creek is gone from our sight
A big lake covers where we once called home.
But again will Mama show us pretty waters
When we're by the river flowing from the throne.

As the song implies, the original farm is now gone, because the entire area has since been covered over by water, submerged at the bottom of what became Belews Lake.

In the mid-1960s the state of North Carolina and the electric company embarked on an aggressive collaborative state-park project, whereby the Shelton farm and other portions of property in the area were purchased, or seized, to create a lake and supply additional electricity for Rockingham and surrounding county customers. Until the inevitable happened, Henry and Mary Lou nourished the hope that the electric company would change their plans.

Mary Lou and Henry and their children had lived near Stokesdale, along Pretty Creek, for over forty years at the time they were forced to move.

Charles, Connie's oldest brother, had been severely mentally handicapped since birth. His mother nearly died during childbirth.

53

It's suspected that there was a lack of oxygen and other complications during Charles' birth.

When Connie was a very small girl, they listened to Saturday afternoon preachers on the radio. One time, after listening to a program for a while, Charles took Connie by the hand and led her to the piano. He wanted her to play hymns just like those he heard during the Gospel Hour. Connie attempted to pick out a melody while he imitated the preacher he'd heard on the airwaves.

Connie's dear brother, Charles

It was in those days of pretend play with her brother that Connie first showed a budding interest in piano. Tinkering around on the ivories after weekly radio shows was how she first became interested in music.

On the farm, Charles' main job was to carry water to the planter when the family was planting tobacco. He did it by himself, and this was a task he did well. Claude also recalls how he worked especially hard on other jobs, adding: "Charles worked alongside other members of the family. He worked just as much and as hard as his brothers, doing things he was capable of doing. For example, he tied out the cows, fetched water and spread fertilizer."

"Charles had right good common sense, but when it pertains to formal education, he never could learn much of anything," said Billy Shelton, his brother.

"He also had an unusual talent for keeping time. When I used to be plowing with the mules in the field, Charles would bring water from the spring for me to drink. When he'd came up to me, I'd always ask, 'Charles, what time is it?' Sure enough, he could tell me—without a watch. If I checked my own watch, I was always amazed that he never missed the time by more than five minutes!"

Connie believes Charles' uncanny ability to tell time was due to an extra-sensitive internal clock. She compares him to other mentally challenged individuals who have unusual natural abilities or display a brilliant aptitude in music or mathematics.

Connie told an interesting story that illustrates Charles' gift: "Some years ago, in 1996, Charles had a leaking blood vessel and had to have minor brain surgery. My sister happened to tell his doctor about Charles' mysterious capacity to tell time. The doctor didn't believe her."

Charles had the surgery and afterwards slept for more than twenty-four hours straight in recovery. When he finally started to rouse, the doctor came in, smiled slyly and asked, "So, Charles, what time is it?"

At that point Charles, who was still groggy from the sedative, opened his eyes, looked at the doctor and told him the exact time— down to the very minute.

The astonished surgeon became an instant believer in Charles' natural talent.

"Another knack Charles had was for remembering people and faces. He never forgot a person once he met him or her," Billy added.

Connie said, "In more recent years, my brother Jack eventually moved back into the homeplace with Charles. They lived together for a long time. Jack was not in such good health, and, of course, Charles was handicapped.

"My sisters, Hilda and Wilma and I took turns making weekly visits to the house for many years," Connie said. "It was important to do little things for Charles that he couldn't do for himself."

Charles and Jack lived together for more than fifteen years, up until Jack's death. After that Charles lived in an extended-care facility until his death in 2005, where health care providers assisted with his special needs. Connie and her sisters continued to play a large role in his life. Connie spent a great deal of time with him, up until his passing.

"It's been personally touching and encouraging for me to see how Connie has devoted herself to her brother over the years," said Dennis Sparks, the Hoppers' booking agent. "Outside of the family, I doubt anyone recognizes how much time and effort Connie gave toward Charles at the rest home. It was as if Charles was not just her brother but, in a sense, her child, for she always lovingly cared for him."

Chapter 10
Connie's Hollow Leg

The light in the eyes of him whose heart is joyful, rejoices the heart of others...

— Proverbs 15:30

One day the Sheltons, with children Wilma and Connie, were traveling across the county to visit grandparents of the children. Along the way, the kids, who were small children at the time, begged their father to stop and buy candy. Finally, in desperation to end the pleading and bellyaching, he stopped at a country store and bought each of the children "a nickel's worth of candy."

Connie

"I remember it was some unusual flavor or type of gumdrops. I can't remember what they were called now," Connie said, laughing as she recalled the incident. "All I remember is how I didn't like the candy at all! Of course, I wasn't about to tell Daddy since we had begged and pleaded for him to stop in the first place. So I thought to myself, 'I'll just sneak and throw this candy out the car door.' "

They were riding in a 1940 four-door Chrysler with what are now termed suicide doors that open toward the back. Connie quietly opened the door. Within a split second, she was whisked out and thrown to the dirt and gravel road!

"The episode cut my head open and I temporarily lost consciousness—blacked-out! All I remember is putting my hand on the door handle. When I came to, I was on the ground. I tried to get up because I realized Mom and Dad's car was leaving me.

"As they drove on, Mama said, 'Henry, I feel a draft.' She turned around and exclaimed, 'Where's Connie? She's gone!' "

Henry hit the brake and frantically turned the station wagon around. The family raced back to Connie, who was standing in the roadway bleeding. Once they reached her, Henry and Mary Lou grabbed her up and helped her back into the car.

"Mama held me on her lap. We went directly to our family doctor's house and then on to the hospital."

Connie squirmed, wiggled and hollered as the doctors fought to get her to lie still so he could stitch the wound. They finally asked Henry to leave the room, since he was also getting upset over the commotion.

"Daddy later said it took six adults to hold me down on the table," Connie said, grinning. "And I was only four years old! I can still remember lying on that table in the emergency room and the doctors putting ether over my face."

Hankering For Corn Pie

"I remember there was a spice apple tree in our back yard," Wilma recalled. "In the summertime Connie and I climbed to the very top of the tree and sat on the limbs. Nobody knew we were up there, because we were so high that no one could see us. Once my brother, Don, happened to be in the loft of the barn. He discovered us in the tree and got excited and hollered, 'Wilma! Connie! You're going to get killed!' He went directly to Mom and Dad and told on us! Well, we didn't climb the tree anymore after that."

When Connie and Wilma came home from school, their parents were usually in the field. The girls went into the house and prepared a simple snack before they went to the field, too.

"I remember one time when Connie was in the seventh grade, we came home and she couldn't find anything she wanted to eat, so she scrambled two eggs and made toast. She sat down and ate that, and then got up and scrambled a couple more eggs. Then, after that, she scrambled even more! Though she had a healthy appetite, she was always extremely thin, with long legs. I guess she was going through a growth spurt. I remember Dad used to tease her about her appetite and said she had a hollow leg," Wilma said.

"Connie captivated people wherever she went. I recall one occasion when we were teenagers, she couldn't find anything that appealed to her on the menu at a restaurant in Madison. After the waitress asked her what she'd really like, Connie said, 'Well, I'd really like to have corn pie.' After Connie described how it was prepared, the cook tried to prepare it especially for her.

"Corn pie was a dish Mama made us in the summertime. Mama took fresh baked bread and slathered it with butter, and poured creamed corn over the hot bread. Sure enough, after Connie asked for it, the cook cheerfully fixed corn pie to her specifications."

"Connie was always independent, too. I admire that in her. When she saw something she wanted to do, she had the confidence to go for it!"

As soon as Connie could drive, she got her license and landed a job at the movie theatre in Madison, working at the concession stand. She seemed to have the inner confidence to reach out of her comfort zone and accomplish objectives.

The Passing Of A Generation

Unfortunately, as the years have gone by, Connie has lost several of her loved ones.

"Mom and Dad have since gone on to Heaven — Daddy in 1981, and Mom in 1986," Connie said, trying to describe what a great loss it has been for her and her family.

In a letter, dated December 22, 1980, Connie's father, Henry Shelton, scrawled a poignant note to his family, which he then tucked away in his worn Bible.

To my family:

This is my message of love to you all.

You have been so good to your mother, Charles and me through all the years as we have grown older. By the grace of God, I feel sure that all of you will—all through your life—never be burdened with more than you can bear.

We were never promised life would all be easy, but by faith in God we can accomplish many things in life. I want you to know that I love every one of you: sons and daughters, sons-in-law, daughters-in-law, grandchildren, great-grandchildren and I pray God's blessings on every one.

I don't think we can hate anyone in this world and love God; we are taught to love each other and our neighbors as ourselves. Vengeance is mine saith the Lord; I will repay.

Henry Evan Shelton

"Daddy told me about the letter the night he was taken to the emergency room. He said that he had not completed the letter; but I'm thankful for what he had written. He passed away four days later," Connie said.

Heaven is even sweeter knowing that loved ones are there, in Christ's presence, anticipating a great reunion day. "I know we will all be together again," Connie said softly. "The rest of my siblings live nearby, except for one brother who lives in Greenville, South Carolina."

The Shelton children have many years of warmhearted memories about life on the farm and with family. Though the homeplace is no longer standing, those vivid recollections live on.

The Shelton family enjoy being together at home. Music was always a part of their lives. Above, Connie plays the piano as the others sing hymns.

59

Chapter 11
Sears and Roebuck Guitar

Music washes away from the soul the dust of every-day life.

— Berthold Auerbach

When Claude Hopper was a young teen, he asked his older sister to drive him to a cousin's home to buy a folk guitar that was for sale. He had picked many buckets of blackberries and helped crop tobacco for weeks to earn the seven dollars needed to buy the Sears and Roebuck Silvertone guitar.

Claude and his guitar

It was a traditional box style, made of varnished natural wood—attractive but extremely difficult to play. The heavy-gauge guitar strings were so far from the fret-board that Claude's short fingers, which barely wrapped around the fret board, would sometimes bleed from pressing the strings down.

He finally figured out how to shave down the bridge, thereby lowering the strings to make playing the Silvertone a little easier. From the day he purchased it, he practiced on the front porch every chance he could—first thing after school, during breaks between farm duties and while his brothers went to supper.

"While he strummed his guitar, all of our laughing and snide comments fell on deaf ears," Claude's brother, Wayne, recalled as he shook his head. "At that time, the sounds that emanated from the instrument were far from pleasant."

During the same time period, Claude often listened to WCKY Radio, broadcast out of Cincinnati, Ohio, where Lonnie Glosson and Wayne Raney had a popular Saturday night program. A certain commercial advertisement during that radio show offered an instruction-

Claude

al booklet on how to play guitar.

Claude saved enough money to order the book. The lessons in that book taught him how to play chords, at least enough to play fairly well. He continued to practice diligently and his abilities grew. Soon he was good enough to sing and play at high school functions, talent shows and even musicals.

"My friends and I liked to get together and hold jam sessions. One friend had an electric guitar and I had my Sears acoustic, so I accompanied him, strumming rhythm. I only knew basic chords, but I had a great time!"

Besides playing and singing for school assemblies and events, once Claude was given the opportunity to travel to Raleigh to play and sing during the annual convention of the Future Farmers of America.

"I'd play and sing at barn dances, hayrides and functions like that. I even attempted to play on the school bus on the way to and from school," Claude recalled with a grin.

Dating In High School

Wayne Hopper, more than any of the other siblings, is the family storyteller and jokester. He's the first person in the Hopper family to get everyone else laughing uncontrollably. It's said he can begin to tell a story and by the time he's done, everyone in the room is nearly rolling on the floor in laughter. His comedic timing is superb and he has a gift for telling tall tales laced with tinges of sarcasm.

In his own words, Wayne described how as a teenager it was always his desire to go on double-dates with his brother, Claude:

Claude was always extremely popular in school; he dated the prettiest girls. He also had a car! Since he had the girls and a car (and since I didn't), I hung around him! Besides, I figured that eventually one of his girlfriends might have a sister.

Lo and behold, one night Claude took me up on my double-dating idea. He told me about a certain girl he was going to take out, and

61

that she had a sister she wanted to bring along.

Of course I shouted, "I'm in!"

That evening when we arrived at Claude's girlfriend's house, he and I went inside and there she was ... Claude's date was beautiful! We stood in the kitchen and talked with her for several minutes. Finally, I was getting overly anxious, so I nudged Claude and whispered, "Hey, where is her *gorgeous* sister?"

Claude ignored me for a minute or two. After several more nudges, he finally asked his date, "Well, Wayne's dying to meet your sister. Is she still coming along?"

She smiled and said matter-of-factly, "Oh, yes, but she's still upstairs ... uh ... shaving!"

My mouth dropped open when her sister eventually entered the room. From the dark shadows on her chin and over her lip, it was apparent it wasn't just legs that needed shaving! *Oh no!*

I'm not saying she was exactly homely, but if this girl applied for a national ugly contest they'd tell her, *"Sorry, no professionals!"*

I never had Claude's luck with the ladies. I guess [like Rodney Dangerfield] I never got any respect.

Chapter 12
Billy Crash Craddock

I now know with certainty that God was watching over me and that's the way it should have been. I wasn't meant to go to New York.

— Connie Hopper

Looking back on her childhood, Connie Shelton loved all forms of music. From the earliest age she enjoyed country and western, bluegrass, church hymns and eventually even rock-n-roll.

"We were fortunate that the electric company strung wires in 1940, and ran electric wires to our house at the time I was born. So, Dad turned the radio on to hear the news and of course we got country music.The first thing Daddy did when he got up in the morning was turn on the radio, around 5:30 or 6:00 o'clock," Connie said.

"Daddy once took us to hear a local Gospel group at Huntsville Elementary School. I was in grammar school at the time. I had never heard a singing group in person, and I really liked it."

Before that occasion, the only time Connie heard anything like Gospel quartets or groups was on the radio when Gospel songs were played daily around lunchtime, or on extended programs on Saturday nights.

"I always tried to pick out tunes on our piano," Connie said. "Finally, I got to where I could play a little bit with two hands."

"We lived in a four-room house when I was very young," Connie's sister, Wilma, explained. The upright piano was in the sit-

Connie at the Shelton homeplace

ting room and before Connie's fingers could span any distance at all, she was playing tunes.

"Mom decided I needed piano lessons," Wilma said. "Connie sat on the floor right outside the living room as I earnestly practiced. I tried and tried to play, but it never sounded quite right. When I finished my practice, Connie would come in and sit down on the piano stool and play the same song I'd just tried to play. Her version sounded just like it was supposed to sound!"

The family sensed Connie had a special gift from the beginning; soon Connie figured out how to play the piano on her own. Two of her older sisters had taken formal lessons earlier, and Connie learned to read music by studying their instruction books. "I memorized all those little sayings, like 'Every Good Boy Does Fine,' 'F-A-C-E,' and 'All Cows Eat Grass,' which helped me learn my notes. Then I somehow figured out where those particular notes were on the piano.

"Daddy also had the Stamps-Baxter 'do-re-mi' shaped-note method books. I eventually learned music from those, too," Connie explained.

When Connie was about eight years old, her father, Henry, became superintendent of the Sunday school program at their church. When the regular church pianist occasionally missed a Sunday, Connie was asked to be the substitute.

"I even played for the preaching service," Connie remembered, "but I could only play in a few keys. I can still recall a time when our pastor wanted me to play 'My Faith Looks Up to Thee.' I knew the hymn, but I didn't know it in E-flat, like it's written in the hymnal. I only knew it in the key of C, so that's where I played it!

"I was embarrassed when I looked up at the preacher, after I started playing the song. He was gazing down at me as if he were thinking, 'Just what key do you have this in, little girl?'"

The congregation noticeably had difficulty singing the hymn in the much lower key. They struggled through what seemed like four especially long verses.

As Connie grew older and learned more, she eventually played piano for her father and his singing group at church.

Connie said they didn't really sing the type of songs that the Gospel groups were singing. Instead, most of their repertoire came directly from the church choir book or hymnal, note-for-note.

"Then one of my cousins started singing with a group and he told me the Hopper Brothers had a singing group, too. I occasionally went around to hear them, usually at churches in the county. I remember that the brothers really seemed to enjoy what they were doing and I liked them.

"Even as a pre-teen, and later as a teenage girl, I cherished the hymns of the church, but I also loved pop songs. The hit songs of the day were really good tunes, like 'How Much is That Doggie in the Window?'"

Singers of that period, in the early 1950s, included artists like Patti Page, Teresa Brewer, the Ames Brothers, the Four Aces and Nat King Cole. Frank Sinatra was still producing hit songs even though the height of his popularity was in the 1940s.

Then Elvis Presley and the dawn of rock-n-roll came along. Of course, as a teenager, Connie enjoyed this new music that was captivating a generation.

"Our older brothers forbade Wilma and me from going to Five Oakes Dance Hall, so we didn't," Connie said, remembering how they both loved music.

The Crush On Claude

Connie recalls one particular summer day when she was a young teenager that her cousin, Tucker Shelton, came to the house to bring her father's banjo back after working on it. He brought along his friend, Claude Hopper, who would have been a junior when school resumed in the fall. "Tucker was older than Claude and a neighbor to the Hoppers," Connie said. "He was not as accomplished on the banjo as Daddy but he played a while on that occasion and then handed the banjo to Daddy. Then Tucker and Claude played guitars."

Claude, as a teenager

Connie couldn't help herself. She immediately picked up the tune and started playing it on the piano inside. The two fellows moved into the house to join her. Connie had never met a boy from the high school (Tucker was out of school), although

65

Connie was impressed with Claude

she was preparing to start her freshman year.

"I had this immediate crush on Claude!" Connie admitted, with a smile. "We played songs for some time that night, and I really thought Claude was something. He made quite an impression on me," she said, as she chuckled. "Then, after summer was over, I started high school. It was then that I saw how all the girls hung around Claude. He was two years ahead of me and very popular! So, I figured right then that nothing would ever come of it. I gave up on my Hopper crush after that. I remember that Claude was eventually voted most popular in his senior class."

Even as a high school student, Connie really had no grasp of the fact there was a separate field of music called Southern Gospel. In a *Singing News Magazine* article, she once said: "It never dawned on me that the field of Gospel music even existed, where groups traveled and performed. I thought those types of songs were only sung in church (or on the Radio Gospel Hour)."

At the same time, Connie started playing the piano for a mixed pop group in high school, performing a mixture of 1950s pop and rock-n-roll tunes, like "Little Darlin!" They were considered quite talented and gained a certain amount of notoriety in the area, even performing at the Plantation Supper Club, in Greensboro.

"I remember auditioning at the Plantation Club. After we finished our list of songs, the owner, Mr. Koury, didn't say much to the rest of the group. He came over to me and said, 'Ma'am, I'm working with this new artist and his name is Billy Crash Craddock, from Greensboro. Billy is going to do some record demos in New York. It's hard to find a good piano player who can play like you're playing. Would you consider going, too?'"

Connie blushed and looked warily toward the floor as she stam-

Connie

mered, "Well … uh … I don't know."

Connie never called Mr. Koury back as he'd asked, and she never heard anything more about the trip. Craddock, however, went on to record a string of number one pop singles: "Rub It In," "Ruby Baby," "Broken Down In Tiny Pieces," "Easy As Pie," "Sweet Magnolia Blossom," "Ain't Nothin' Shakin'" and "Dream Lover." Connie never played at the Plantation Supper Club, for the fellows in the group went their separate ways shortly after the audition.

Connie later said, "In retrospect, I know with great certainty that God was watching over me and it all went the way it should have gone. I wasn't meant to go to New York. The Lord had something else in mind for my life.

"After high school graduation, I still enjoyed playing the piano, but my greatest aspiration was to get a job so I could make money! I was in my late teens and I wanted to have two pairs of shoes!" she said with a chuckle. "We had everything we needed at home, with all the necessities. But I guess I just wanted some money to jingle in my pocket."

Chapter 13
Leaving The Farm

To accomplish great things we must not only act, but also dream; not only plan, but also believe.

— Unknown

Claude said that one of the greatest personal struggles of his life happened when he was a teenager. It was when his father told him it was time for him to be on his own. A heartbreaking episode at the time for Claude, the conversation occurred right after his high-school graduation in 1957.

"Dad didn't actually come out and tell me to move out. Instead, he looked at me sternly and said, 'Son, this farm is not big enough for all of us now. Do you understand?'

"I definitely understood. I realized then that I had to 'root-hog or die'," Claude said. "Actually, looking back at it all, Dad was right. The farm wasn't big enough. Yet I was absolutely distraught for the moment. Dad temporarily took away my dream."

Surely Archer knew how much his son, Claude, loved the homeplace. Likewise, he knew Claude's desire was to one day inherit a portion of the property. From his earliest memories, Claude yearned to make farming his lifelong occupation.

Perhaps Archer thought pressuring his son into going out on his own was what it would take to persuade him to grow up into a responsible adult and further his education; or maybe it was just a bad period of time for farming and Archer overreacted

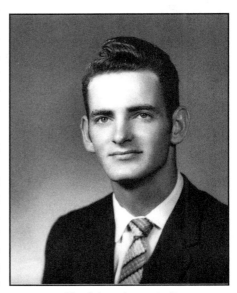

Claude's senior portrait

to the financial pressures of keeping the farm running.

Regardless, Claude didn't fully understand his father's reasoning at the moment, but reluctantly went out on his own. He borrowed enough money from his older sister, Virginia, to attend college for one year. He entered Elon College near his home, which turned out to be a positive experience. He also worked for the college library to help pay his way. He eventually paid Virginia back for the loan as he continued to support himself.

"I learned a valuable lesson in life from my history teacher while I was in college," Claude reminisced. "The professor was from Germany and spoke broken English. He graded us on pop questions, which represented much of our overall grade. When the course began, he told us that if we weren't prepared for a pop question, we were to tell him before class.

"One Monday morning I walked into class and he said, with his heavy German accent, 'Mista' Hoppa, zould you take the nexta question please?' I responded, 'Oh, sir, I am not prepared.'

"He said dryly, 'Zid you tell me before class zat you were not prepared, Mista' Hoppa?'"

Claude hung his head and answered, "No, sir, I forgot."

"Well, Mista' Hoppa, you gambled and vhen you gamble zometimes you vin and zometimes you lose. Today you lose and dats a ZERO," the teacher said, as he called on the next student, "... Nexta!"

Clauded learned from the experience, and added: "Since that day, I have always tried to be prepared, regardless of the circumstances in life, so I won't get a 'zero' again."

In keeping with Claude's lesson, in 2 Timothy, we are are told to "Preach the word; be instant in season, out of season; reprove, rebuke, exhort with all long suffering and doctrine." Being prepared is important in life and in service to the Lord.

Claude has also gained a different perspective since the long ago difficult experience of being asked to leave the farm: as painful as it was for him at the time, he sees now that it helped him learn to rely upon Christ.

"In hindsight, this was really the greatest thing Dad taught me: independence and reliance on Jesus for the future. Dad made me realize that I needed to get out and find my own destiny. Through the process, I also grew in confidence and faith."

Chapter 14
First Gospel Concert

The music and the message affected me so much that
evening that I began to weep.

— Claude Hopper

By the early 1950s, WSJS Radio, out of Winston-Salem, North
Carolina, played Gospel music programs at various intervals during
the day. Most of the time the signal was crystal clear on Claude's bat-
tery-operated radio. The batteries were large and cumbersome (nearly the size of a car battery) but they made the magic of radio possible.

It was on the radio that Claude first heard legendary Southern
Gospel groups like the Chuck Wagon Gang. He was impressed with
the group's tightly woven harmonies and the meaning behind their
lyrics. It's worthy of note that both Claude and Connie, coincidentally, were inspired by this famous group.

"In 1956, I went to my first live Southern Gospel concert, held in
Winston-Salem, at Reynolds Auditorium," Claude remembered.
"While I had heard some of this kind of music on the radio before, I
had never gone to a concert and experienced it in person.

"That night I saw the legendary Statesmen, the Blackwood
Brothers, Homeland Harmony and the Speer Family. I was dating
another girl at the time, and she went with me."

During the evening, the music and the message affected Claude
to such a degree that at one point he began to weep. "You know, I
could hardly contain myself, and I thought, 'This is exactly what I
want to do!'

"As I think back on that moment, I don't really know what my
date thought of me—nor did I care. There I was weeping and crying
over the words and the music. It obviously wasn't affecting her in the
same manner. Nonetheless, I was never the same after that night!"

It was at that concert that Claude sensed some sort of calling on
his life. He didn't totally understand it at the time, and he surely had
no idea what the future ramifications would be. Yet, Claude knew the
Lord seemed to be directing him toward spreading the Gospel

through music, if only on a local basis.

He also detected the Lord's confirmation after he talked about the concert with his brothers the next day. Claude's enthusiasm and passion for Southern Gospel music proved to be contagious.

Steve, Will, Claude and Monroe

Brothers Begin Singing

Not long after experiencing his first concert, Claude talked his brothers into singing with him around the kitchen table at home.

"We were singing 'Farther Along,'" Claude remembered. "After we sang for a few minutes, I became so excited that I got on the telephone and called my sister, Virginia, and said, 'Hey, I want you to listen to this!'"

Claude held the phone receiver at arm's length while his brothers sang another verse of the hymn. Virginia listened and was amazed that her brothers sounded so good. This was the informal beginning of the singing group.

"After that time we started practicing every Friday night. Within weeks, we began talking about singing in front of others," Claude said. "From then on we officially started calling ourselves the Hopper Brothers."

Claude wrote this letter to Virginia shortly after the Hopper

Brothers were organized:

> Virginia,
>
> We are singing and getting a number of invita-
> tions. Richard is good as the lead and we are all learn-
> ing. Monroe and Paul are improving; and Will and
> Steve are doing good. I'm so proud of them!
>
> I know the Lord is with me every time I sing
> because it is the greatest feeling that I have ever had.
> Nobody knows the power of the Holy Spirit until they
> have experienced Him. The Lord has wonderfully
> blessed and watched over us.
>
> I don't think I have ever felt more welcomed and
> more at home than I did on Sunday evening at Fancy
> Gap Baptist Church, in Virginia. The boys really sur-
> prised me. I have never heard them sing the way they
> did on Sunday night since we have been singing
> together.
>
> The congregation was so responsive to us. The
> more we sang, the more they wanted us to sing. It was
> the first time my hand got tired from shaking hands
> with people. You just can't beat those mountain peo-
> ple. I think everything happens for good to those who
> love the Lord. A big change has come in all of us since
> we have been singing, and I hope we never break up.
>
> Love,
> Claude

Monroe explained how, as tobacco farmers, he and his brothers
had assignments to stay at the barn and cure tobacco at night. It was
during those long evenings that they sang while Claude picked his
guitar.

Eventually word about the fellows got around the Rockingham
County area and preachers began to invite the Hopper Brothers to
homecomings, revival services and church picnics.

"Most of the time all we received was a meal in exchange for singing — if we were lucky," Monroe laughed, "but that was really okay with us! We just enjoyed singin'!"

Then as the Hopper boys improved, they entered singing competitions with other Gospel groups, like at the Grove Sing in Benson, North Carolina.

"I remember we once won a singing competition in Fayetteville. After that, we won several other contests in the area," Monroe added. With each win, the Hopper Brothers' confidence grew. The boys soon became completely engrossed in music. It was exciting to sing together, and people seemed to enjoy them, for their voices blended so well.

In the beginning, the group consisted of brothers Claude, Will, Steve, Monroe and Paul. Wayne also participated during the first months but soon stepped aside when he went on to college.

Wayne joked about his brief involvement with the group: "You know, I'm proud to say I started out singing with my brothers. But before too long, the fellows stopped telling me where they were practicing [or if they did tell me a place, when I arrived, everybody was already gone]. All you could hear was the distant sound of crickets chirping!

"I don't understand it," he said, as he chuckled. "You know, I still think I was pretty good! Okay, maybe 'good' is the wrong word to describe it. Actually, I was loud—good and loud! Maybe I was half-a-bubble off key, but I was always good and loud!"

The original Hopper Brothers were accompanied by piano and guitar. Claude said: "I played guitar, and our first piano player was a girl by the name of Ann Johnson. She played strictly by sheet music. I never dated Ann, but I do recall that we often went to Greensboro together. We headed for the music store to find new sheet music for the group. When we could afford them, we especially loved Stamps-Baxter songbooks."

In due course, the brothers went to see a music teacher in Madison, Mrs. C.T. Sutherland. She was a kindly woman with a great deal of knowledge about music. She helped them understand more about singing

Steve Hopper

73

Claude

separate parts.

"I was singing tenor, but Mrs. Sutherland switched me to lead," Claude said. "Will was singing bass; she switched him to tenor, and Monroe and Paul to bass. Steve sang baritone."

Mrs. Sutherland started pulling the harmony together for the boys.

"Later, Steve suggested we try to get this girl, Connie Shelton, from Stokesdale, to play for us," Claude recalled. "I definitely remembered Connie from high school when she played piano in some of our assembly programs and with her pop group. I also knew she was an excellent basketball player."

Unbeknownst to them, God's plan was unfolding before their very eyes.

Chapter 15
Life-Changing Stoplight

There are many things in life that will catch your eye.
But only a few will catch your heart...

— Ben Crenshaw

After Connie Shelton graduated from high school and the pop group disbanded, she presumed her piano-playing days were over, so she set her sights on working and becoming independent.

"In my thinking now, this shows how God is. He had something far different in mind," Connie reminisced. In the fall of 1958, she was driving through the little downtown section of neighboring Madison and noticed Claude Hopper standing on a street corner, near the intersection. When she stopped for the red light at the intersection, she glanced over his way.

Claude, remembering the serendipitous encounter, elaborated: "At the time I was working part-time at the A&P grocery store. I was on my lunch break when I saw Connie pull up to the stop. It was my big chance to ask her to play piano for us!"

Claude smiled from the corner and motioned for her to roll down the car window. Claude hollered: "Hey, Connie! My brothers and I are singing together in a Gospel quartet. Would you be interested in playing for us?"

Connie answered, "I'll have to think about it." Seconds later the light turned green and she found herself blurting: "Uh-oh-okay!"

"From the first day she started with us, Connie knew more about shaped note parts and quartet-style than anyone else we knew. She started helping us instantly! We started going to Connie's parents' house to work on vocal arrangements," Claude remembered.

Eventually, Claude took Connie to her first live Southern Gospel concert, where professional groups performed.

"I didn't even know those types of events existed. I fell in love with the music I heard. I won't say I immediately knew I wanted to do that kind of thing professionally, but I do recall thinking that if I was going to continue to play piano and sing, I wanted to play and

"We always had a great time when we were together," Connie said.

sing what I heard on stage," Connie once told a *Singing News Magazine* reporter.

Looking back, Connie can see God's providential hand in all that was happening. She had been bitten by the music bug years before, and instead of letting her go down a path of potential trouble (in the rock-and-roll industry), the Lord closed some doors and opened others. One of the doors that opened was the opportunity to be involved in Southern Gospel music with the Hopper Brothers.

"I recognized immediately that it was a whole lot more than just playing and singing songs. It's about the powerful message more than it is about the music."

Claude's sister, Virginia, recalls the first time she met Connie: "I remember when she first started playing for Claude and the boys. They were scheduled to sing at Little Valley Church. I've got a lovely photograph of Connie walking down the driveway that evening. Her hair was short, you know, kind of like she wore it when she played basketball. I had long heard of her father, Henry Shelton, and his singing group. They sang at funerals and other occasions for years."

Claude And Connie's Courtship

Claude was a snappy dresser in the 1950s. On special occasions, he wore wide-lapels, pinstriped suits, suede shoes and the typical 1950s-era "ducktail" haircut and every strand of hair carefully positioned with Brylcreem. Personable and charming, Claude seemed to easily gain the attention of young ladies on campus.

Connie was tall and athletic with dark, short stylish hair, deep brown eyes and a bright smile. She had a gentle and sensitive disposition with a superb sense of humor. She was an attractive young woman, but usually quiet and reserved.

"Not long after I joined the group, Claude asked me out on a date. By that time, however, I had long recovered from my Claude

Left to right, Will, Steve, Claude, Monroe and Paul, with Connie at the piano

Hopper crush. I even had a boyfriend I was sweet on at the time," Connie recalled, with a laugh. "Of course, Claude had several girl-friends then as well."

At the time she started playing for the brothers, Connie had already moved away from home and was working in Winston-Salem. She traveled from Winston-Salem to Madison every weekend for group rehearsal, and often to sing somewhere. She either rode a tran-sit bus, or her father picked her up and drove her to Rockingham County.

"Claude didn't give up! He persisted in asking me out. I remem-ber one particular evening, at one of our rehearsals, he asked me to go to a ballgame with him," she said. "I guess he just wore me down. I finally accepted. We really had a great time on our first date! From that point forward, he asked me out more and more often. I usually accepted each invitation."

They occasionally went to movies or took a drive up the Blue Ridge Parkway. Yet, for the most part, their time together consisted of preparing for and going to Gospel music sings.

"I have to be honest. I fell in love with Connie's spirit and her

brown eyes first, and in the feeling in her voice when she sang," Claude reminisced about the early days. "Later, I really fell in love with her!"

Once they started going out frequently, Connie and Claude seemed to always have a great time. Feelings steadily grew for one another from that point.

"It wasn't one of those love-at-first-sight things you read about or see in the movies. I just came to a point where I knew that this is the man I wanted to spend my life with," Connie said.

Claude recalled a particular time when he visited Connie at her parents' farmhouse. Connie told her mother they were going to walk down to Pretty Creek, and her mom immediately became upset and put a stop to their plans.

"I tried to explain that I was just going to show Claude the creek," Connie said, smiling, "but Mama didn't exactly buy it. In fact, she forbade us from going down there. Things like that just weren't done in those days. You didn't walk into the woods with a man you weren't married to."

Claude and Connie's love continued to grow. They were soon engaged.

In the earliest days of the group the singing dates were mainly scheduled on Sunday evenings and on an occasional Saturday night. The group's practice night was always Friday evening.

"At first, Claude was in college. He had to leave after his last class on Friday and drive home. Steve was still in high school, so if he had a football game, we had to reschedule rehearsal. Monroe, Will and Paul were married and lived nearby, so their schedules usually worked out," Connie recalled. "I came home from Winston-Salem to be there."

As "the Boys" (as Dossie Hopper called them) practiced, their harmonies began to blend and they were achieving an unmistakable style—a sound that was recognizable.

After college in 1960, one of Claude's first jobs was with the R. J. Reynolds Tobacco Company on the Green Leaf Market. Claude wanted to travel and this seemed like a perfect opportunity.

"I was a factory foreman. We packed tobacco into things called hogheads. Then these containers were shipped to a re-drying location. I enjoyed traveling with the market. I went to the only market the company had in Indiana—coincidentally Madison, Indiana—and here I was from Madison, North Carolina!"

He journeyed back and forth to sing with the group on weekends. Claude explained that at the time he had a strong suspicion he was going to be drafted in to the service. "A friend of mine who happened to be in the Indiana National Guard suggested, 'If I can persuade you to sign up, we can split the $300 they give me.'

"Since I expected to be drafted anyway, I signed up for the Indiana National Guard; when I got back to Rockingham County, there was a government letter waiting on me—my call to the United States Army. I soon went to boot camp at Fort Leonard Wood, Missouri," Claude said.

"I guess I never really realized to what degree I loved Connie until I joined the Army, in 1960. During basic training, I used to save up quarters to call her on Sunday nights," he said. Claude had actually already given Connie an engagement ring about a year before he went into the Army.

"For a while, though, there was no talk of a wedding date," Connie remembered.

"Claude had a lot of great qualities that I admired. Even before we fell in love, he was my best friend—and he still is."

It was on one of those Sunday night "quarter calls" from boot camp that they decided they didn't want to wait any longer. Claude and Connie set a date for the wedding: after he'd get home from basic training—April 14, 1961.

The ceremony was held at Eden Methodist Church, with Reverend Ronald Overcash officiating. Connie's dress was later described in the local newspaper as a gown of brocade taffeta with a Chantilly lace bodice, embroidered with seed pearls and sequins. It included long lace sleeves and a princess skirt with back streamers appliquéd with pearls and sequins. She carried a bouquet of white

Wedding Day—Henry and Mary Lou Shelton, Connie and Claude, and Dossie and Archer Hopper

roses and white lilacs.

Connie's maid of honor and only attendant was her sister Wilma. Claude's best man was his oldest brother, Monroe. Ushers were Paul and Will Hopper.

Virginia recalled the wedding ceremony: "Connie's mama had a dry sense of humor and could say some of the funniest things! At Claude and Connie's wedding, after the reception was over, they were getting ready to leave. Connie's mother came down the center aisle of the church and she hollered, 'Tell that Claude Hopper to come back here! He hasn't signed the marriage certificate! He's not taking my girl nowhere until he signs it!'"

Claude laughed, and ran back and signed the certificate, making everything legal. Then the couple left the reception and began their life together.

Claude left for Fort Jackson days after the wedding. He was enrolled in EIB (Expert Infantry Badge) School. After specialty training, he was back home by August and was a proud member of the North Carolina Army Reserve. "Going into the Army was one of the greatest things that ever happened to me. It taught me self-respect and discipline," Claude said.

The Army became a positive experience for Claude

One of Connie's first holidays with her new husband was when they planned their first Thanksgiving dinner together. She wrote about the experience in the *Singing News Magazine:*

> Recalling my first Thanksgiving dinner as a young bride and a new cook is not very memorable. Claude's job had moved us to Kentucky temporarily. Normally on Thanksgiving day, the Hopper brothers (all eight of them) and their dad would go hunting in the morning, returning in the afternoon to enjoy a delicious feast that Mom Hopper had prepared. This particular year, it was just Claude and I in a small apartment far from home. I attempted preparing my first Thanksgiving dinner.
>
> I had watched my mom many times as she baked chicken or turkey and the most wonderful dressing in the world. I thought I'd try to do it just as she did. I knew that we'd need a small chicken, though I had never seen a small one prepared. I fully intended to boil my three-pound chicken just as many hours as Mama boiled her 10-pound hen. After a couple of

hours, the meat was perfect for chicken casserole.

I had never heard of chicken casserole forty-four years ago! The local supermarket there sold pole beans instead of green beans. I had never eaten any so I thought I'd give them a try. I could hardly stand the odor as they were cooking. Needless to say, nobody gobbled them up. I don't remember what I did to the yams, but I do remember the look on Claude's face when he came in from work (not from the customary hunt) and we sat down to that wreck of a Thanksgiving dinner.

He was kind as he smiled and nibbled at his food. I smiled and nibbled too.

Claude and Connie often laugh nowadays when they recall such moments as newlyweds. Thankfully, in subsequent years, Connie's cooking greatly improved and many family memories have been cultivated around the Hopper kitchen table.

Even after the marriage, the Hopper Brothers and Connie continued with weekly rehearsals and weekend Gospel sings. However, in spite of their busy schedule, it wasn't long before the newlyweds started thinking about starting their own family.

Chapter 16
Those Early Years

Finish each day and be done with it. You have done what you could; some blunders and absurdities have crept in; forget them as soon as you can. Tomorrow is a new day; you shall begin it serenely and with too high a spirit to be encumbered with your old non-sense.

— Ralph Waldo Emerson

Connie made a world of difference to the Hopper Brothers—now called the Hopper Brothers and Connie—by continually helping the boys to improve their singing parts. Before she joined, the brothers could have been described as a rough bunch of Rockingham County farm boys who just happened to sing together.

"We were still singing some of our songs in unison when Connie joined the group, then she helped us learn actual singing parts. Afterwards we were still fun-loving farm boys, but Connie added a touch of class and a great talent to the group," Claude remarked.

"The Hopper Brothers knew basic harmony and who should be singing what part. Mrs. Sutherland had already helped them make the transitions," Connie recalled. "I helped them as we continued to learn new songs."

The guys soon discovered Connie sang wonderfully, too. Early on she sang classics like "When I Lift Up My Head," by Dottie Rambo. In the late 1950's and early '60s, a lot of the groups on the road sang the same songs during any given concert, especially if the song was a crowd-pleaser. Much like the other groups of the era, the brothers chose to learn some of those best-loved songs. The brothers soon featured Connie on even more songs.

Claude added, "Connie pulled us forward in a new direction. She played a big part in the Hopper Brothers' success."

Connie also recalled that Claude and Steve switched on the lead and baritone parts. If Steve had the solo, Claude sang baritone; like-

A publicity photo of the Hopper Brothers and Connie

wise, if Claude had the solo, Steve switched parts. They both had strong voices which are needed to lead a song. For a teenager, Steve had an especially big voice with exceptional breath control.

Also, Will's tenor voice was an important component of the Hopper Brothers and Connie sound, for he could hit the high notes that thrilled the audiences.

"Monroe might not have been able to hit the lowest notes that some of the veteran bass singers could sing, but he sang his part well and in perfect pitch. His stage presence and charisma with the audience on and off stage left nothing lacking. His persona onstage reminded me of Big Chief of the Statesmen, who was one of the greats," Connie said.

"The practice sessions were paying off. I may have played a small part in arranging and working parts, but these boys delivered the songs," Connie said.

At first, the Hopper Brothers and Connie drove to various sings in their cars. They later graduated to a Volkswagen van. They hauled a little suitcase-style public address system packed tightly in the back.

"I remember singing one time in a church in Detroit," Will said. "This congregation made up entirely of wonderful black folks had a different way of worshipping than we did, but we just loved it! Beforehand, the people at the church fed us. They seated us at this long, long table in the fellowship hall. They had women there to serve us, dressed in white uniforms. Somehow, at the time, I got tickled because we were positioned in such a way that it reminded me of *The Last Supper*.

"We ate well, set up our equipment and sang. We had a long trip ahead of us after the sing, but as far as the congregation was concerned, the night was *young*! The service was just getting started! We sang for hours. We sang nearly everything we knew, and repeated several of our best songs," Will continued. "Finally, we told 'em kindly that we had to finish up and start tearing down equipment to get to the next sing. By the time we left at ten o'clock, the congregation was still singing, clapping their hands, and enjoying the night.

"We finally left for our next stop, but we really enjoyed the experience and appreciated their precious hospitality."

Will recalled another occasion when the group was singing in Modesto, California. After the guys set up for the evening, they strolled down the street looking for a bite to eat, when they came to a quaint-looking barbeque restaurant that they noticed when first driving into town.

"We went in and met the owners of the establishment, who surprisingly were originally from Mayodan, North Carolina, which is right up the road from our hometown," Will said. "For twenty-five years, this couple had run that restaurant. We sat down there and talked and talked for hours.

"Actually, the couple decided to go to our singing appearance, and took us back to the concert. They also brought along a container of barbeque for all of us."

Will said that while on the road, things like this occurred often, where they coincidentally ran into acquaintances, old friends, or people from their neck of the woods. Through years on the road the group has met thousands of people from all walks of life who have extended innumerous kindnesses to them, for which they are always grateful.

Not long after Claude and Connie married, the group decided to go to Salem College to take music lessons from an instructor, Dr. Peterson. He coached each one in voice.

"My brothers and I had never learned notes — absolutely none!" Claude said.

The time spent with Dr. Peterson was quite valuable, and the brothers continued to grow in ability and experience. About that time, Clyde Baker, the son of Claude's great aunt, started promoting the Hopper Brothers in the local area, including Roanoke, Madison, Reidsville, Danville and in the surrounding areas. Clyde was instrumental in helping the Hopper Brothers and Connie for the first decade of their singing career, beginning in 1961. He also started adding them to other programs with well-known Southern Gospel artists.

"For example, by the ate 1960s and early 1970s, we often sang on programs with J.D. Sumner and the Stamps Quartet. I remember that on occasion J.D. would graciously place Donnie Sumner in with us when we sang. Donnie played bass guitar for us; Bob McCallum occasionally worked with us stressing the importance of stage choreography and presentation.."

The Hopper Brothers came to realize early on that when you are in ministry for Christ, you must work toward being as professional and trained as possible. They believed, and still believe, that it is important to work hard, study, grow and give the Lord one's utmost for His glory. But most notably, they have always relied upon the Spirit's anointing.

Rick Warren, the well-known pastor of Saddleback Church, in Lake Forest, California, once wrote: "Living to create an earthly legacy is a short-sighted goal. A wiser use of time is to build an eternal legacy." It is this eternal legacy that the Hoppers have attempted to construct since their beginnings. They are motivated by eternity in their hearts.

"Certainly the Lord deserves our best," Claude stated. "As far as musical ability goes, it wasn't until I was thirty-five years old that I finally took my first piano lessons. I took them from my cousin and I accomplished what I wanted to do. I yearned to be able to pick up a hymnbook and instantly recognize what key the song was written in," Claude said.

The Hopper Brothers and Connie have always watched for any opportunity to improve their talents or their ability to minister to others effectively.

In the early days, the group looked up to premier groups like Hovie Lister and the Statesmen Quartet, the Speer Family, the Rebels, the Florida Boys, the Oak Ridge Quartet (later Oak Ridge Boys), the Harvesters Quartet, the Happy Goodman Family, the Harmonaires, the Singing Rambos and the Blackwood Brothers. They were also enormous fans of individuals like Jake Hess, George Younce, Glenn Payne and J.D. Sumner.

They especially noticed the abilities of groups and soloists that were able to excel at that unique quartet sound.

"The fellows and I sang in those days because we loved to sing Southern Gospel and because we loved the Lord. It was exciting and awe-inspiring to see people respond to Christ's message during a concert," Connie said.

In those days there were no track recordings, as many groups use today. The Hopper Brothers and Connie used only live musicians. Claude played rhythm and occasionally bass guitar. Connie played piano and later electric bass guitar on certain occasions, too. There were other musicians who joined along the way as well.

Little Rex Foster was the Hopper Brothers and Connie's first full-time pianist; he started in the late 1960s.

"When Rex first began with us his mother had to bring him, because he was too young to drive," Claude explained. "He was fifteen years old. At first he played on songs where Connie sang, and Connie played all the others. Then as time went on, he started playing on more and more songs. He played with a distinct Eva Mae LeFevre style, and Connie accompanied him on bass guitar," Claude said.

He later played for the LeFevres, the Rex Nelon Singers and the Proclaimers. Little Rex went home to be with the Lord on Tuesday morning, June 19, 2001, after a period of declining health.

"The Lord was always good to the Hopper Brothers and Connie. We had generous donations," Monroe said. "God looked after us completely. When you consider people like Jake Hess and the other old-timers, and what it was like when they first started, we had it easier than some. The old-timers made great sacrifices to sing full-time for Christ."

The Hopper Brothers did not always have an easy go of it either. It took all of their combined financial resources and gifts from fans to keep them on the road. No one in the group was paid for the first thirteen years. Nevertheless, they continued, for they sensed a heavenly calling on their lives. Connie, Claude and the brothers believed the Lord had particularly selected them for this type of ministry. Though the hours were sometimes grueling, they still enjoyed the camaraderie, the traveling and the opportunity to establish new friends across the country, too.

"We were very close as a family. We enjoyed it. We laughed and had lots of fun during our travels. It seemed like we were always getting ourselves lost and trying to find where we were going! I remember one time we were going to Mount Airy, North Carolina, and Claude was driving his car. I followed him in my old Dodge, which I purchased from two old-maid schoolteachers who never drove it except on Sunday," Monroe said, as he chuckled, "and I had it loaded down with musical equipment. We were up there [on the mountaintop] trying to find this church."

Pilot Knob, which is in the vicinity of Mount Airy, rises more than 1,450 feet above the densely wooded countryside of the upper Piedmont plateau.

"We searched all over that ol' mountaintop for a certain hillside, and I'll never forget my brother Paul saying dryly, 'We're not lost because I can still see the knob!'

"We were going around, around and around it," Monroe said. "Finally we found the church, but not until we had spent hours touring the mountain."

Regardless of where the group went, they had to be home in time for work on Monday morning. For this reason, they didn't ven-

The Hopper Brothers and Connie continued to improve in the early years.

ture too far from home. Seldom did they stay overnight. Yet, occasionally they stayed all night with someone from a church where they sang. More often, though, they changed clothes in a Sunday School room or church bathroom in preparation for a concert or revival service. After the sing, they drove home or on to the next booking.

"The Lord put the right personalities and temperaments together from the beginning," Connie said. "I've never been treated nicer by any group of people than I was by Claude's brothers when we traveled together. For being a bunch of rowdy boys, they were always kind and polite to me.

"We spent a lot of time together and there were probably times when it became stressful for everyone, but it never manifested itself much. Most the time we just had loads of fun together," Connie remembered. "I recall Bill Gaither once emphasized that you have to have fun in this business. I think he's absolutely right! There shouldn't be tension-filled circumstances while driving to a concert stage or church building. All of the Hopper brothers have a great sense of humor. They love to laugh. So it was usually a grand old time for all of us on the road."

Chapter 17
Recording In The Garage

Always bear in mind that your own resolution to succeed is more important than any other one thing.

— Abraham Lincoln

It was in 1962 that the Hopper Brothers and Connie recorded their first professional record album. Connie and Claude were virtually newlyweds and were anxious over the possibilities of making a record.

Don Mattney, a recording technician in Thomasville, North Carolina, helped them record the project. Don was an unimposing-looking man who had been a disc jockey for years and was active in Southern Gospel music.

"Don wore very thick Coke-bottle glasses and was an interesting fellow. He had a small recording studio," Claude recalled. "His recording and mixing board was located next to the kitchen sink in his home. We actually sang in his adjoining garage. Don peeked out at us through the kitchen window as we sang into the microphones. The kitchen window looked directly into the garage.

"We were more than a little nervous, being that this was our first opportunity to work on a recording project. Yet we all survived the experience."

Connie laughed and said, "When we finished each song, Mr. Mattney peeked out the window and excitedly hollered, 'That's a cut, boys!'

"He never wanted us to re-record or sing any parts over; he'd just lean over the sink and yell, 'That's it! That's a cut!'"

On this first recording, the Hopper Brothers and Connie chose one of the first songs Bill Gaither ever wrote: "I've Been To Calvary."

Oddities On The Road

Life on the road can sometimes be peculiar. As with other groups, there were moments, in the first years, when the Hopper Brothers and Connie were traveling and thought, "We shouldn't even be here!"

For example, there was one particular time when the group booked a church and then couldn't find it. It's the only time in a half century of ministry where they never did find the location.

"Another time we booked a church in a secluded area—a small town in West Virginia. Somehow—it was very bizarre—we ended up in the wrong town in the wrong part of the Mountain State," Claude said. "After studying a map, we finally realized there were two towns in the state with the same name! By the time we figured it out, we couldn't get to the other place in time to sing. We were in northwestern West Virginia and the church we were supposed to be at was in the eastern panhandle of the state. I called the pastor and said, 'I'm so sorry. We're in the right state, but wrong town.'"

The pastor was gracious about the situation and was able to explain the snafu to his congregation. The concert was rescheduled.

On another occasion, the group was scheduled to sing in Douglas, Georgia, and unintentionally ended up in Douglasville, Georgia, instead.

"Douglasville is just west of Atlanta. Douglas is toward Valdosta. I called the promoter and said, 'Hold on, we're on our way!'" Claude said.

They drove like maniacs and got to Douglas before the concert was over. The Inspirations were also scheduled for that evening. "Thankfully, they sang until we finally got there," Claude recalled with a chuckle.

Claude recalled a particular concert at Jewel Valley Presbyterian Church, in Virginia: "These dear folks at the church had been wanting us to come for several years and it finally worked out with our schedule. I remember it was on a Sunday night. At the time we were driving a 1972 Eagle bus.

"To get there, we had to go up from Kingsport, Tennessee, and travel across the Kentucky and West Virginia state lines. We crisscrossed in and out of several states to get to Jewell Valley, and it was a very, very crooked road."

Claude laughed as he continued: "I've never been afraid of my own driving, but this time I was frightened. Sometimes I nearly met my taillights going around a hairpin curve! When we eventually got to the church, we barely had enough room to pull our bus off the side of the road. I looked up on the side of the mountain on the hill where the church was located—and I'm not exaggerating—our bus was larger than the whole church! I bowed my head and said, 'Lord, what are we doing here?'"

By the time the musical equipment was set up and the group started singing, the church was full with 41 people; some of the neighborhood children also had their faces pressed up against the windows of the church to get a better look at the singers. "Their little coal-dusty faces were shoved up against the windowpanes," he said, smiling. "I'll never forgotten what the pastor said that evening. He told me, 'I appreciate you folks coming here. These folks never get to hear the Gospel the way it's being presented here tonight.'

"The people were so appreciative that we were there. We really had church! Later that night, the congregation took up an offering and gave us a love gift of $410," Claude said. "We were just over-whelmed. That was a phenomenal amount of money for us at the time. We all wondered how this could even be.

"The Lord used that experience to teach me something vital. Don't measure the importance of a church by the number of members on the roll or the size of the structure. God often uses small places and the small things in this life to bring about His grand purposes," Claude surmised.

"Our role, and the role of all Christians, is to be faithful to His call. I was reminded that night that it's Christ who provides and blesses."

Connie added: "Through the years, we have never said we weren't going somewhere because it was too small, or for any other reason. If churches called, we went as long as dates were open. Claude's philosophy with the group has always been that if we schedule a date to sing, we go, regardless of outside circumstances. Part of the notion of having faith means being faithful."

Chapter 18
Winning At The NQC

Small opportunities are often the beginning of great enterprises.

— Demosthenes

In the late 1950s and early '60s, the Hopper Brothers and Connie continued to improve and grow. They participated in sings and contests held in Zebulon and Fayetteville, North Carolina, in their courthouses. At the Fayetteville sing, Southern Gospel groups sang live from the judge's chambers—an activity that would now surely be considered controversial by some.

They also competed in a Southern Gospel music contest held at the W.F. Sessom's Memorial Sing, in Roseboro, North Carolina, and sang at the legendary two-day North Carolina State Annual Singing Convention at Benson, North Carolina, an affair that first began in a tobacco warehouse in 1921.

"We entered a local contest in Thomasville, North Carolina, sponsored by a local promoter, C.R. McClain. By winning that particular contest in 1962, we were given the opportunity to sing at the coveted Reynolds Auditorium," Connie reminisced. "This was part of Claude's initial vision for the Hopper Brothers. One of the first times I practiced with them, he said, 'One day we will sing at Reynolds Auditorium,' which was considered a major accomplishment. I was always amazed by Claude's steadfast vision and perseverance toward attaining a goal."

Little did they realize at the time that things were about to change dramatically for the Rockingham County music group.

The National Quartet Convention (NQC) has long been considered the premier event for the entire Gospel music industry. It was in 1964 that the Hopper Brothers and Connie first went to the NQC, which at that time was held in Memphis, Tennessee.

"I suppose we got popular enough regionally that it was suggested we go to Memphis for the big quartet convention," Monroe recalled.

Although they were all nervous about the prospect of singing before such a large number of music fans and peers, they knew they were at a point that this was the obvious next step. Since they couldn't afford to travel to the convention on their own, the people of Madison and their home church, Ellisboro Baptist, collected donations to make it possible for the group to fly to Memphis and enter the NQC International Championship.

The group consisted of five Hopper brothers with Connie playing the piano at the time. "We were one of eighty-five groups participating in the contest that year," Monroe said, explaining how the competition was grueling and their nerves were frayed for the duration of the event.

Monroe also remembered that Elvis Presley performed at the convention that year. He came on stage with two bodyguards, one on each end of the stage. He sang "How Great Thou Art" to open the program.

Connie added: "The convention was held at old Ellis Auditorium. It was packed, and we'd been there literally all day long. Remember, we were only part-time singers. When our turn came, we sang the song, 'The Answer Came,' a popular song written by Henry Slaughter. I remember how special it was for all of us when they later announced our name as the overall winner!"

Normally, when artists take first place at the convention, they are apt to celebrate with a certain air of dignity and decorum. However, when the Hopper boys heard they'd won, they stood onstage slapping one another on the back, laughing uncontrollably and hooting and howling with joy. Unlike the typical professional group of singers, they more resembled a group of buddies excited over the final seconds of a close football game. Connie

94

and the boys were completely surprised and overjoyed by the moment; they were just celebrating in typical Hopper farmboy fashion.

"Since it was an international championship there were groups from all over the United States and several foreign countries," Monroe said. "We won the trophy and Jimmy Davis (the songwriter who penned the song, 'You Are My Sunshine,' and who was also the governor of Louisiana), gave us the key to Baton Rouge and a recording label.

"On the way home, it was kind of funny because we could hardly get our trophy onto the plane. Then, somehow, as my brother Paul was holding it during the flight, it broke. We glued it back together when we got home, and everything was okay."

It was a wonderful milestone in the career of the Hopper family. After they won this big competition, the group stopped entering contests altogether. It was around that time that they started performing on stage with many of the most popular professional groups. The Hopper Brothers and Connie noticed a positive reaction, especially from other groups, after their triumph at the convention. Due to the prestige of the NQC win, their stature grew in the industry.

"We had two main goals from our inception: to sing at Reynolds Auditorium, and to own a bus," Monroe recollected, noting they had accomplished the first goal before the NQC win. "Then, not long after the convention, our transportation goal was met. In 1965, we bought a 1948 Silverside bus. The mileage log on it read four million miles! We gave $4,500 for the bus, as is," he said and chuckled.

Although it had a great deal of age and mileage, the group couldn't have been more pleased. They felt they had finally attained an important objective. The Lord made a way for them to travel together.

"We had never ridden on a bus too much, let alone drive one," Monroe added. There was a lot for the brothers to learn about maneuvering and parking a full-size bus. You didn't need a special license to drive it at the time, but you needed to know a little bit about weight and clearance. We had to drive by mirrors instead of just looking out the window. We all learned to drive it: Will, Claude and myself. My brother Steve was younger and was probably the only one of us guys who didn't drive the bus."

After the NQC win, the group continued working with Clyde Baker Promotions, singing at most of his concerts. "That's really how we became familiar with artists like the Singing Rambos, Speer Family, Statesmen, Blackwood Brothers, the LeFevres, Goss Brothers, Chuck Wagon Gang and the Happy Goodman Family," Claude said.

"Since those early days, the Goodman family has visited in our home. This has been a great blessing for our family. We knew them even before Rusty Goodman joined with them. In the early days, Rusty was singing with the Plainsmen Quartet, and it was just Sam, Howard and Vestal Goodman. They were tremendous Christians and a wonderful family who inspired the Hopper family throughout the years," Claude said.

Chapter 19
Belews Creek To The Hopper Farm

Claude and I actually built our first home on a portion of the Shelton farm after we married. So we started our married life living near Pretty Creek.

— Connie Hopper

Claude and Connie built their first home outside Stokesdale near Connie's parents' homeplace, although Claude daydreamed about someday owning and working on the Hopper farm.

His father, Archer, could be a very inflexible individual, and he'd stiffen if anyone even suggested he sell the farm. "However, God used Mama to influence him and mediate behind the scenes," Claude said.

Whatever it was that Dossie said eventually softened Archer's feelings on the subject, and as Claude noted, "God's timing is always perfect." At the time

Dean with his grandparents

Connie and Claude were living in their Stokesdale home and assumed this is the way it would always be.

Then one day Archer walked up to Claude at the farm and understatedly said, "Claude, I'm going to sell you a portion of the homeplace."

Claude's mouth dropped as he was overcome with emotion. He never suspected he would get such an opportunity. Archer even seemed encouraging about offering him fifteen acres, and smiled when he saw the excitement on Claude's countenance. Archer was true to his word. He sold a portion of the farm to Claude at that time, and later sold him another tract of the original farm.

During the same time period, the young couple welcomed their first child into the world. Dean Hopper was born on October 24, 1962.

They couldn't have been more pleased with how the Lord was blessing their union.

Dean and Grandma Hopper

"One day when Dean was small electric company representatives came to our house to talk. They described their plans for creating Belews Lake. They told us what was going to happen to the whole region, along with our property. They wanted to construct the lake to provide more electricity," Claude remembered.

Claude and Connie were told they had a "decision" to make: sell their home to them, or the electric company would condemn and seize the property anyway.

So, reluctantly, they sold the house and started planning their next move. They were extremely broken-hearted over the loss of Pretty Creek and all they had built together.

"I personally doubted we'd find another place I could call home," Connie said. "It was devastating to me. For a long, long time I didn't go back over to the homeplace, especially after it was submerged. My childhood memories were there, at the bottom of the lake. I remember lying at night sobbing over thoughts of the homeplace being taken."

Through this experience, and after time elapsed, God tenderly taught Connie something important. It was as if He whispered softly to her, "Connie, don't get too attached to this world."

"I have never forgotten that whole experience," she recalled. "I now know from experience that Christians can lose worldly belongings, very important things, and yet still go on. We can still be happy, too. The Lord had a special lesson for me. I am often reminded that I still have my memories. My precious recollections can never be lost, seized or smothered beneath lake waters."

"Connie, Dean and I moved from our first home. Fortunately, we had a place waiting for us, since Dad sold us the farm sometime before. We headed directly to the Hopper farm and moved into a singlewide trailer, situated alongside Dad and Mama's home, until we could build our own house," Claude recalled.

"Meanwhile, Mike was born in the fall of 1969 while we were still in the trailer. He never got to see my parents' home, or our first home on Belews Creek," Connie said. Belews Lake became a reality in 1971.

"Although the move was heart-wrenching, I knew the relocation would ultimately be positive for all of us," Claude said. "Although our time living next door to the Shelton family ended, God miraculously opened this new door."

They eventually erected a new house exactly where the Hopper log cabin had once stood. Everyone in the family was involved with the formation of the new farmhouse.

Dean

Dean recalled the experience: "Dad and Mom started building the new house in 1969; we actually moved into our home on the farm in 1970 when Mike was just a baby and I was in second grade."

Once the house was completed, Connie and Claude dedicated the farm to the Lord. Claude remembers standing inside the structure and praying, "Lord, whomever you send by we'll try to make feel welcome." And so they have.

The home and grounds are chock-full of sentimental reminders of the Hopper family legacy. For example, the living room of the attractive, yet modest, two-story home (where they still live to this day) has a fireplace constructed from the original foundational stones from the old log cabin homeplace. The walnut tree where Claude and his siblings once played stands regally beyond the back patio, as healthy as ever.

Connie and Mike

The sparkling clear brook, with its bubbling spring, where Claude and his siblings once waded and kept perishables cold before refrigeration, still flows freely alongside the farmhouse.

Inside the home, they built an additional living area in the basement, with a separate bedroom, kitchen, living room, dining room and small fireplace for visiting guests.

A barn and outbuildings exist from the original farm, including a rough-cut corncrib. The well-manicured grounds and beautiful landscaping are the result of one of Claude's greatest passions, and there are hearty trees that have survived through the decades.

The original Hopper cabin is still within view, located across the meadow at the same place Claude's father moved it prior to their move.

"On the north side of our farmhouse lived my Grandmother and Grandfather Hopper, adjacent to our property," Dean explained. "So, once we moved to the farm I was able to spend a lot of time with them while Mom and Dad traveled. There were a lot of times when I got off the school bus at their house. I spent time with my Grandma and Grandpa Shelton, too, especially before we moved over to the farm, since our first home was closer to them."

Dean said they tried raising a crop of tobacco—only once. Later, while the group was singing in Baltimore, Maryland, on a Sunday night, one of the barns burnt down while the tobacco was curing inside.

"Dad felt a little funny about raising tobacco in the first place. He knew, after the fire, that we weren't meant to raise tobacco anymore. So Dad switched to raising beef cattle. Cattle are sort of low maintenance. We feed them and they raise their young. We eventually sell those off. They even keep the grass eaten down in the pasture."

The Hopper farm might be described as a perpetual work in progress. "Connie helped me raise hogs and cattle on this farm—but

Dean with his snare drum

she raised a lot of cane, too," Claude joked.

Dean and Mike spent much of their childhood working and playing hard on the spread. The farm represents a full family commitment and a source of great joy for all the Hoppers.

"Dad and I built our first barn behind the house, with the help of another worker. All the wood for that barn was cut out from the woods on our property. The beams, the lean-to and everything else came from the farm. Dad bought old tin from another farmer that was used as well. The shed stores hay and supplies for the cattle," Dean said.

"Then I later helped erect another barn when I was twelve years old. I assisted Dad and Grandpa Shelton. Grandpa was a skilled carpenter. We rented this post-hole digger, which was like a gasoline-driven auger. I hated that machine because it vibrated so badly. But we eventually dug all the holes and sank telephone poles. Grandpa guided us as we completed the exterior of the barn.

"So as you might imagine, I have a great number of memories at the farm. It seems that everything there has special significance for me. I know it's the same for Mike, too," Dean said.

"It's been a blessing to be working this old farm and see the Lord grant the increase. Of course, my childhood memories are here and the Hopper family heritage is all here," Claude said.

"This farm is now home for me and a source of fond memories for our entire family," Connie added.

Mike: aspiring graffiti artist?

101

Chapter 20
Steve Leaves The Group

There are two dilemmas that rattle the human skull:
How do you hang on to someone who won't stay?
And how do you get rid of someone who won't go?

— Danny DeVito, *The War of the Roses*

Even the best of families have struggles. The Hoppers are really no different.

Steve Hopper, the second to the youngest of Claude's siblings, had been an employee at Salem Steel since graduating from high school. Then shortly before the Hopper Brothers and Connie started talking about committing themselves to full-time ministry, Steve—considered the most powerful male voice of the group at the time—left the group.

Surprisingly, at a point between concert dates, Steve told Monroe, his oldest brother, that he had decided to quit the group. On the day of the Hopper Brothers and Connie's next singing engagement, Monroe pulled Claude to the side and whispered to him what Steve had said. Later that day, when everyone else gathered to board the bus, they realized Steve had already taken his clothes and belongings off. Although everyone else was prepared to leave for a scheduled concert, Steve never showed.

The other members were confused and upset and the loss caused a significant hardship since Steve was featured on many of their most popular songs. His untimely departure was a devastating blow for the up-and-coming group. Claude was particularly distraught and bewildered. However, he knew—as did Connie and the other members—that, as always, they must go on for the sake of the call on their lives. So they sang without him that weekend.

Later, Steve's only explanation to his brothers was that he had a financial opportunity that seemed too good to pass up. The next few months were difficult for the remaining members and emotions ran high.

Connie recalled one night shortly afterwards: "Once, we were going to Raleigh for a big concert at the huge civic auditorium there. Steve was gone. Monroe couldn't go because he was in the middle of an important task at his farm. For the first time, I felt like we'd be just a big flop. Will, Claude and I had not been singing together like that before. We went on anyway, and a friend from another group on the program filled the bass spot for us that night. Perhaps it wasn't the greatest night of our career; but we went and did the best we could. That's one thing Claude has insisted on. If he tells someone we will be at a church or function, *we go*. A few times we had to form a make-shift group at the last minute in order to fulfill our commitment. "

In the meantime, Steve joined a booming business on a full-time basis and was successful in a relatively short time; unfortunately, just as quickly, he lost a great deal of his earnings through poor investments.

"One night, several years later, Steve called me while I was home at the farm," Claude recalled. "I suppose I was still a little bitter internally because of the way Steve left us. It was difficult for me to talk with him civilly. Of course, I came to realize later that I had a wrong attitude toward my own brother. I guess I was living on emotions, walking in the flesh, at first."

Steve said softly, "Claude, God told me, through the Holy Spirit, to call you and you'd give me a job."

Claude paused for a moment or two. He then responded by saying, "If the Lord told you that, then you should come home."

Steve returned in 1975, not as a full-time singer, but as part of the Hoppers' organization nonetheless. Steve has since shared his testimony on stage, telling how at the time he swallowed his pride and called his brother. He had hit rock bottom some time after leaving the group, and when he came to the end of himself, so to speak, he returned home to his family and roots.

"I put Steve in distribution, which we called Hopper Distribution. Today, Steve owns Hopper Distribution and does a wonderful job. Of course, he sings with us during our annual Hopper Brothers and Connie Homecoming, in Eden. He is a great talent and a wonderful brother, and we all love him dearly.

"I suppose there are no perfect families. Yet, regardless of the difficulties that have occurred, we are a big family and we stick together. We all remain very close."

Chapter 21
Full Time In 1970

If you think you can, you can. And if you think you can't, you're right.

— Henry Ford

In the late 1950s and early '60s, singing became an every-weekend proposition. In fact, up until 1970, the Hopper Brothers and Connie ministered on a part-time basis, singing somewhere nearly every Friday, Saturday and Sunday night. The schedule could be grueling and expensive. However, they continued to persevere. From the group's inception, not one member ever received a salary.

"Through the years, we had several private business enterprises on the side, just so we could eat, such as raising cattle and crops on the farm. No income was ever derived from the singing, up until the time we went on the road full-time," Connie said.

At the time the decision was made to enter full-time ministry, Will had a good job at Sears, and Claude worked at Madison Throwing Company.

Paul and Steve had already left the group, being eager to see what they could do in the business world.

"However, Claude always stuck with the singing," Connie said. "His brothers, Will and Monroe, also stayed and of course I did. Claude eventually quit the Throwing Plant. Will quit Sears in 1970. We were now full-time. Nearly every penny we took in was used to pay off our bus! All donations, record and 8-track sales, sheet music and any other income on the road paid for stage clothing, the sound system and incidental operating costs. Members of the group paid their own personal expenses for many years."

"We needed some type of salary to live on, now that we were full-time. So we allotted fifty dollars a week for each member," Connie remembered. "Everything else—if anything else was left— went toward ministry expenses like gasoline and other needs."

By 1970, the Hopper Brothers and Connie had already spent

In this photo, at left, Archer and Will Hopper look on as Connie and Claude are recognized at a concert date.

years on the highway and knew what it would take to make the ministry a full-time proposition.

"Singing was what we really wanted to do. We felt we must do it. So we stepped out in faith and did it," Connie said. "Through years of performing on a part-time basis, we were fortunate enough to have built a following by the time we committed ourselves to full time."

Claude, being a man of integrity, wasn't going to allow anyone assisting the group to go without being paid, and he wouldn't allow bills— whether at home or for the ministry—to become delinquent either.

"In 1970, I attended the Stamps School of Music, in Waxahachie, Texas, to study piano technique, theory and voice. I was one of the older students, but I still enjoyed the school," Connie recalled. The 1970s became an especially fruitful era for the group, as they continued to improve and strengthen their vocal talents. They saw many souls come to the Lord at concerts during this era, and many re-commitments were made for Christ.

105

In 1972, they made another major decision: to purchase a brand new bus. Songs by the Hopper Brothers and Connie started receiving nationwide attention during this time period. In April 1974, "I Believe He Died for Me" reached the *Singing News* charts; "When I Wake Up (To Sleep No More)" charted the same month. In October 1975, "When I Cross To The Other Side Of Jordan" was being played on national Southern Gospel radio stations.

Les Butler Reminisces

At the time of this writing, Les Butler is the director of promotions and programming for Solid Gospel Radio Network and director of business operations for *Singing News Magazine*. He was the founder and owner of Family Music Group and Butler Music Group and is well known in the industry as a versatile musician.

Les Butler

Les was born and raised in Chicago. He said, "We had several Southern Gospel groups come through that region of the country. One such group was the Hopper Brothers and Connie."

Les was a young teenager when he first met the Hoppers. It was an occasion in the mid-1970s, at a church in the Chicago area. A few years later, in 1977, Les worked at a Southern Gospel radio station and became familiar with their newest recordings. The Hoppers serviced their own recordings at the time, visiting radio stations during their travels. They encouraged stations to play their records at these meetings. That is how Les had the opportunity to get to know them much, much better.

"I became close friends with Claude and Connie. From 1978 to 1983, I often sat in on their concerts, playing along with their band when they came into the area, since I play piano, bass, drums and other instruments.

"When Claude and Connie would come to town, they often invited me to perform. They were very open to this snot-nosed teenaged boy; maybe they saw a little bit of talent in me."

Les was especially touched by their sincerity: "At the end of their concerts, they always had an altar call. I remember how Connie

Dean

would go down to the altar and pray with people. That carved a special place in my heart for the Hoppers.

"By 1982, Dottie Leonard Miller, of New Day Christian Distributors, hired me to be the first radio promotion person in Southern Gospel music. That position was to help promote independent artists. Her company was structured to help Southern Gospel groups get retail exposure. Of course the Hoppers were independent artists at that time.

"I worked on their radio singles for two or three years in the 1980s, and assisted them with concerts and promoting their music to radio. It was a great relationship and they were wonderful to work with. They were very successful.

"I remember Dean before he started singing, when he was their drummer. I guess we sort of climbed the ladder together; Dean did it with such integrity and grace.

"The one visual picture that readily comes to mind when I reflect on the Hoppers is that in the late 1970s and early 1980s, they performed at some of the smallest and medium-sized churches in

Dean behind his drum set

Chicago. They may have only made enough to pay for their gas. They never complained. They were just happy to sing.

"Even today, I still see Connie at the altar praying with strangers. Even though she is a woman who has won all the awards you can win in Southern Gospel music, she is still humble. She has the humility and the heart of a servant. The Hoppers made a wonderful impression on a teenage boy—that's for sure!"

There were lots of singers and musicians who came and went during the 1970s, but the signature Hopper Brothers and Connie sound, with Christ-centered lyrics and powerful arrangements, remained constant.

Roger Talley, and later his talented younger brother, Kirk, sang with the group. Roger joined the group in 1974. Kirk eventually joined on a full time basis in 1976, right after high school.

Lee Chilton sang bass around this same time.

Around 1977, Dean, fifteen at the time, boarded the bus as the full-time drummer. There were many discussions with his parents until he finally persuaded them to allow him to complete school on the road through American School's correspondence course. The decision turned out to be a good one in that Dean excelled in his home school studies while learning a great deal on the road, too. Once the decision was made for Dean to join the family on tour, he took his role seriously.

"As far as schooling, the road life has always been an education. I learned things like flexibility, being ready to improvise at any given time, and common sense methods of problem-solving while traveling."

One of the first albums featuring Dean as a full-time member of the group was *Something Going On,* released on Supreme Records in 1978.

Dean's Growth

"First I started as a drummer, as a teenager, and then I started taking care of the sound, too. Uncle Will, who is such a sweet man with a humble spirit, decided around that time that he no longer wanted to take care of sound. When difficult sound issues came up, or things became tense, it would work on Uncle Will's nerves."

Dean singing with Kirk Talley

Dean, in contrast, had always been interested in sound quality, so he was excited to learn all he could about the soundboard. Eventually he started driving the bus, as well.

"I even became the unofficial on-road mechanic, so to speak. I have a little bit of a knack for that kind of thing anyway. I took care of things like oil changes, oil filters and general maintenance. However, there were times when I changed alternators or fan pulleys, and worked on heaters and tougher situations," he said. "I remember occasions when we would be stranded in the middle of nowhere, and the bus was dead. I would wind up lying beneath the bus with my cell phone. I called people I knew who could help troubleshoot the problem. They could often guide me through certain situations and we would eventually get back on the road.

"When I look back on those days, it's hard to believe how we did some of the things we did to stay on the road. There were times when it was really, really hard."

It wasn't long before Dean started singing.

"At the time we traveled with Roger and Kirk Talley, those two would prod me into singing a little. My first moment on stage singing was back when I was twelve. I sang 'Where The Soul Of Man Never Dies' with Roger and Kirk. Later, Debra Talley joined the group. That's about the time I started getting more serious about my singing. I remember being featured on one of Squire Parsons' songs around that time, entitled 'He Came To Me.'"

Although the Hopper Brothers and Connie were traveling constantly, they still didn't have the name recognition or fame that many of the bigger and better-known groups had during the same period. However, they were blessed to sing with many of the top groups of the day and loved what they were doing.

"The more established groups seemed to be so supportive of us; many encouraged us to stick with it, too," Connie said.

Claude and Connie remember those days when they'd see new groups or soloists coming along. "I think it's so important for older, well-established groups to encourage and befriend new artists who are just beginning on the road," Connie said. "We need to help and support them as much as possible. After all, we've been where they are, and the road can be a very hard and lonely place to be without encouragement."

It's true that when the Hopper Brothers and Connie first began, fewer Gospel groups were on the road. Most of the traveling groups saw each other regularly. It was like a family atmosphere.

"Today there are new groups coming out all the time. Praise God for that, for this is one way the Lord's message is being spread across the nation and world in song. But sadly, sometimes the new artists jump into a full-time situation without thinking about the ramifications," Connie continued. "If I could advise others about choosing this lifestyle, I would strongly suggest a firm commitment to the Lord and to His people from the outset. To succeed, there must be an unquenchable desire to minister, and God has to make the way possible!"

The first day the Hopper Brothers and Connie went out on the road, they never worried that they might not be as polished as others. "We didn't compare ourselves with others," she said. "We just gave it all we had!"

Claude added that real success isn't measured in CD, DVD or videotape sales at a ministry table. Real success is more than any of these things. Success in this ministry—and in life—is based upon whether you're fulfilling God's purpose for your life. "Even if album sales plummet and donations dry up, if you're in God's will, you're still a success!" Claude said.

Chapter 22
Watermelon Park Camp Meeting

Watermelon Park was always a fun time for me. Being
a young child, I traveled with family and spent a week
to ten days at the park. I made friends that I only got
to see once a year.

— Mike Hopper

In the 1960s and '70s, there were several important Southern Gospel
outdoor events and singing conventions in the country that drew
enormous crowds. One such event, conceived by Claude, in 1972,
was held at Watermelon Park, located near Berryville, Virginia.

His concept of the Watermelon Park camp meeting was pat-
terned to a great degree after a godly gentleman, Harry Peyton, from
Hinton, West Virginia. Harry was preaching his own revival services
when Claude first met him. He had morning, afternoon and night
services. Guest singers were a part of the services, and he had nightly concerts as well. He provided something noteworthy for everyone
in the family.

"We participated in three services a day for the whole week in
Hinton with Harry," Claude remembered. Not long after the Hinton
camp meeting, Claude met John Miller, the owner of a bluegrass and
country music park called Watermelon Park.

The park had once hosted such renowned artists as Johnny
Cash, the Statler Brothers, Bill Monroe, the Country Gentlemen and
even a young Merle Haggard. Yet, by the late 1960s, the park was in
disrepair.

"I'll never forget that first year we sang at Watermelon Park, it
may have been in 1970 or 1971. We were invited to sing with the Oak
Ridge Boys, the Rambos and several other popular groups. We were
there for other promoters at the time, which included Myles Cooper's
group," Claude remembered. "Right after that, discussions began
with John Miller, the park owner, about promoting an annual event
ourselves."

After coming to a business agreement with Miller, Claude started planning an event that would start out, initially at least, on a Thursday and continue through Sunday. The name chosen for the outdoor sing was The Spirit of the Shenandoah Camp Meeting, at Watermelon Park, since the beautiful Shenandoah River meandered through the property.

It was somewhat odd that Claude and Connie had already been looking for a suitable place to hold an outdoor sing when the subject first came up with Miller. This park seemed to have everything they were seeking. It had ample hookups for recreational vehicles and campers. Also, families could enjoy the picturesque beauty of the region while having the opportunity to fellowship with others.

"It turned out to be a glorious experience. Hundreds and hundreds of Gospel music lovers, camping enthusiasts and church groups gathered together for the event each year," Claude said.

Claude carried Harry Peyton's idea to Watermelon Park. Claude learned through his time in the military that if you keep people busy they never get bored. He added a wide variety of activities to the plans, creating a unique event and environment.

The Hopper Brothers and Connie, along with other Southern Gospel artists, sang at regular intervals during the event. A morning lesson was held by Bible school teacher Rev. Nathan Myer, followed by old-fashioned preaching in the afternoon and concerts at night.

"Eventually we had a precious lady, Peggy Bauher, from Maryland, hold a Bible School program for children," Claude continued. "The idea came along when she introduced herself to us. She said she noticed all the children running around with nothing to do. She volunteered to begin Bible lessons on their level. From then on, she came every year and brought lessons, crafts and games. There was also a

This tattered photograph shows a baptism at Watermelon Park

young man who started a youth group.

"Our Sunday morning preaching service, which happened to be the last service of the week, was always conducted by a young evangelist and longtime friend of the Hoppers— Rev. Phil Hoskins," Connie said. "The Watermelon Park people loved him, and both Dean and Michael made professions of faith under his ministry. He is now pastor of Higheer Ground Baptist Church, in Kingsport, Tennessee, and receives eminence as a sought after speaker for Bible conferences and Christian functions.

"Maybe the most important thing about the Watermelon Park project was that we had crews made up of great friends who volunteered every year to make the camp a success!"

Limbs, brush and trees always needed trimming before the event could be held, and the campgrounds needed to be landscaped and manicured. Helpers painted, provided electrical and carpentry skills and ran chain saws in order to make the property acceptable.

"These beautiful people gave of themselves so the Word of God could be preached," Claude said.

Years before, a flourmill stood in the center of the park. It was at that beautiful setting, where huge oak, cypress, sycamore and weeping willow trees bowed alongside the riverbank that baptisms were performed on the last Sunday of the camp meetings.

"Thirty-four souls were saved and eighty-four were baptized in the Shenandoah River that first year! Others rededicated their lives to Christ," Claude said. "It was awesome!"

"Dean was ten years old when we first started Watermelon Park," Connie said. "Mike was only about three. It was a family affair."

In Connie's book, *Heart of the Matter*, she gives a vivid firsthand account of Watermelon Park:

It is now nearing the midnight hour. The last song was sung and the closing prayer was offered about 11:00 p.m. Still many people linger to fellowship with old friends, or maybe new friends they have met this year at Watermelon Park. Some are determined to shake hands with the famous Speer Family before leaving the park tonight.

The campers have been arriving steadily for the past few days. The campground is already filling up for so early in the week. Many who live close enough will drive in to the concert each night.

As I talked with friends here today, many have said, "It's like coming home." Others expressed, "It's like coming to a peaceful spot of the world, apart from everything." As I stand here in the softly lighted atmosphere under the big oak trees, I am aware of the serenity and the peacefulness of this place.

Through the night I hear laughter, chatter, and the sounds of children having that last fling of play before Mom says, "Bedtime." Just a few hundred feet from where I stand flows the beautiful Shenandoah River. God's beauty invades this place. The steady flowing river seems to confirm the fact that we can know for sure that there is a steadfast, unending source of strength available to us through the Person who spoke this river into being.

One of the greatest blessings to me each year is to see all the little children who attend Bible school. There was also an overwhelming attendance for the morning Bible study. People came with Bible in hand to hear the Bible prophecy teaching of noted speaker Dr. Nathan Meyer. Pastors, laymen and congregation alike clung to every word as he proclaimed the timely message. We are thrilled to have Dr. Meyer for five days of prophecy teaching.

Rev. Joe Cordosa is also involved in presenting wonderful moments of Biblical teaching.

The Speers were great tonight and a blessing. We

look forward to the Kingsmen and the Kingsboys tomorrow night, the Cathedrals the next night, and many great groups throughout the week.

God is already here at Watermelon Park. Lives have been touched spiritually and physically. We are expecting great things from God this week.

Each morning sixty-five children and teens emerged from that vast family campground to join in Bible school studies. Then on Sunday morning, some of those same precious children came to a stage front and asked Jesus to come into their hearts.

Mike was always adventurous, even as a child

Watermelon Park obviously meant different things to different people who attended. Mike Hopper, who attended the event with his family, talked about his own memories of that time period, saying that Watermelon Park was a fun time. Being a young child, he traveled with his parents and spent a week at the park, arriving early to make preparations for the event. He made friends that he only saw once a year. So, it was very special in that way. He described it as something like going to camp every year.

Looking back, he said it was inspiring to see people moved during the services. It was also touching to see how the Lord did great things at the park. "Many lives were touched. Souls were saved. It was a great time for our ministry."

The Blinded Eye Shall See

One year, a particular fellow came nightly to the singing services at Watermelon Park. During the days, and for the duration of the afternoon preaching, he fished along the riverbank.

"The next year, this gentleman unexpectedly came up to us during the Singing in the Smokies concert at Bryson City, North Carolina. He wanted to talk," Connie recalled. "He said, 'Folks, you probably don't recognize me. I was sitting out there in that audience last year at Watermelon Park. I was totally blind in one eye. When you all were on stage singing the song, 'The First Look,' lo and behold, a bug got in my good eye. I closed my eyes to get the bug out. After I got it out, I opened my eyes and was able to see you all perfectly with both eyes! My blinded eye was instantly healed! I know it's been almost a year, but I had to come up here and tell you about it!'"

Some time after the miracle occurred, he started preaching.

Drama At Watermelon Park

Connie told about another episode that happened one night many years ago. It all began when a dramatic play was planned at Watermelon Park, titled *The Cross, His Own*.

The youth group who met daily were led by a young lady named Sabrina. The youth volunteered to be members of the impromptu cast. They practiced and memorized their parts, and then performed the drama on the last night of the outdoor sing.

"Near the end of the presentation, a teenager was brought out on a cross, depicting Jesus. The youth group performed a song, 'I Saw Love,' while the boy was brought out slowly through the middle aisle of the outdoor congregation. I remember as the boy was carried forward, one fellow, under conviction, ran out of the park weeping. He just couldn't take it," she said.

"Later, someone who o knew this fellow told us that he wasn't a Christian and it was his son who was playing the part of Jesus on the cross! Someone followed him out of the park that night and shared the Gospel with him. He got saved! We saw him later that night and he was praising God!"

Wendy Bagwell Witnesses A Miracle

Another time at the Spirit of the Shenandoah Camp Meeting, Wendy Bagwell and the Sunliters were performing onstage. In between songs, Wendy stood at the center microphone talking to the audience. All of a sudden, a strong breeze started blowing and something caught his attention: a long, broken limb [almost a foot in circumference], was swaying and dangling precariously from the top of

116

one of the tallest trees above the people sitting in their lawn chairs. Wendy gasped as he realized that it was certain to fall into the crowd below.

Before he could shout out a warning to the crowd, the limb came toppling from the tree with a loud crack! Astonishingly, however, instead of landing directly on people sitting underneath it, in rows of chairs, the limb was slightly diverted by the wind, crashing into the narrow center aisle—fortuitously falling without touching or hurting anyone in the crowd.

Wendy was noticeably moved by the experience, as he boldly proclaimed the happening as a true miracle from God.

Dean, although young at the time, remembered that Wendy told the story for months afterwards at other venues. It deeply affected him.

The event was always exciting and inspiring

Chapter 23
Lifelong Friends

The better part of one's life consists of his friendships.

— Abraham Lincoln

There is an old adage that says gems may be precious but friends are priceless. The Hoppers are the first to admit that any accomplishments or triumphs they've enjoyed over the years are a direct result of the Savior's blessings and grace and, the support and devotion of God's children.

Through the years there have been many special friends who, through their kindness, thoughtfulness and assistance, have helped the ministry grow. Perfect examples of these special friends are those cultivated directly as a result of Watermelon Park.

Ellis Klahre, of rural Bedford County, Pennsylvania, is such a friend who has meant a great deal to the Hopper organization and family. Ellis is in the lumber business and has known the Hoppers for many years.

"I got saved one Saturday night before Labor Day in 1971. After the Lord came into my life, I had a desire to hear Gospel music. Not long afterwards, my wife Marge and I went to Chambersburg to hear the Hopper Brothers and Connie sing. There, we met them all," Ellis said.

"We saw them several times over the next year or so. One day I asked Claude if he'd consider coming to Everett, Pennsylvania, for a concert at our church. Claude immediately smiled and said, 'Yes, I will.' He agreed, never mentioning a price. They just came. From that day on we have been great friends," he added.

Soon after that experience Ellis and Marge volunteered to help with the Watermelon Park project, organizing crews and helping build a portable stage. For years they assisted with the extensive mowing, clean up detail and improvements to the park in preparation for the annual Spirit of the Shenandoah event.

"Other friends who helped make the homecoming a success included Melvin and Bessie Godfrey, Dean and Catherine Keeney,

Don and Polly Winters, Dave and Gertie Kuhl, Martin and Lib Panak, Sandy and David Newell, Debbie Panak, Charlie and Louise Smith, Orville and Mary Long, Nathan and Retha Keener, Bob and Jan Maraugha, Ray and Doris Hostetter, John Kennedy, Ronald Harvey, and Conard and Dot Deeds. Dot had beautiful handmade banners displaying the name of the event to accent the stage. There were many others who also helped.

"These folks remain our dearest friends. We will always be grateful for each of their sacrifices and to all the others who participated along the way," Claude said.

Watermelon Park Floods

The annual Spirit of the Shenandoah Camp Meeting continued to grow for many years until the mid-1980s, when a great flash flood, which took many people's lives in the region, washed Watermelon Park away entirely.

"During the flooding, even the new stage supported by sturdy wooden beams was washed off—everything gone! Nothing was left after the calamity but a deep hole where the stage once stood," Claude said. "That was the sad end of Watermelon Park for the Hoppers.

"Scrambling for a replacement location, we chose Pipestem State Park, located in the mountains of West Virginia, near Beckley. I worked out a deal with the Department of Natural Resources, at Charleston, WV. We tried to get a Gospel sing started there, similar to the Spirit of the Shenandoah Camp Meeting. We tried to have a revival atmosphere, but unfortunately, the Pipestem Camp Meeting was never as popular as Watermelon Park had been.

"I remember they had a nice campground at Pipestem, but it was limited. Thankfully, some of the same crew came that helped us at Watermelon Park. We had morning Bible study along with programs for children. After lunch we had old fashioned preaching and at night we had the main concerts."

In September 1986, Claude authored a commentary in *Singing News Magazine*, describing his personal excitement behind the group's first appearance at Pipestem State Park, in July of that year:

With a mixture of fear and trembling, and yet overwhelming

119

anticipation, we drove onto the grounds of Pipestem State Park, high up in the beautiful mountains of West Virginia. It was only one day until our 14th Annual Camp Meeting would officially begin.

In our hearts, it had begun months ago, as we had to make new plans, new arrangements for a different location due to the complete devastation of Watermelon Park's recent flooding. We, along with many of you, joined hands together daily in prayer for God to have His way throughout the entire week. Our hearts were deeply touched as we parked the bus and walked the short distance to where our loyal friends had already begun to assemble the beautiful stage that overlooked the most serene setting.

Little did we realize to what extent we were on the very threshold of being "high and lifted up" as God manifested Himself through the Word, the singing and so many individuals!

The Hoppers at Watermelon Park

Chapter 24
The Work Ethic

Plough deep while sluggards sleep.

— Benjamin Franklin

It was always Claude's intention to teach his boys early in life about the importance of being reliable and dependable. To that end, he would seek out small opportunities to train them in this direction. "One thing I never figured out, when I was a child, was how Dad seemed to always create something for me to do when I got home from school," Dean said and laughed. "There was never a chance to just come home from school and watch television, or take it easy around the house. He always had something in mind for me to accomplish each day.

"I once asked Dad, 'So, how come you always have jobs for me to do...and regardless of how much I do, there is always more and more and more for me to do?'

Claude replied dryly, "Because, son, there is always something to do on a farm."

Claude was actually right, for the duties seemed endless. The work may be mending a fence, putting up new railing or cleaning and closing up the barn. Dean added: "I also might have to put up hay, feedbags or supplies into the shed.

"I wouldn't take anything now for the times I spent on the farm; but it was really difficult at the time. Farm life teaches a person a lot of common sense and values that can be applied to everyday life: things like a strong work ethic, patience, endurance, perseverance and resolve."

Claude confirmed that Dean, even though he was especially hyperactive and always on the go (much like his father), was an exceptionally hard worker as a teen. Mike, although younger, worked right alongside his brother on most occasions. The two boys were close friends as well—as they remain today.

For pleasure, Dean enjoyed riding mini-bikes and dirt bikes and all manner of outdoor activities. Mike's restless nature also seemed to lead him toward extreme sports, such as motocross and later jet-skiing.

"Both the boys have always had delightful personalities, good manners and other strong qualities," Claude said, "and I always had confidence that they could and would accomplish anything they set their minds to do. Both have an abundance of energy and a love for people."

Claude recalls advising both sons, when they were young, not to enter Southern Gospel music just because Mama and Dad were involved. Fortunately they seemed to gravitate toward it anyway. To give them incentive to consider other alternatives, Claude prodded each of the boys to choose a college they'd like to attend. He told them that he and their mother would do everything in their power to try to send them to that school. In a sense, the family situation resembled something out of America's early beginnings when a child would continue his education by joining his father in the family business, or by learning the father's vocation. In the age-old American practice of apprenticeship, Dean and Mike were unconsciously being mentored in the ministry by their parents.

"I suspect that's where they really gained their education: I've actually included them in on just about every aspect of the ministry, especially once they became adults," Claude said. Besides having hands-on involvement in the Hoppers' ministry, Dean is also involved in a Southern Gospel promotional organization, Abraham Promotions, which includes his brother-in-law, Tony Greene, Tony Gore, Ray Flynn, and Roger Talley. The business is primarily responsible for the Annual Gatlinburg Gathering every Labor Day, in Gatlinburg, Tennessee, and the annual Singing in the Sun event, at Myrtle Beach, South Carolina, each spring.

"My brother Mike, Les Beasley and I are part owners of the annual Great Western Fan Festival, in California, also," Dean explained.

Connie added: "If the Hoppers ended today, I would like to think that Dean and Mike would be able to continue in the Gospel music industry in any variety of capacities. In addition to having their own unique musical abilities, they know a great deal about recording, computer technology, promoting, and many other areas of endeavor."

Chapter 25
Enjoying Gospel Music

In years to follow, I watched these fellows constantly strive to do their best for the Lord and the fans. The Cathedral Quartet set the bar for all other Southern Gospel music groups.

— Dean Hopper

It was in the early days of the Hopper Brothers and Connie's ministry, when they had opportunities to spend quality time with Southern Gospel artists such as the Happy Goodman Family, Singing Rambos, the Hinsons, the Downings, Cathedrals, Singing Americans, Speer Family, Dixie Echos, Rex Nelon Singers, Florida Boys, and other legendary greats. During this time period Dean and Mike became inspired musically.

"For example, even as small children my boys, Dean and Mike, started picking up a lot by watching Howard and Vestal's son, Ricky, play drums on stage. Dean, who started playing drums when he was seven, learned a great deal from the Oak Ridge Boys' drummer, Mark Ellerbee," Connie remembered.

Dean added that as a child he got the chance to travel with his parents on occasion. He remembered flying with the family to several locations in those days, since this was the time when children could fly for just a few dollars. He went to California for the first time when he was eight years old. By that time he was already playing drums for the group when there was no school, or during summer vacation.

"On that California trip, I recall that we had eighteen consecutive dates, with seven or eight dates scheduled with the Oak Ridge Boys. We were appearing at all kinds of major concert halls. I don't think anyone really knew who we were at the shows, for it was the Oak Ridge Boys that drew the crowd. Yet, it was a great experience for me."

As a boy, Dean studied drummers while on the road, like Ricky Goodman, Billy Blackwood and Ronny Sego. "It was all a big attraction for me; I really wanted to be a part of it all," Dean reminisced.

"I grew up around mostly older folks. Many of Mom and Dad's friends became my friends as well."

By the time Dean was ten, he had the opportunity to play drums with a variety of groups on stage. "I played drums with the Cathedrals on many different occasions. It seemed like every time I was playing for them, George Younce sang, 'Everybody Will Be Happy'. Because he had the rhythm going on, he just wore that song out! He was always great!"

Dean

Dean said George made people feel like a part of his family: "Back then I guess it was a friendship between a young boy, his family and two gentlemen: George Younce and Glen Payne. In years to follow, I watched these fellows constantly strive to do their best for the Lord and their Gospel fans. The Cathedral Quartet set the bar for all other Southern Gospel music groups. That bar is still being used today as the benchmark whereby all others are measured."

Dean recalled other moments with the Cathedrals, too. George particularly loved to tell funny stories and play practical jokes. In fact, one night, in Virginia, the Hoppers and the Cathedrals were in concert together. Throughout the evening, George comically picked on Connie. Finally, in the spirit of good fun, Connie acted as though she'd had enough and came from backstage with a broom she'd found, acting like she was going to hit him with it! Quick-witted George said, 'Connie, the last time I saw you with that broom, you were riding it!' The audience burst into laughter, and so did Connie.

124

That was a great memory for them all.

In addition, Dean once played drums with Cleavant Derricks, the black minister and artist who wrote "Just A Little Talk With Jesus" and "We'll Soon Be Done." When Joe Bonsall and Richard Sterban [now of the Oak Ridge Boys] were with the Keystones, he performed with them during the International Gospel Song Festival, in Nashville.

"In both cases, Dean happened to be there and was asked to play," Connie added. "That was such an exciting opportunity and encouraging for a child!"

Mike Hopper and Music

As a youngster Mike, too, found he had a knack for the drums, although he never really practiced until the rest of the family left on tour and he was home alone, with his nanny. Dean had an old Ludwig set in the basement of the farmhouse. The family also had an old sound system stored in the basement, having replaced it with a newer system on the road. The speakers, which were as tall as Mike, sat next to the drum kit, along with Dean's stereo system nearby.

Mike, Richard Sterban and Claude

"Dean had an 8-track tape of the pop-rock group, Bread. I started playing the 8-track through the P.A. system. I was also a big Elvis fan; his drummer, Ronnie Tutt, was awesome."

Mike laughed mischievously as he remembered those early practice sessions, saying it must have driven the babysitter crazy. He added, "Before long, she knew every word to every song on every 8-track I had by heart."

It was in the basement that Mike first discovered various rhythm patterns and what drums can do to accentuate a musical perform-

125

ance. As he played along with various records, he attempted to figure out what other musicians were doing. His own sense of rhythm was astonishing.

"I guess I was around seven years old when I first started playing Dean's old set," he said. By analyzing and imitating other musicians and practicing long hours, Mike grew in ability. It would be a while, however, before his parents discovered his secret pastime and the degree of his talent.

Mike practicing

In concert

Chapter 26
Learning From Others

The secret of joy in work is contained in one word—excellence. To know how to do something well is to enjoy it.

– Pearl S. Buck

At one point the Hopper Brothers and Connie leaned on the expertise of Lee Roy Abernathy, sometimes known as "Professor" by folks within the Southern Gospel community.

Lee Roy.
Abernathy

When Claude and Connie first met Abernathy in the 1960s, when he sang with another gentleman, Carroll "Shorty" Bradford. The two sounded like a full quartet when they performed, giving the illusion of four-part harmony.

On occasion the group stayed all night at Lee Roy's home and slept on the floor of his living room. Throughout the night, he worked with one of them at a time as a voice coach.

"Of course you have to have a talent—the more the better—and commitment. Yet, Lee Roy taught my brothers and me that performing Gospel music was ten percent singing and ninety percent attitude," Claude recalled, underscoring that he never forgot his comments. "When he said that, I thought to myself, 'I certainly love to sing and, I can have a good attitude, too!'

"Rather than just being a good singer, pianist and teacher, Lee Roy's greatest gift was that he was a Southern Gospel psychologist, so to speak," Claude said. "He could psych you up in such a way that you found yourself singing extremely low parts and exceedingly high parts you never dreamed you could hit. He somehow made you believe it was possible, and sure enough, he was usually right.

"He showed us, by using the scale, how to get the right tone with each note. For him it was all about tone quality. He was a real genius," Claude added.

"In my estimation, one becomes whom one associates with. So, it was by observing, by listening, by attending and by being on the Southern Gospel programs with other artists that the Hopper Brothers and Connie analyzed what others were doing and were inspired. We tried to improve, without mimicking others, and grew as singers and ministers."

J.G. Whitfield

Jesse Gillis Whitfield, a legend in Southern Gospel circles, was instrumental in helping the Hopper Brothers and Connie grow in Southern Gospel music. The Hoppers met Mr. Whitfield when he was primarily a Gospel music promoter. He was a prominent player in the origin of the popular television series, *The Gospel Singing Jubilee,* and founded the premier Gospel magazine *The Singing News.*

J. G. Whitfield

"By promoting us in the North Carolina area, we became acquainted with him," Claude said. "He eventually took a liking to us and booked us in faraway places like Mississippi and Florida, and elsewhere in the South.

At that time, Whitfield promoted the biggest all-night Gospel sing in the country, at Bonifay, Florida. The first time the Hopper Brothers and Connie performed there, Connie was eight months pregnant with Mike. They took the stage as the sun was coming up. Claude described it as "an amazing experience that I'll never forget."

"You know, Mr. Whitfield really didn't need us at the time. He was well known and successful! We were complete unknowns and nobodies. However, he gave us a chance," he said.

J.G. passsed away on April 9, 2006, at 90 years old.

Above, Will, Steve, Claude, Monroe and Paul Hopper and Connie Shelton.
Below, the Hoppers Brothers and Connie in the 1960s.

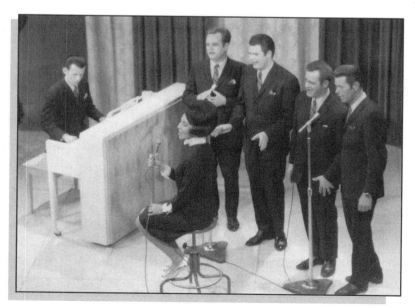

Connie, in her Madison High basketball uniform, was one of the standouts for the local team. Below, left, this is Connie's senior portrait, at Madison High School; and, below, right, an early snapshot of the Hopper Brothers and Connie (Monroe, Claude, Connie, Will and Steve pose before a Gospel sing).

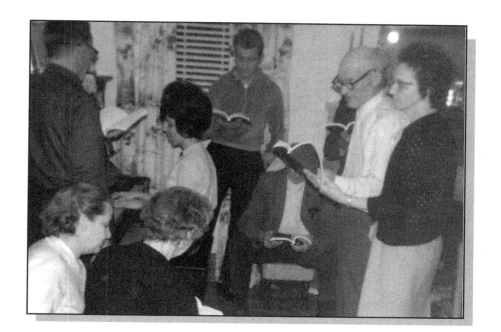

Above, Connie, at the piano, plays and sings along with her family. The Shelton home was always full of music. Her father, Henry (above, second from right) also played the banjo and sang in a local Gospel group. Her mother, Mary Lou (abbove, far right) was also musically inclined.

Below, at right, Henry Evan Shelton and Mary Lou Flynn Shelton, Connie's parents, owned a tobacco farm outside Stokesdale, NC.

From the union of Archer and Dossie Hopper (shown above) eleven children were eventually born. In birth-order, they were: Virginia, Monroe, Octola, Catharine, Paul, Will, Claude, Wayne, Richard, Steve, and the baby of the family, Dewey. Below, the entire Hopper family gathered together for this photo in the 1970s.

Claude Hopper

Above, this was a group
shot of the Hopper
Brothers and Connie in the
mid-1970s. At right,
Connie oftentimes played
bass guitar for the group
in the 1960s and into the
early 1970s.

Dean Hopper

Mike Hopper

Connie and Mike at
Watermelon Park

Dean

Left to right, Will, Connie, Claude and Lee Chilton sing at Watermelon Park, along with Kirk Talley on bass and Roger Talley on piano.

At left, the Hopper Brothers and Connie, including Will Hopper, Debra Talley and Connie and Claude sing at *The Spirit of the Shenandoah Camp Meeting.*

At right, the Hoppers—Dean, Kim, Connie and Claude—sing at one of the last camp meetings held at Watermelon Park. The park was later devastated from a major flood, and an event was started in Beckley, WV, at Pipestem Park.

Claude's sister, Virginia Hopper Steele, and Claude at a concert

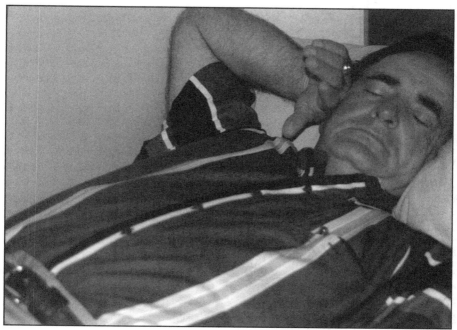

Claude catches a few winks while traveling on the Hopper bus. The Hopper family spends a great deal of time on the road as they keep a full tour schedule.

The original Hopper homeplace, where all the Hopper siblings were raised, remains in a pasture adjacent to where it was originally located.

Claude and Connie's home, built on the exact location of where the cabin was originally located. Several of the foundational stones from the cabin were used to make a stone fireplace.

Here is Claude's prize bull, *Shoutin' Time.*

The Farm, Dean and Mike's recording studio, located inside this barn, near the entrance to Claude's farm. The facility offers a state-of-the-art digital recording studio. This is actually the third recording studio for the Hoppers; the first was destroyed by a tornado, and the second studio burned.

The old corn crib still stands on the farm. It was hewn from trees on the property.

It was several years ago that Bill Gaither, Guy Penrod, Mark Lowry and David Phelps harmonized in Connie's kitchen—singing for their supper. Below, David, Guy and Bill tour the farm (while Mark is sound asleep on the couch in Connie and Claude's living room).

Here is another view of the beautiful Hopper farm, located near Madison, NC.

The Hopper Brothers and Connie today. Left to right, Will, Steve, Claude, Monroe and Connie Hopper. A rare reunion of the original group is always a treat.

Connie Hopper singing during a Hopper Heritage Tour date

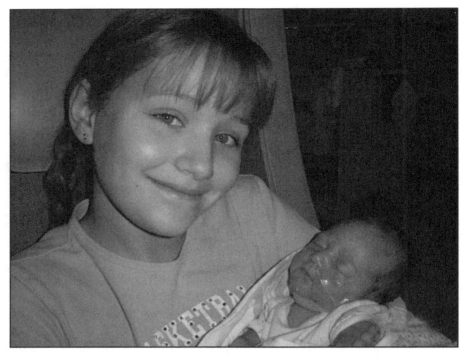

Big sister, Karlye, tenderly holds Lexus Jazz Hopper, only days after her premature birth. Lexi was born at 12:39 a.m. Tuesday, January 4, 2005.

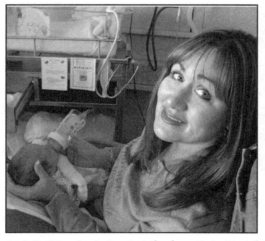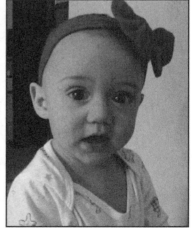

At left, Kim feeds Lexi at the hospital. At right, this picture of Lexi was taken in 2006.

Above, an early photo of the Hopper Brothers and Connie. Below, the eleven Hopper siblings gather for a family picture. The Hoppers remain a close family.

Chapter 27
Singing At Sea

It's turned into a great time of fellowship for everyone, with plenty of great music. We always look forward to the cruise.

— Connie Hopper

In 1974, Skylite Talent, of Nashville, and several of their artists embarked on a new venture, a Gospel singing cruise. The Kingsmen and the Hoppers were at the top of the list. The endeavor was an ocean cruise coupled with a concert series aboard a first class luxury liner.

By this time, the Hopper Brothers and Connie consisted of Connie, Claude, Will, and Dean, along with Roger Talley. Monroe had retired from singing full time shortly before the first cruise began. Roger was fresh out of college and had been with the group less than a year.

The idea behind the sea cruise was for Gospel groups to encourage friends and fans to join together aboard a ship for several days of great fellowship, relaxation and Southern Gospel music.

"I remember that first cruise," Dean said. "I was eleven years old. The Kingsmen and our family initially got the trip started. The Scenic Land Boys and the Hinson Family traveled with us on that luxury cruise."

After the first cruise, Eldridge "Foxy" Fox, of the Kingsmen, suggested that the group of artists go with Wilcox Tours, of Asheville, North Carolina, for their next cruise. Claude agreed and worked alongside Fox. Maurice Templeton was the representative for Wilcox Tours at the time. The new venture was called *Singing at Sea*.

"The result was that the Kingsmen and the Hopper Brothers and Connie went on the first *Singing at Sea* cruise," Maurice recalled, "where we

Maurice Templeton

had about a hundred and thirty guests booked by singing groups. Well, after that I started looking for new ways to make this venture grow and realized that we could potentially fill a whole ship with Southern Gospel fans!"

That second cruise turned out to be a rousing success and included the Hopper Brothers and Connie, the Kingsmen, Dixie Melody Boys and the original Singing Americans.

"Then the third year was an ominous year when we experienced a horrible tropical storm at sea," Dean said. "We were at a port at Freeport, in the Bahamas, and it had rained all week long. Earlier in the week the weather had been just awful at Nassau, and it was still terrible.

"I remember we were shopping at the World Bazaar and our cruise director appeared and hollered excitedly, 'If there's anyone here from the *Emerald Seas*, we're leaving!'

"After we asked what was going on, he told us the ship was leaving two hours early due to a storm that was sucking all the water out of the channel."

The *Emerald Seas* was originally a World War II vessel. It had once been a supply ship delivering provisions to the allied troops. After the war, additional decks were added and it was transformed into a luxury cruise liner. The ship, which may have seen better days, had a permanent lean, unfortunately.

"After we all got back to the ship, it began to move out of the channel," Dean remembered. "There was a tugboat on each side of the liner to help us move on out to sea. A full-blown tropical storm was brewing and rough water moved into the area. The waves were incredible. Due to the rough seas, the tugboats were just trying to keep us from capsizing. As the ship leaned toward one direction, a tugboat rammed against the ship's hull to counteract the tilt. Then, when the ship wobbled and slanted in the opposite direction, the second tug butted the other side."

Where were Mike and Dean at the time of the tropical storm? They were out on the top deck in full exposure to the wind, rain and waves, running and laughing along the deck without a care in the world. As the angry waves crashed against the hull of the ship, they became interested in watching the prop lift up, down and in and out of the water. At first it seemed extremely thrilling for two fun-loving boys looking for excitement. However, as the storm picked up its force, Dean began to feel ill as he watched rolling water. He tried to keep his footing onboard. The boys finally went inside to wait out the storm. It so happened that Dean was bunking with several friends while Mike headed for his parent's cabin.

"While Dean and Mike had been running around on deck, I was in our cabin deathly sick. I could not leave my bunk!" Connie said.

"Michael finally came into our cabin and found a place to cuddle up on the floor. While he was lying there, the ocean water splashed up against our room window. We were fairly high up on the ship, so it was extremely scary."

The ocean liner rocked and swayed to the angry mood of the tempest. After several minutes Mike mumbled, "Mama, do you think the ship is going to turn over?"

"I tried to pat his head and calm him down," Connie recalled. "However, I was so sick I figured if the ship did turn over, at least it would put me out of my misery!"

Roger and a few others were able to stand the storm's effects without getting nauseous. Those who were able assembled a jumbled troop of artists to sing and entertain guests who were brave enough to come out of their rooms.

"By the time we got back to Florida, I kissed the ground!" Connie said with a chuckle. "It took a long while for me to get over that adventure. However, in all fairness, for all the years we have participated on cruises, that was the first and only time we ever experienced a storm like that. I don't want to go through that again."

"The Hopper family formed a business relationship with Wilcox Tours to book cruises annually," Claude explained. "Eventually, Maurice Templeton came to see me in Charlotte. He told me he was no longer with the Wilcox organization. Maurice started his own cruise company, Templeton Tours," Claude remembered.

He had been a longtime friend to the Hopper family and to many other artists. Claude later met with others involved with Singing at Sea to discuss which direction they should all go. Should they continue with Wilcox, or move the annual cruise over to Templeton's new organization? A decision was finally made and all future cruises were scheduled with Templeton Tours, now one of the largest Christian-based tour companies in the world.

Jumping Overboard

"I can remember many years ago when we would go into the port at Nassau and there would be native children who would ask folks from the ship to toss coins into the water," Mike recalled.

With a heavy accent, the children would yell out, "Hey, George—they called everyone George—toss a coin into the water and watch me dive for it!"

When a quarter was tossed into the water, it spiraled downward and one of the native boys would dive in to snatch the coin before it spun to the bottom. Some of the youngsters were even brave enough to climb up on the thick ropes of the ship and high-dive for coins. Once any of the boys collected five dollars or so in change, he'd leave. Another young diver would take his place. On one particular occasion, after watching these shenanigans, several young fellows onboard the ship got a bright idea. Glen Payne's son, Todd, Eldridge Fox's son, Greg, and Mike Hopper decided they could do the same thing!

"We waited for the right moment [when no adults were looking]; then we did it! We dove into the water from the side of the ship! It was great fun, but we got into a little trouble afterwards. Since we were only wearing swimming trunks, we didn't have our boarding passes with us. So we didn't have access to get back onto our ship. Had it not been for Maurice, we would have never gotten back onboard, and our parents would have killed us!" Mike laughed. "Maurice vouched for us and got us all back onto the ship without any more problems."

The cruises have come a long way since those early days. In the 1970s, singing groups and fans were positioned in an isolated section of a ship, away from the regular tourists and travelers; today, Southern Gospel music fans typically book the entire ship.

Voyages now hold as many as 1,800 Gospel music lovers, and today's hottest groups participate annually. Most tours are sold out months in advance of the cruise date.

Chapter 28
Learning To Give

We make a living by what we get; we make a life by what we give.

—Winston Churchill

Sometimes God sends special individuals or circumstances our way for a purpose. Perhaps it is to get our attention, or to teach us important principles. Christians walking sensitively in His light often recognize the fingerprint of the Almighty in unusual occurrences.

Through a series of circumstances, after singing at Sappony Baptist Church, in Stony Creek, Virginia, Claude and Connie felt led to do something out of the ordinary, in making a financial commitment to help a young man complete college and go on to seminary.

"It was the fall of 1976, and to be honest, although we were certain we were being led to assist this fellow, we were concerned about the magnitude of such a commitment. We sensed the Lord's prodding in this as never before. The tuition was a phenomenal amount of money for us, but we began to pray and trust," Claude said, "and we turned the college fund commitment over to Christ."

It was amazing that in future weeks, God blessed the ministry in ways that made the ongoing assistance possible. Donations from the Lord's people increased at concert dates over the following months, and Claude and Connie could see exactly what was happening: the Lord was meeting the need and teaching them something new.

"After our commitment, then friends from Sappony Baptist Church began giving to this young man's college fund, as well God really blessed.

"The Lord led us into a deeper relationship with Him by giving to this young man," Claude recalled. It was at this point the group came to recognize it's really impossible to receive the Lord's entire blessing if you don't give generously and cheerfully to His work.

This fellow, named Hugh Mays, entered Richard Bland College on a full-time basis by September. On June 4, 1978, during the 205th

Homecoming at Sappony Baptist Church, Hugh was licensed to preach. He was later ordained at Sappony Baptist and accepted at Southeastern Baptist Theological Seminary at Wake Forest, North Carolina, graduating Magna Cum Laude in December 1980.

"Hugh became a pastor, and we were thrilled," Claude said. On July 26, 1981, he was invited to proclaim God's Word at Watermelon Park. It was a wonderful experience for the Hoppers and for Hugh, and a glorious culmination of the group's yielding to the Lord's desire for them to give abundantly.

This Is How God Works

"Sadly, as the years went by, we lost contact with Hugh. However, one day he just popped in at our office at Madison. It was a wonderful moment to see him again and to hear what the Lord was doing in his life," Claude said.

"Coincidentally, around that same time period, we had just invested in a computer," Claude said. "Hugh asked us what we were doing with it and I explained, 'Nothing really. We don't know how to use it yet.'

As they came to find out, besides being a pastor, Hugh was also a gifted computer programmer. As he examined the new hardware and got a feel for what the Hoppers' special needs were, he offered to set up a workstation and program the computer. He would also train the staff on how to use his customized software.

For a while, Hugh traveled to the Hopper office one day a week as he developed various programs and backup systems to modernize and transform the Hopper organization.

"Hugh set up systems and methods that helped save us time in many areas of the ministry, and developed an extensive royalty program for our publishing company."

Every now and then, he still drops by the Madison office to update the various programs and visit with the family.

"It's a God thing," Claude concluded. "This is how the Lord works, in that the Hoppers made a small gesture many years ago, but God just keeps giving, giving and giving back to us. The Lord has given everything back to us hundreds of times over. It taught us a vital lesson on giving: you just can't out-give the Lord!"

Chapter 29
Overcoming Illness In 1979

We all appreciate an arm around the shoulder or a kind word. When the Holy Spirit leads you to encourage someone, go ahead and do it. Be an encourager.

— Dave Egnor

An edition of *Our Daily Bread,* a devotional publication of Radio Bible Class, contained this quote: God can transform tragedies into triumphs!

How true this proclamation is. When a child of God enters into a dark valley, or drifts into a violent storm, the best remedy is to cling tightly to Jesus. In her inspiring book, *The Peace That Passeth Understanding,* Connie Hopper wrote about her personal storm.

It was 1978 and Claude and Connie had set out on a grueling eleven-hour flight to Amman, Jordan, to embark on an inspiring tour of Israel and the Holy Lands. The next few days were glorious as they walked streets where Jesus had walked.

By the time she returned home to Madison, Connie was totally exhausted. She didn't feel energized or rested by the vacation. She was unusually tired.

One of the first concert dates for the Hopper Brothers and Connie, after their return home in November, was at Winkler's Grove Church, in Hickory, North Carolina. That night Connie was physically and mentally drained as she struggled to make it through the evening. She began to worry that something was wrong.

Connie in the Middle East

Not long after that sing, they were home one evening when Connie casually walked by a mirror and stopped to smooth out her dress. As she passed her hand over her right breast, she realized something wasn't normal. She thought she felt a lump!

The next morning she called her gynecologist. Dr. Barker was out of town, so Connie reluctantly spoke with his nurse about her

On a Holy Land tour

findings. The nurse, who wasn't overly concerned or compassionate about the situation, said the doctor typically recommended a specialist or a surgeon in such situations. After the call, Connie hung up the phone and decided to wait awhile before doing anything drastic.

After the holidays, she went back on the road with the group. Even though she was weary most of the time, nightly concerts kept her mind occupied and off her health concerns.

By late February 1979, during self-examination, she found the lump again. This time there was no doubt about it. It was there. It even seemed larger than before.

That night in bed she confided to Claude about finding the abnormality; and, of course he did his best to reassure her that everything was probably fine. They agreed that she would call the doctor. Early the next morning, she called Dr. Barker's office again. This time she spoke directly with him and asked to be checked. Instead, he recommended she call a particular surgeon, Dr. Abrams, located in Greensboro. After the conversation, Connie got down on her knees and prayed before calling the surgeon.

She talked to his nurse about her circumstance. The nurse said, "I'm sorry. Dr. Abrams can't see you today. Perhaps he can see you tomorrow."

The nurse quickly added, "However, Dr. Farley is here and can see you today. He is our senior surgeon."

"Fine," Connie replied. "I would really like to see someone today!"

That afternoon she drove to his office. In this excerpt from her book, Connie describes the encounter:

> Dr. Farley was a nice, gentle man. He asked me all the things that doctors ask of new patients. He examined me and confirmed that I did have a lump in my right breast, but said chances were good that it was benign.
>
> Very carefully and tactfully, he explained, "The thing we need to do is put you in the hospital and do a biopsy and see how it turns out. We'll do a frozen section and send it to the lab where it will be tested immediately. If it is malignant, we will go ahead and do the surgery then. If it isn't, you'll walk out and forget about it."

Connie agreed halfheartedly, realizing she had no other choice. Dr. Farley explained that his nurse would telephone the hospital, make all arrangements and notify her when everything was set. Connie went back home and waited for the phone call.

Finally, a day or so later the nurse contacted her and said preparations were made at Wesley Long Hospital in Greensboro on Monday, March 5th. After pre-op tests, the medical procedure would be done early Tuesday morning.

Connie described that next week as a "nightmare," as she attempted to prepare for the operation. She continued on the road and even attended a recording session with the group that week. Yet, her stamina seemed to dissolve as she struggled to keep going.

On the Sunday night prior to the surgery, the group was scheduled to sing at a Church of God in Lumberton, North Carolina. When the pastor called on those in the congregation who wished to be anointed, Connie stepped forward and stood in line to be prayed for.

For the next few days, Connie was at the lowest point of her adult life, as she awaited the surgical procedure.

The day came to check in at the hospital, and since Claude was temporarily tied up with a telethon program, Connie's sister, Wilma, drove her over to the facility. After Connie settled in to her hospital room, visitors stopped by during visiting hours and helped her keep her mind off the impending procedure.

That evening Dr. Farley walked into her room to discuss the details of the biopsy, confirming that it would be done the next morning. His relaxed nature helped to calm Connie's worries.

The next morning she woke up early and spent quiet time with the Lord. She had come a long way in the last day or so, spiritually speaking, and felt ready for the operation. She had turned the entire situation over to the Lord and found His peace and comfort in the situation.

At 11:00 a.m. Connie, who looked especially fragile in the hospital gown, was wheeled into the operating room and the doctor, wearing his surgical garb, walked over beside her. She tried her best to focus on the doctor's face but her eyelids wanted to droop due to the medication she had already received. She managed to look up at him and mutter, "God's going to help me through this." Dr. Farley smiled, nodded toward his assistant, and waited for Connie to fall completely asleep so that the procedure could begin.

Two and a half hours later, Claude and the rest of the family were still sitting in the waiting room. As the time went by, they all became extremely anxious. The procedure lasted longer than anyone expected. Finally, Wilma walked over to the nurse's station to inquire. The nurse called into the operating room and found out that the operation would take still a while longer. At that point everyone realized the truth: the biopsy had been done, tested, and found malignant.

Dr. Farley began a mastectomy once the cancer was confirmed. During the painstaking surgical process, an artery under Connie's arm was unintentionally severed and she lost a great deal of blood. Yet during the entire process, her vital signs remained strong and consistent. The operation lasted a little over five hours.

After they wheeled her gurney into recovery, Claude was allowed into the room to see her although she was still fast asleep.

The rest of the day was a complete haze for Connie as the anesthesia slowly wore off.

Connie wrote:

> When I woke up, I cannot express how I felt. I was an entirely different person. That was when I learned I had had a mastectomy. That is when I should have been depressed.

The Lord had performed a miracle in Connie: she felt empowered by the presence of the Holy Spirit. Even though she waited to hear whether her cancer had spread, she found perfect peace.

She was later told that Dr. Farley performed twenty-one different tests during the surgery to determine the extent of the cancer. Those test results would return within four to five days. In the meantime, she was to wait.

Connie was hospitalized for the next twelve days, and she said, "There was always someone coming in to cheer me up." She made new friendships with employees in the hospital wing, and even Claude was astounded with her positive attitude. She experienced very little pain and had a healthy appetite. Even though her arm was in a sling due to the severed artery, she remained in good spirits.

Five days after the surgery, Dr. Farley entered the room to talk to her.

"Well, I have good news," he said, as he clasped her hands in his. "We received the results from the tests. Every one of those tests came back negative! I think we got all the cancer."

Connie burst into tears and praised the Lord!

The next few days would have its share of difficulties. By Sunday, Connie's ninth day in the hospital, the doctor wrote an order so she could finally shower and wash her hair.

It was then, after she undressed, that she came face-to-face with the consequences of the operation: a part of her body was missing. She sobbed for the next half-hour until at last she sensed the Lord's presence. At that moment it was as if Christ softly spoke, saying, "Connie, this is not a loss. This is gain. By losing a portion of your body, you have gained further life."

Connie recalls she momentarily stopped crying as she felt God's reassurance. After her shower, she dressed and went out into the room where a nurse was waiting. Realizing the seriousness of the moment, the nurse reached her arm around Connie's shoulder. They both sat on the side of the bed and wept.

Later that same day an attractive, kind-natured woman, Ann Mills, stopped by Connie's room and introduced herself. She was a volunteer representative from Reach To Recovery of the American Cancer Society. Ann had had the same medical procedure earlier. Connie felt comfortable with Ann and was able to ask her a variety of practical and personal questions that filled her mind since the procedure. Ann's visit was a pleasant and valuable experience for Connie.

While she was still in the hospital, Dr. Farley suggested that Connie might consider being a volunteer for Reach To Recovery. She immediately accepted, hoping that she could share with others what the Lord had already done in her life.

After her recovery period, she attended the American Cancer Society's school for Reach To Recovery volunteers. After completion of the training, she started receiving occasional phone calls and referrals from doctors. She then began visiting the hospitals and talking to patients.

Ironically, the Lord used the early counseling opportunities to aid Connie as she also healed—physically and mentally— from the trauma of the operation.

It's now hard for Connie to believe that her battle with cancer—and the testing of her faith—took place over twenty-five years ago. For her, it seems like only yesterday in so many ways. As a cancer survivor, she has since been used in countless ways to speak to others about her experience and God's healing power.

By overcoming her bout with cancer and seeing God's healing power in her life, she realizes she is commissioned to reach out to others in need.

Above all else, Connie Hopper is now an encourager.

Chapter 30
The Reagan Inauguration Ball

Under one such marker lies a young man, Martin Treptow, who left his job in a small town barbershop in 1917 to go to France with the famed Rainbow Division. There, on the western front, he was killed trying to carry a message between battalions under heavy artillery fire.

We're told that on his body was found a diary. On the flyleaf under the heading 'My Pledge,' he had written these words: 'America must win this war. Therefore I will work, I will save, I will sacrifice, I will endure, I will fight cheerfully and do my utmost, as if the issue of the whole struggle depended on me alone.'

The crisis we are facing today does not require of us the kind of sacrifice that Martin Treptow and so many thousands of others were called upon to make. It does require, however, our best effort and our willingness to believe in ourselves and to believe in our capacity to perform great deeds, to believe that together with God's help we can and will resolve the problems which now confront us.

And after all, why shouldn't we believe that? We are Americans. God bless you, and thank you.

— President Ronald Reagan, *Inaugural Address*

The words published above were the concluding words of a triumphant speech uttered by the "Great Communicator," President Ronald Reagan, on January 20, 1981. On that extraordinary day in Washington, Ronald Reagan, at sixty-nine, stood before thousands of supporters and onlookers. His hand was placed upon his mother's

Bible, and it was opened to the seventh chapter, fourteenth verse of II Chronicles:

> If my people, which are called by my name, shall humble themselves, and pray, and seek my face, and turn from their wicked ways; then will I hear from heaven, and will forgive their sin, and will heal their land.

He then took the Presidential Oath of Office.

Reagan, formerly a sports radio personality, Hollywood actor and Republican governor of California, defeated President Jimmy Carter by a huge margin, as the nation leaned toward a more conservative perspective. Members of the president's inauguration committee wanted to have Southern Gospel music featured at one of the inaugural balls. The Hopper Brothers and Connie were invited to perform.

The new year of 1981 started out on a wonderful note for the Hoppers. The group traveled from Madison to Washington, D.C., to

Claude briefly speaks at the inaugural ball

represent Southern Gospel music at the celebration for President Ronald Reagan, held at the armory. Debra Talley had joined the group by this time, beginning a few years earlier when Connie was recuperating from cancer surgery. The rest of the group included Claude, Connie, and Dean, with Roger Talley. Kirk Talley had already moved on to the Cathedrals.

It was a well-organized program, with the master of ceremonies introducing each group. The facility resembled a large gymnasium, but the inaugural committee made sure it was decorated appropriately for the new president. An acquaintance and friend, Ken Cox, oversaw the event.

142

"I recall Michael was little then. We have great recollections of that experience that we'll never forget," Connie said. "We remain grateful and humbled to have been invited."

"I really looked forward to seeing President Reagan," Mike recalled. "The facility had a large roll-up metal door and those in charge made very specific preparations about what they were going to do when President Reagan came in. Security was extremely tight."

The Reagans had several inauguration balls to attend that night and were expected to make their rounds. Mike added, "The plan for our ball was that at some point in the evening the presidential motorcade would drive right into the armory, up to the back stage area. Reagan would get out and greet the people.

"When we first arrived, I got to know several guards at the door. Early on I begged them to let me get President Reagan's autograph. I had my official program book with me. I just wanted a chance to get close to the new president. Finally, one of the guards said, 'Look, son, sit here by the door! When the president gets here, don't jump up or security will be all over you! I will try to get you up to him to get the autograph.'"

The inaugural started early and lasted into the night. For the duration of the ball, Mike sat quietly next to the door waiting for his chance to meet history. Unfortunately, to his dismay, the president never showed. "Apparently, he had so many parties to attend that he wasn't able to make it to every inaugural ball," Mike added, shrugging his shoulders. "What a dissapointment!

"Even though the president wasn't able to attend, it was a wonderful experience to be a part of," Mike said. "After the event was over, we drove over to the White House. Dean had just purchased a nice camera and planned to take a few photographs. Our bus pulled up to the White House gate and we jumped out. Dean began to set up his camera. Instantaneously, a stern looking guard raced over to us carrying an M-16 rifle. We got really subdued," Mike said, as he chuckled. "We then respectfully, and ever so politely, said, 'Sir, we're only here to take a few pictures.'

The guard motioned for them to continue quickly. After Dean took a couple of pictures, the Hopper bus left Washington.

Nearly a year after the performance for President Reagan's ball, the Hoppers appeared at the National School Prayer Day Rally, held at the Capitol Mall. The activity was designed to rally support for a constitutional amendment to return voluntary prayer to the public school system.

Through the years the group have promoted and encouraged moral issues and principles such as prayer in public schools, after-school Bible clubs, public posting of the Ten Commandments and other matters designed to strengthen societal morality.

Times Are Changing

As the 1980s came, it was a time of evolution for the Gospel group, and their sound became much more polished. Claude and Connie would soon make the decision to shorten their name from the Hopper Brothers and Connie, to just the Hoppers.

The group continued to receive national recognition. By then many of their releases were making the *Singing News* charts. The decade was also a time of internal change.

For example, Will [a member from the beginning], who had been considering leaving the road for a while, decided to officially retire in June 1981. The name change [the Hoppers] officially came into being when Will stepped down. There were even more changes ahead.

"I was nineteen when Uncle Will retired," Dean said. "On one particular night while on the road, Dad asked me to drive the bus. He also suggested I put on my headphones and listen to music for a while. Meanwhile Dad, Mom and Roger Talley discussed the future of the group.

"As I drove, I kind of acted like I was listening to the radio," Dean said and laughed, "but I was actually listening to every word, every syllable, that was said in the back."

That night the three members discussed options for a replacement for Will. Roger was first to make the suggestion that it was time to bring Dean to the forefront as a singer. By the end of the conversation, the decision was made.

"I was really excited about the opportunity. I was definitely willing to try," Dean said. "Soon afterwards, I started singing fulltime and continued on ever since."

"In January 1983, I started playing full-time with the group," Mike said. "During the preceding year I played drums part-time.

That's around the time Mom started working things out with the public school system so I could join the family on a full-time basis."

At first the transition was difficult for Claude, who was now singing and traveling for the first time without any of his brothers onboard. Yet he still had the camaraderie of travel-

Roger and Debra Talley wait for Gospel music concert performance.

ing with his immediate family: Connie, Dean and now Mike.

Then, Roger and Debra made the decision to venture out on their own. The Hoppers entered a challenging new chapter of rebuilding.

Chart-topping songs during the decade included "Home Is Where The Heart Is," "Come To The Wedding," and "Walk Right Out Of This Valley". By 1985, "When He Comes Down" and "I'm On The Rock" were popular releases. "Smoke of the Battle" charted in 1987. Others during this period included "Foot Of the Cross," "Don't Give Up The Fight," "Stand For Jesus" and "You'll Be There."

Chapter 31
The Talleys And The Hoppers

Remember, no man is a failure who has friends.

— Jimmy Stewart, *It's a Wonderful Life*

The Hoppers experienced a number of personnel changes and additions, as, one by one, the brothers retired from touring and vacancies had to be filled. In the 1970s and '80s, it was an especially creative era for the Rockingham County group. Roger, Kirk and Debra Talley were great assets to the group and each became lifelong friends. The progress made by the group at the time had a lot to do with their influences.

"I know during the ten years Roger toured with the group, he greatly improved our sound," Connie commented. "He is well-known in the industry as a true musical genius, and he certainly helped with our vocal and musical arrangements while with us."

Roger & Debra Remember The Hoppers
Roger recalled that he had just graduated from college a short time before and had worked nearly a year for the Farmers Home Administration at the time his life changed.

The Talleys—Debra, Roger and Lauren Talley

It so happened that the Hoppers were taping a television program one night in Bristol, Tennessee. Claude asked the host if he knew of anyone in the area that might be interested in playing piano. The host remembered a young fellow, Roger Talley, who had just played on a session at his studio a few days before. Claude jotted down Roger's name and phone number.

"I didn't know anything! I was as green as I could be, but he told Claude I had potential. Claude later called me out of the blue and said, 'Hey, Roger, this is Claude Hopper!'"

"He wanted to know if I could go with them one weekend and

fill in as a try-out. So I did. After that weekend, he offered me a job. I had just received a promotion where I was working, but I thought, 'Nah, I'm not thrilled with this job anyway. This music group will be fun for a while and someday I'll go back to real life.'

"I started with the Hoppers. Since I didn't know anything; I just did whatever they told me to do!"

Roger moved from Bristol and found a mobile home for rent for

$90 a month, in Madison. He recalled that he only had a couple of boxes to carry with him when he moved, adding, "It was whatever Mama packed for me: basically a few dishes, towels and washcloths."

He lived in the singlewide mobile home for a couple of months. The former piano player for the Hoppers, Johnny Porrazzo, also lived in a mobile home behind Will Hopper's house. Roger eventually made a deal with Johnny, since he was ready to move on, to take over payments on his trailer.

"That's where I lived when Debbie and I met. When we eventually married, she joined me in the trailer. It was so small she didn't have anywhere to put her clothes at first. I already had the closets full."

Roger reminisced: "I guess the most important thing I learned through those years with the Hoppers was to try to have a positive mental attitude about things. When I first went with them, Claude said I was always negative. He'd laughingly say, 'You are so negative we could send you out and get you developed!'"

Roger's attitude in life began to change through those years.

"Claude and Connie have also been examples to me of what hard work and dedication can accomplish.

"I have heard them say that they aren't the most talented singers ever, but they have something real to offer people. They are smart enough and have always worked hard enough to make things happen!"

Debra Talley added: "I traveled with the group for four years and learned a lot, too; like Roger, I had never been anywhere either. Roger and I met, got married and I soon joined the Hoppers. I don't think they ever anticipated having another girl [because it had always been the Hopper Brothers and Connie]. Nonetheless, they thought the sound was okay with me and they kept me. Looking back, it's not that I ever contributed much to them; however, I learned so much from Connie and from all of them. Claude was and is a very wise businessman, and you'll not make it in this business if you're not," she added. "We realized when we started singing on our own with Kirk that it was what Roger had learned from Claude's example, plus the things Kirk had gleaned from the Cathedrals, that helped us get our trio underway. At the time, we didn't really know how to put a group together."

Debra came to realize through the years that Claude was a tenderhearted man as well. "He helped a lot of people that nobody knows about. He has given freely to people when he knew they needed it. I've personally seen Claude tear up and weep just thinking about, or talking about, someone's difficult situations. He will then go out of his way to help that person who is hurting.

"You know there are a lot of people who will help others when they think they are going to get something out of it for themselves. Claude isn't like that at all. Claude has given and helped hurting individuals expecting nothing in return," she said, "and his motivation has always been to love others and please the Lord."

Debra and Roger said that through their years of being with Claude and Connie, they learned about perseverance, dedication, having a good heart and doing everything for the right reason. Debra says she now understands why Claude emphasized the business aspects of the group and the importance of faithful stewardship.

"Seriously, Claude doesn't have to do all this touring and singing anymore," Debra said. "He and Connie could retire, stay home and take it easy at this stage in their lives. However, they continue singing because they know it's what they're supposed to be doing! They sing for the right reasons: for the Lord and His coming Kingdom."

Chapter 32
Behind The Scenes

All of a sudden there would be a curve and I'm lean-
ing over on two wheels and everyone is scared to
death!

— Roger Talley

Roger and Debra Talley have lots of humorous memories of touring
with the Hoppers. Roger laughed as he recalled a time when they had
all been at Watermelon Park for an entire week.

"We really worked like dogs while we were there! It was so hot,
too. Many nights, I'd be in my best suit getting ready to sing, and I
would still have to run down to the entrance gate and park campers.
I frantically ran back to the stage when it was time to start playing!
Things like that went on for an entire week, and then we packed
everything up and drove home on Sunday night. I really looked forward to getting home to rest."

About 8:30 Monday morning the telephone rings and a voice on
the other end of the phone says: "Roger, there's a semi-tractor-trailer
down here at the farm. It's full of songbooks that need to be
unloaded. Claude bought everything Stamps-Baxter had in their
warehouse, and he wants them stacked in the hay barn."

"Specifically, he wanted them placed up in the top of the hay
barn," Roger said, as he grinned and rolled his eyes. "I had to get out
of my bed and go down there immediately. By the time I got to the
farm Claude's dad, Mr. Hopper, was excited, saying, 'There's a giant
18-wheeler full of songbooks down here! My gosh, where are we
going to put them?'

"I know we sold those songbooks for at least the next ten years!
Three for a dollar every night! Every week I'd be designated to drag
another three cases out of the barn. I'd lug them onto the bus. We'd
break open the case and sell books three for a dollar! We were selling
songbooks forever!" Roger emphasized and laughed.

"Claude gave me a lot of responsibility from the start," Roger said. "I was immediately put in charge of the publishing company, inventory of all the products, and I don't even remember what else. I think I was the first one in the group they ever trusted to mix their recordings."

Traveling On The Bus

The best part of traveling on the Hopper bus was that as soon as the singing ended, fellowship and fun began.

"Once we got back to the bus, Connie took off her wig, every-

body changed clothes, and we got ready for some fun," Roger said, explaining that there was a tiny lounging area with two seats on one side and two on the other side.

"We'd pull a trash can to the center, and we had a smooth board that made a great tabletop. We'd place the board on the trash can and somebody would say, 'Deal 'em!'

"We played Rook for half the night! They were all hilarious when they played Rook, especially Connie!" Roger chuckled, as he recalled those moments.

"Whoever wasn't driving was usually playing. When Claude, who was usually driving, finally got tired of hearing us cackle [we were up playing until two o'clock in the morning or later], he'd lean over and look in the rearview mirror and say something like: 'Ahh, aren't some of ya'll getting sleepy back there yet?'

"That was our cue to end the game! Claude and Will did most of the driving then. Claude asked me to drive a time or two," Roger said, laughing. "He'd look down and I'd be going 75 or 80, and he'd say, 'Roger, that 85 is the interstate number, not the speed limit!'"

Freezing Half To Death

"I remember we once borrowed a bus from another group — an

old bus. Ours was in the shop at the time. That jalopy was a 1935 or 1940 model," Roger said, grinning. "It had thick blue shag carpet on the floor, up the walls and over the ceiling! It looked like it was going to smother us!

"It turned out to be really cold that particular weekend. It was Easter and we were experiencing an unexpected winter storm. As if things could not get worse, there was no heat in the bus! We nearly froze to death! We could actually see our breath!"

Claude bought a kerosene heater and set the apparatus in the middle of the bus floor. The group members nuzzled around it. "We tried to sleep on the floor in our clothes, with other clothes layered on top of us for warmth. We tried desperately to sleep," Roger reminisced.

"I remember if we were too close to the heater, we burned up and, if we were more than three feet away, we froze—especially when the bus was traveling down-wind. While moving, there was so much air seeping inside that it was like being inside a 40-foot-long deep freezer."

"Every time we hit a bump, someone would have to jump up and re-light the heater," Debra laughed as she also remembered, "and only later did we realize how dangerous that really was. My, it could have blown us all up!"

Roger also remembers earlier days when accommodations on the Hopper bus were not really wonderful. He said, "We'd go to the church early on Sunday morning. We would try our best to wash our hair in the restroom sink. The water was usually ice-cold! Then we tried to find an empty Sunday school room to use as we dried our hair and finished up. All the while, people were already starting to come into the church. Talk about embarrassing!" he said, chuckling as he recalled the humbling experiences.

"At that time the Hopper bus had no generator, no electricity and no water! It had nothing but beds and a very tiny toilet in the back."

All Hoppers Wear Belts

"When I first went on the road with them I had been in college at the University of Tennessee," Roger recalled. "That was at the very height of the hippie movement and the Vietnam protests. I remember

I had these worn-looking bell-bottom jeans; Claude called them 'those Hoover pants.' He joked about that because he thought they looked like something a poor kid would wear back in the Great Depression.

"I responded by saying, 'Claude, these pants are in style!'

"What do you mean?" Claude asked with a puzzled look.

"Everybody wears them!"

Claude dryly replied, 'Well, they don't here!"

Roger also recalled that he'd occasionally come out of the bus without a belt. While in college no one wore a belt.

"Claude would catch it right away and say, 'Uh, Roger, uh, where's your belt?'

Roger answered, "Belts are not in style, Claude."

Claude responded, "Belts are in style with the Hoppers! Now go get yourself a belt!"

"We joke about it a lot now. Occasionally, for a really good laugh, when we see Dean one of us will say: 'Belts are in style with the Hoppers!'"

Passing Of A Saintly Mother

"I left the group shortly before Lauren was born," Debra remembered. "One Thursday Roger left with the Hoppers to go sing somewhere. Unexpectedly, Claude's mother passed away in the night. So they immediately turned the bus around and came back home to Madison. It so happened I was around ten days overdue at that time.

"Roger was getting ready to go to the funeral home for the viewing and wouldn't you know, that's when I went into labor!

"Roger went on to the hospital with me and wasn't able to make it to the funeral home. Lauren was born the day Mrs. Hopper was buried," she said.

In *Heart of the Matter*, Connie described the passing of Claude's mother:

> Two weeks after Thanksgiving Day (1982) time stopped for my beloved mother-in-law and eternity began. Much was accomplished through her life and likewise, much was accomplished through her death,

because in the funeral service, five precious souls opened their hearts to the Lord and received Him as their personal Savior. I know that Mrs. Hopper would have wanted this more than anything. I know her heart would have overflowed as four of her sons — four of the original Hopper Brothers — sang "Never Grow Old," and all eight of her boys were pallbearers.

A grandson and a son-in-law, who are ministers, helped officiate at the service.

Mrs. Hopper loved Gospel music and was extremely proud of the "boys," as she called them. If there was a sing close by, she was there if possible. She traveled with us on the bus quite a lot when she was younger. She went with us to the National Quartet Convention in Memphis and enjoyed every minute. She loved to go to Watermelon Park. She enjoyed the fellowship there.

"Under the circumstances, I never expected any of the family to come to visit me in my hospital room, but Connie and Claude both came," Debra said. "I was especially touched that Claude came, due to the great personal loss he had suffered.

"I feel even closer to Claude nowadays than I did when I traveled with the group," she added. "In those days, he was the businessman and group manager. To my way of thinking, that's an authoritative position. He's the boss! I was probably a bit intimidated, I guess.

" I have always liked Claude, and we always had a good relationship. But it was that hospital visit that meant the most to me! He walked into my room and stayed for quite a while. Then before leaving, he walked over to my bed, where I was sitting up. He leaned over and hugged me a little and slipped something into my hand, and then left. He had given me a rather large bill as a gift for Lauren.

"You know, he didn't even have to come, much less give a gift like that! Through the years, they had more than given us enough, for they were always very good to us!

"At that time, I began to recognize another side to Claude. He didn't always let it show—but when he did, it meant something to me!"

Pertaining to his mother's passing, Claude said, "You know, Dr. Charles Stanley once wrote about mothers. I do think he said it best, and I agree with his sentiments: 'My mother taught me many lessons about perseverance, a servant's spirit and obedience. The one that has the most impact on my ministry is the importance of encouragement. Through her constant encouragement, she helped me be the man I am today. I carry a part of her with me in everything I do.'"

Also, Dwight D. Eisenhower was once asked who was the greatest man he ever met. His answer was "It was not a man; it was a woman, my mother."

Regardless of the years that go by, Claude and his siblings still miss their mother, Dossie, greatly. It was Dossie's unconditional love, work ethic, humor and consistency in living a Christian life that inspired and influenced all of her children.

Steve Keen, James Rainey And Shannon Childress

After Roger and Debra Talley's exit, Steve Keen replaced Roger as pianist. Later James Rainey, who was from West Virginia, took his place.

After Rainey, Shannon Childress joined the group and remained for nearly a dozen years, from 1987 to 1998. Besides being an accomplished pianist, Shannon wrote several of the group's most popular songs of that era, including "Anchor to the Power of the Cross" and "Milk and Honey."

Recollections Of Kirk Talley

"In 1974 Roger came over to me at a concert and said he had a younger brother, Kirk, that could also sing," Connie reminisced. "Claude said to bring him on! So, he joined us one Sunday morning in Pennsylvania and he tore the service apart. There was not a dry eye in the place. It was really incredible!"

Kirk joined the Hoppers on a full-time basis in 1976, actually on the day he graduated from high school. He continued with the group through 1979. Claude recalled taking Kirk out and buying him his first suit: an all white double-knit with wide lapels and flared slacks, complete with a pair of white buck shoes.

Kirk grew into a gifted songwriter and powerful tenor during his tenure with the Hoppers. In 1979, Glenn Payne and George

Kirk Talley

Younce asked Kirk to sing with Cathedrals.

"The decision was a big one for me, since Connie and Claude had taught me so much, and they had always been so good to me," Kirk said. "Yet, after a time of thought and prayer, I decided to join the Cathedrals."

"The day Kirk went with George and Glenn, the Cathedrals' bus pulled alongside the Hoppers' bus. He stepped from one bus directly into another," Claude remembered.

"When Kirk decided to leave the Hoppers, I gave him back every song he ever wrote," Claude said, explaining that he held the publishing rights on the songs at the time. "He got them all back, with the exception of one special song that Kirk never recorded. I still have that song. It's a sentimental thing for me. That was his *first* song."

Chapter 33
Geez, They're Not in the Army

I have never let my schooling interfere with my education.

— Mark Twain

When Dean and Mike were young, Connie often thought Claude was too hard on the boys. She thought Claude treated them a little like his father had once treated him [but not quite as severe].

"I remember thinking, 'Gee whiz, Claude, they're not in the United States Army, ya' know!' Now I realize I was wrong. I now see how his method paid off. The boys know that when there is a job to be done, they do it. I am extremely proud of them and how they conduct themselves publicly and privately. They are both responsible young men, and both love and serve the Lord."

Early on, Claude made it a point to give the children certain absolutes. He expected the best from his sons in all areas of endeavor. His sons were given farm duties and other chores to accomplish throughout the week, much like what was expected of him when he was young.

Claude has since said that he hopes his style of working with the boys instilled self-esteem and self-reliance. Dean and Mike knew they had responsibilities as members of the family. When they completed their farm tasks, Claude wanted them to realize they were capable, and they were accomplishing things that were meaningful.

He said, "The boys were contributors to the family's welfare, and I wanted them to know it."

As the great Ethel Waters once said, "God doesn't make junk." To this end, Claude wanted the boys to recognize that they were valuable in his eyes, and in their Heavenly Father's eyes, as well.

Mike's Childhood Vs. Dean's
Michael's situation was altogether different than Dean's when it came to choosing to go on the road. Connie chuckled and said, "Instead of Mike pleading with us to let him go on the road [like

Dean did], we nearly had to manhandle him onto the bus to make him go with us!"

Mike explains his feelings at the time:

> There were certainly times when I missed my parents while they were on the road, but I guess I adapted especially well. I enjoyed what was on the farm, and it was the only life I knew. Dean, on the other hand, remembered when Mom and Dad were home more, before they went full-time in ministry. Perhaps it was more difficult for him to get used to the change that had taken place.
>
> On occasions when I was expected to travel with the family, it was hard for Mom and Dad to get me to go. I just liked being home. There were lots of things for me to do on the farm.
>
> Most guys my age had dirt bikes. I was no different. I enjoyed riding my dirt bike around the property.
>
> In my opinion, I also had a great childhood because I had this awesome opportunity to spend time with my grandparents—my Mom's parents and my Dad's folks. Mom and Dad left on Thursdays and come home every Sunday night. Before they left, they dropped me off with Grandma and Grandpa Shelton for the weekend, or I rode the school bus to their home.
>
> During these times Grandpa Shelton would take me fishing. I spent a lot of time with him at Belews Lake. I also spent time with my Uncle Charles, Mom's oldest brother. Those were really wonderful memories for me.
>
> Of course, later on, I visited Grandma and Grandpa Hopper a great deal. When Grandma Hopper passed away, Grandpa and I became especially close. We were very tight.

Mike admittedly was sometimes considered a "handful" for the babysitter. His ornery vitality and insatiable curiosity constantly got him into unusual predicaments.

For example, in a 1982 article in *Singing News Magazine*, Mike told a story about an unorthodox tea party that took place at the farm. As he originally told the story, while his parents were away and his babysitter had gone to the store, he called neighborhood friends and invited them to a tea party. Nothing was particularly wrong with such an invitation except for the unusual location of the party: the roof. Michael hauled a table and several chairs up to a flat segment on the roof. Friends who accepted his invitation were expected to climb on the top of the house to join him before they could drink tea. Before long there were several rowdy boys gathered on the rooftop.

Mike explained in the article that it was a very irate Grandpa Hopper that found him out and later told his father! The rest, as Mike said at the time, was history. He declined to comment about the type of punishment that ensued.

As an adult, only recently, Mike decided to come clean when asked about the tea party incident [hoping that the statute of limita-

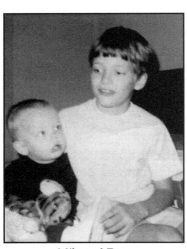

Mike and Dean

tions had long run out]. He chuckled as he finally clarified the truth, spilling the beans about the long ago episode. "Actually, the whole tea party was a cover-up story! The truth of the matter is that my buddies and I were launching bottle-rockets off the top section of our house! We were aiming for the cows in the pasture," he confessed, trying to contain his grin.

"Technically, though, because it was hot outside, we did have iced tea with us. So, after being caught red-handed by Grandpa Hopper, and due to my fear of severe punishment, I told Grandpa we were having a tea party."

Mike Joins The Family Group

It was not long afterwards that Connie and Claude started thinking that Mike should be on the road, too. "I guess Claude and I had come to the point where we felt that it would be better to have our entire family together," Connie explained.

Connie and Mike visited the school guidance counselor together to discuss the situation, and the counselor finally said, "Mrs. Hopper, take Mike with you. He is going to learn much more living it than by reading about it in a book."

Mike was halfway through his eighth-grade year when he went on the road full-time. He continued school through the same home-school correspondence course his brother, Dean, had used to earn his diploma.

This took place the same year Roger and Debra Talley left the Hoppers.

In a June 2000 interview with the *Gospel Voice Magazine,* Mike discussed his joining the family with a bit of

Mike

humor. "In a nutshell," he said, "I once rode dirt bikes all day, and then one day Dad said, 'Get on the bus!'"

Before long, something started taking place in Michael's life. He played drums for the group full-time. As time went on, he came to love the Southern Gospel people and the music, as well. His creative energy became intensely focused on music and eventually on various recording techniques and business endeavors.

Over time, his percussion skills grew, so much so that he is now considered one of the most innovative drummers in Gospel music, and was the first percussionist to win the *Singing News* Favorite Musician Award in 2001. It has been said that his sense of rhythmic precision and professionalism behind a drum set is nothing short of astounding.

Like his father and brother, Mike gravitates toward the business side of the ministry. Today he fully accepts and understands the calling on his life. He continues to grow in Christ and depend upon Him for guidance.

Chapter 34
The NQC is Sold

If you want one year of prosperity, grow grain. If you want ten years of prosperity, grow trees. If you want one hundred years of prosperity, grow people.

— Unknown

"If you can dream it, you can make it happen!" has been one of Claude's favorite sayings through the years; and in Proverbs 23:7, the Bible says, "For as he thinketh in his heart, so is he..." Through right thinking, a positive self-image and application of these principles, all coupled with an insatiable drive toward success, Claude has been involved in a variety of successful business enterprises.

"I usually remember James 4 when making a decision: it says in part, '...ye have not, because ye ask not. Ye ask, and receive not, because ye ask amiss, that ye may consume it upon your lusts.' Although positive thinking is wonderful, I recognize that my prayers and dreams must be in keeping with God's perfect plan. If we have the mind of Christ, and ask according to His plan, we can confident-ly ask and receive," Claude said.

Connie and Claude remember well going to their first National Quartet Convention, in 1964, where they found themselves drawn to the nightly concerts, artist display tables and the amateur contest that surrounded the event. It was a great place to meet legendary per-formers and other people in the industry, as well as thousands of fans. Through the years, the National Quartet Convention became something the Hoppers supported every year.

In the fall of 1982, Claude was given an opportunity to invest in the NQC enterprise. He was hanging around the box office during the convention, casually looking around when he noticed J.G. Whitfield in the corner of an aisle way, weeping. Claude walked over to console him. As he inquired about what could be wrong, Whitfield explained, through tears, that his feelings were hurt by one of the artists attending the convention. At the time Whitfield, the Blackwood Brothers and J.D. Sumner were equal partners in the convention business.

As the two men talked further, Whitfield finally composed himself enough to say: "Claude, this is becoming too much for me. Let me sell you my portion of the NQC and be done with it."

With a puzzled look on his face, Claude asked if he was serious. "Yes, I am!" he answered. "I have never been more serious."

Because of the unusual circumstances, Claude recommended Whitfield go home and talk everything over with Hazel, his wife, whom he lovingly called "Mama."

Claude assumed that the emotions of the moment coupled with the exhaustion from all the work of putting on such an extravaganza had clouded Whitfield's thinking. Claude figured that once he calmed down and thought things over, he'd forget the comment and resume with the convention.

Claude

A week later Whitfield called Claude at home. They talked several minutes before the matter of the convention came up. Finally, Whitfield said, "Claude, I've talked to Mama and she agrees: we think it's time to sell and move on to other things."

Claude asked him how much he wanted for the one-third partnership. Then, he asked the price if he bought the entire convention outright. Since Whitfield had talked with the other owners beforehand and they were willing to sell their parts as well, he was able to give general figures that night. Claude requested that he give him a little time to consider the offer and see what he could pull together.

The first person Claude contacted was his dear friend Rex Nelon.

"Rex, the NQC is for sale," was Claude's opening statement as soon as his friend answered the phone. He added, "Why don't you, Don Shumate and I buy the convention from Mr. Whitfield and his partners?'"

Rex suggested they consult others from the music industry before making a decision. Rex and Claude went about discussing the issue with other individuals and were soon able to assemble a core group of people who were committed to the effort and willing to invest.

The men who joined together to purchase the National Quartet Convention included Les Beasley, Glen Payne, Brock Speer, Charlie Burke, Don Shumate, Rex Nelon and, of course, Claude Hopper.

A board was named from individuals already promoting the event on the road, namely: Rex Nelon and the Rex Nelon Singers, the Hoppers, the Cathedral Quartet, the Speer Family, the Singing Americans, and Don Shumate, who managed a local group at the time.

For the most part, the board members were already in full-time ministry. They campaigned for and promoted the National Quartet Convention throughout the year while crisscrossing the country. Claude said this is how they first marketed the convention—on the road.

From the beginning, Claude said he believed the Lord honored the message in the music as well as the motivation and intent of the board. Although the NQC is a business, the board saw the annual event as a magnificent way to uplift Christ and promote Southern Gospel music.

Yet, for the first few years the venture didn't really go well financially for the new owners, even though the music was phenomenal. But after those initial years it began to grow and fans started coming every year and supported the events.

In time the convention outgrew Nashville. The NQC had to find a larger venue. The Nashville site was somewhat neglected and had poor acoustics. After careful consideration, in 1993 the board chose Louisville, Kentucky's Freedom Hall. Within two years after moving there the facility was packed out on Friday and Saturday nights—with over 21,000 fans each night.

God has continued to consecrate and bless the efforts since the early days following the acquisition. The event is all family-friendly with inspiring entertainment.

"Most importantly, the primary reason for its growing popularity is that the hand of God is on this undertaking," Claude said. "We do not take this flippantly, so all that we do at the NQC must honor Him."

Another reason the event has grown is due to the innovative activities scheduled. For example, the idea of artist showcases at the convention, where multiple Gospel groups perform under the umbrella of a particular recording company or booking agency, was gleaned from several members on the board who first saw the concept at Bill Gaither's Praise Gathering. The showcases and contests are designed as an opportunity for up-and-coming young groups to be formally featured in front of the convention audience.

"The NQC wants new groups to be able to participate, for we were all there at one time," Claude emphasized. "There are wonderful quartets, mixed groups, trios and soloists that deserve exposure and need to be highlighted. The NQC makes this all possible."

Eventually, the idea of special seminars and programs came along. One of these events includes Pianorama, where some of the best pianists in the country are featured together in one magnificent event. There are various morning Bible stud-ies, Bluegrass Gospel festivals and an exhibition hall where nearly everyone in the industry is represented with sponsored booths and displays. In recent years, the NQC brought dynamic pastors and speakers like Dr. John Hagee, Dr. Jerry Falwell, Dr. Charles Stanley and Dr. Jerry Vines.

For the last few years, portions of the NQC have been national-ly televised on the Inspirational Network [INSP], including the pres-tigious *Singing News* Fan Awards.

It was in 2005 that the NQC made another innovative shift. The convention announced the creation of NQC Internet Radio. The 24-hour webcast features performers from the convention along with vintage cuts from Southern Gospel music artists from yesteryear.

The National Quartet Convention is held every September. With the infusion of televised replays on INSP, Internet music programming, and DVD/video copies sold for home use, it is an event that will minister year-round.

"Although it has been over twenty-three years since J.G. Whitfield passed on the torch, we have attempted to hold to the Christian ideals and goals that he and his partners initiated," Claude said. "The National Quartet Convention still exists to promote Southern Gospel music and to encourage talent and Christ-centered ministry. It is here to insure Gospel music continues on for future generations."

> It is gratifying to know that composers and fans will be getting together to enjoy Southern Gospel music. I am pleased that so many Americans are truly dedicated to the religious values this music embodies. Our country was built on these values, and it will continue to prosper as long as we adhere to them. You have my warmest good wishes for a successful and inspiring meeting. God bless you.
>
> — President Ronald Reagan, National Quartet Convention 30th Anniversary

Keep On Singing

At a time when Rex Nelon was still singing bass for the LeFevres, before the group changed their name to the Rex Nelon Singers, it seemed like sheet music was becoming less and less popular. Up until that point in time, most Southern Gospel artists carried a variety of Gospel sheet music on the road to offer at their product tables.

Because so many song titles were becoming available and demand was great for compilations, it was difficult for artists to adequately stock enough inventory for the need. Songbooks were becoming popular and the new trend was slowly replacing sheet music altogether.

At that time, the LeFevres were extremely popular and Rex Nelon owned the publishing rights to a great number of inspirational songs. It so happened that Claude Hopper came up with the concept of publishing sheet-music-sized books that would include a variety of older inspirational standbys, yet feature several of the most popular hits by various Southern Gospel artists. Around 1980, Claude telephoned Rex and shared his idea, asking permission to use several of Rex's songs for his first book project. Rex loved the idea and the two began to brainstorm about the concept. By the time they ended their conversation,

Rex Nelon

Rex and Claude had formed a partnership in the songbook venture, and the *Keep On Singing* line of Gospel music songbooks was born.

Interesting to note, Rex Nelon was already using the name, *Keep On Singing,* and logo before the business venture began, on his own sheet music. The name was originally inspired by the bumper sticker catch phrase "Keep On Trucking." As Claude and Rex initially discussed the new songbook idea, Rex suggested they adopt that name for their new books.

"He had his responsibilities with this venture and I had mine. It worked especially well because we were dear friends, and Rex was a true Southern gentleman," Claude said.

Once the project was underway, the top forty Southern Gospel music songs each year were released in book form. Word Publishing distributes the product and other Southern Gospel groups sell it while on the road, too.

There were fifteen volumes of *Keep On Singing* that were produced up until Rex's unexpected passing on January 23, 2000. He was sixty-eight and in England with the Gaither Homecoming Tour when a heart attack claimed his life.

Judy Spencer Nelon talked about the sudden loss, saying, "The friendship [Claude and Connie] shared with me and my late husband, Rex Nelon, would comfort me through the hard times after his sudden death in England, just hours before the taping of the London Homecoming. Claude stood beside Rex as he left this shore for Heaven, and Connie held me and brought comfort as I was faced with this loss and sadness beyond belief."

Danny Jones, editor of the *Singing News,* once wrote in his monthly column: "If I had to pick just one incident in Southern Gospel music that completely caught everyone everywhere off guard, it would be the passing of Rex Nelon."

Perhaps those words could sum up Claude's own thoughts as well. "It was an extremely painful and personal loss for Connie and me when Rex passed," Claude said. "He was one of our best friends. We had great respect for him, for he was a man of great character and integrity. He was also a man with a big heart and an even greater sense of humor. He is missed by everyone who knew him."

The *Keep On Singing* tradition was recently revived. For example, *The Best Of Keep On Singing, Volume 1*, was released in September 2004, and other editions are in the planning stages. The collaboration between the Rex Nelon Music Company and Hopper Brothers and Connie Publishing Company still produces popular music volumes. They plan to continue the series far into the future.

Ink In His Veins
In the early 1980s, a newspaperman, Ron Williams, was looking for investors to help him develop a Southern Gospel music newspaper.

Claude Hopper, Charlie Burke and Don Shumate joined Williams in the effort, each owning a fourth of the operation.

"I think the publication did many wonderful things for the industry while we worked with it," Claude commented.

The *Gospel Music News* was located in J.D. Sumner's building on Music Row, in Nashville. Williams hired a team of seasoned writers, photographers and salespeople to produce the paper. After several years, the newspaper was sold.

Reach Satellite Network
Another venture that Claude was heavily involved in was Reach Radio Network, a 24-hour-a-day, seven-day-a-week satellite network.

It began when Chris White and Carroll McGruder (of the McGruders) called Maurice Templeton one day with details about a business opportunity, a syndicated satellite radio network.

"Carroll told us that his brother-in-law had started a Bible quiz show, broadcast from Sacramento, California," Maurice recalled. "The show was on satellite and a few stations were picking it up. Regardless of his efforts, he just couldn't get it all to work. Carroll talked him into playing Southern Gospel music in between questions. So he did and the response was better."

166

After a year of broadcasting, the excessive costs of satellite syndication became too expensive for the current owner to continue. He came to the conclusion that he wanted to find someone with a like-minded heart to buy him out.

For several years Claude, Maurice and others in the industry had been encouraging the Southern Gospel industry to improve broadcasting standards, which would include radio quality for the independent Southern Gospel radio stations. To this end, they toyed with the idea of how they could create a high quality radio signal, with professional programming and creative, affordable radio shows.

"Chris and Carroll told me that the network could be the very thing we had been seeking," Maurice said. He then called Carroll's brother-in-law. Carroll's brother-in-law told Maurice that he would be happy to sell the network, since he was hoping to end the costly venture anyway.

After their conversation, Maurice called friends and put together a small elite group of investors who could make this venture work, including Charlie Burke, Chris White, Dave Thomas, Eddie Crook and Claude Hopper.

The men met together in Nashville to discuss the opportunity and unanimously agreed to pool their resources and purchase what would be later known as Reach Radio Network. Their vision was clear, and they started developing the first Christian music satellite network of its kind.

Claude remembered that they soon found that the technical equipment included in the deal was outdated. So, when they brought the network to Nashville, they invested in state-of-the-art gear and hired a new staff to create top-notch radio programming. The organization put together a management team to sell syndicated packages and the enterprise began.

"We produced Christian music radio programming formats at a time when it was a totally new concept," Claude said. "This network could potentially give every station in the country all the advantages of high quality programming, and the best in Southern Gospel music, without hiring additional manpower to accomplish the improved broadcasting."

"So we would go out to all the small radio stations and sell them on this programming," Maurice added. "In fact, WWWC in

Wilkesboro, North Carolina, was one of the first stations to pick up our satellite feed. The quality was superb."

Radio stations could now have high quality programming for a low monthly fee. "We generated a computer signal over the satellite during programming that triggered the cart machines of local stations, allowing them to build their own local advertising into the syndicated shows," Maurice said.

"Station owners found out that while they programmed these

high quality shows, they could also reduce rising overhead at the station," Claude said. "Actually, with the Reach Satellite format in place, radio employees could devote nearly all their time to increasing advertising sales."

Perhaps the strongest point of this new development was also its biggest weakness, however. The newness of the technology, and the difficulties related to promoting it, caused the Reach management team to struggle with sales, which

Dean and Claude accepting an award

stifled the company's growth. In fact, it was doing far less business in the first year than the owners predicted.

Eventually, a new management team was put in place and, sure enough, the sales began to improve. Yet even with an increase in sales, the company did far less than initially projected.

"I was introduced to Jim Cumbee, who was with Disney World, in Orlando, Florida," Maurice said. "After several meetings with Jim, he told me he was interested in getting into Southern Gospel music."

Cumbee wanted to involve himself with something that touched the whole Southern Gospel industry. Maurice told him there were only three entities that involved the whole industry: *The Singing News,* the National Quartet Convention and Reach Satellite Network.

Since the first two were not for sale, he told him he would call a meeting of the Reach Satellite Network Board of Directors and advise them of an interested buyer.

Cumbee's offer was accepted on the condition that certain stockholders remain with him. Claude was among those who continued with the venture.

Claude and the others procured two radio stations to serve as flagship stations for their network: one north of Nashville, and the other in downtown Nashville.

Reach Radio Network eventually grew to become one of the most noted, innovative and respected broadcasting networks in America, delivering daily programming to over two hundred Southern Gospel radio stations.

After the company improved, Stuart Epperson made the remaining owners an offer to buy the network. After careful consideration, Claude and the others sold their stock [including Jim Cumbee]. Stuart Epperson owned Salem Communications Network and was busy acquiring Christian radio stations from around the nation. His feelings were that Reach would align itself well with his vision for Salem.

As a result, Reach merged with Salem Music Network and Salem Communications, which includes several program formats: *Solid Gospel, Today's Christian Music* and *The Word In Praise*. It continues to this day in over 230 North American markets. At this time, Jim Cumbee serves Salem as president of non-broadcast media.

Gospel Music Television Network

"When Gospel Music Television Network (GMTN) began, I was fortunate enough to be involved," Claude said. "As a member of the governing board, the Hoppers and others were able to provide quality concert footage and videos for the television airways."

Two of the missions of GMTN's board were to assist in improving the quality of the station and to inspire an improvement in audio and video quality in the industry. GMTN wanted a wide variety of Gospel artists involved in the network. "Through the Lord's blessing, GMTN now promotes Southern Gospel artists and the industry. I believe it glorifies Christ through its nationwide family-based programming," Claude said.

During Claude's tenure on the board, the network had five world premieres. In August each year in Pigeon Forge, Tennessee, GMTN hosts the popular World Premiere Gospel Concert. This three-day celebration featuring numerous artists is held at the Grand Resort Hotel and Convention Center.

Claude also helped organize and then sat on the board of the Southern Gospel Music Guild, and was named to the board of the Southern Gospel Music Association and the SGMA Hall of Fame.

"When GMTN got off the ground and things were progressing well , I sensed the Lord leading me to step down from my duties and slow involvement elsewhere so I could concentrate on quality and quantity of time with my family.

"I suspect I was so diversified and overextended during this period of my life that I was having trouble keeping up the pace I had set for myself. I met myself coming and going, so to speak, and there was no stopping. It was time to slow down. It has since been apparent I made the right decision," Claude stated.

Chapter 35
Wayne's Struggle With Cancer

Although the world is full of suffering, it is also full of the overcoming of it.

— Helen Keller

Wayne Hopper's sense of humor is legendary in certain circles, and he is a gifted public speaker who obviously loves people. Behind the comic persona, however, is a man who has certainly had his struggles with serious health concerns over the years.

Wayne Hopper

Claude recalled receiving a phone call in 1989 from Wayne's wife, Shirley: "Claude, I need you! Wayne is really, really sick."

Claude and Connie immediately packed and left for the Baptist Hospital, in Lynchburg, Virginia. Wayne was critical.

"Wayne is younger than me," Claude said. "However, when I saw him, it broke my heart. He looked older than my Dad, who was in his late-eighties at the time. They found out he had colon cancer. So we began to pray for him."

As the tears began to flow, one by one, family members joined together and sought the Lord's face in the matter. Many of them remained at the hospital for several days to be with Wayne and Shirley; however, Claude and Connie had to return to the road.

Wayne remained in grave condition and was barely able to speak. Besides, his nurses wanted him to preserve what energy he could muster to fight his battle against illness. Pale and in considerable pain, life was draining out of him with each hour that passed. To make matters worse, he hadn't eaten in days and was being fed intravenously.

"To be honest," Connie lamented, "I was hopeful for Wayne's recovery, but he was so critical, I knew it could go either way. We never stopped praying and never stopped expecting God to touch his body if it was in His will."

A few days later, Connie, who was relaxing in the front living quarters on the bus, called Wayne's room. She was totally surprised when Wayne answered the telephone!

Wayne's voice sounded stronger, and after he and Connie talked for a minute or two, he asked to speak with Claude. With a smile on her face, she reached the mobile phone to him.

Wayne raised his voice, and said, "Hello, Claude! I'm telling you something has happened! I am walking the hallways! I'm feeding myself! It's unbelievable!"

"Praise the Lord! It's a miracle!" Claude shouted, as tears rolled down his cheeks. The bus was instantly full of excitement as everyone jumped up to listen in on the phone call.

So it happened, Wayne saw a complete reversal of his medical condition, and the entire hospital staff was astounded by his last minute turnaround. His stamina was returning and his comical sense of humor was restored. He was eventually released from the hospital and continued the recovery process at home.

Since his close brush with death , Wayne is a much stronger Christian—and an even funnier comedian.

Chapter 36
Archer In His Latter Days

I loved to spend time with Grandpa. We did everything together.

— Mike Hopper

Mike was close to both sets of grandparents, but it seemed that he
had a special bond with his Grandpa Archer Hopper during the final
years of his life. In spite of the obvious generational differences, there
was a special relationship between grandpa and grandson.

"When I was very young, Grandpa Hopper had an old green
pickup truck. He and I made our rounds every Saturday in that truck.
We often visited Aunt Virginia, either at her home or over at her linen
shop (once located where the Hopper office is today). She had a small
kitchen in the back.
Grandpa and I
would drink Cokes
and eat Nabs. We
sometimes played
jacks or other games
together, too."

To Mike, it
seemed like his
Grandpa Hopper
knew everybody in
town. They visited
with older citizens in
the community.
There were other
many occasions
when they stopped
in several stores, in
Madison, to talk
with the owners. In
every case, Mike fol-

Mike and Grandpa Hopper

173

lowed his grandpa inside. He quietly listened as they fellows talked for hours, telling story after story about life in the olden days.

Mike thought his grandpa was a walking history book. It was fascinating to hear Archer describe his own father and grandfather in great detail, going all the way back to the Civil War era.

Even when he was older and began traveling with the group, Mike remained close to Grandpa. When the bus rolled back into Madison, Mike usually spent at least two of the three nights he had off with him.

"After Grandma Hopper passed away, someone stayed with Grandpa

Archer

every night. All of the kids in our family took turns staying overnight with Grandpa. There were many times, due to how much I enjoyed our time together, I'd call a cousin and say, 'Hey, don't worry about coming over. I'll stay with Grandpa again this evening.'"

Grandpa and Mike stayed active when together. Sometimes Mike drove him to Greensboro to look around or go to the movies together. There were even occasions when they went to the circus.

"These were great times for the two of us. I remember first going to a Japanese steakhouse with him. Japanese restaurants were just becoming popular and I talked him into trying the place. Grandpa was in his mid-eighties and his youngest brother, Uncle Irvin, met us for dinner. Uncle Irvin lived in the Sandhills area of North Carolina. The three of us did many things together.

"I wouldn't take *anything* for those precious times with my grandparents. Nowadays, I see younger people—although I still see myself as being young—and realize most don't experience the kind of moments I had as a child. Sometimes extended families aren't very close anymore. It isn't often that families live as close together as we did. I appreciated Grandpa's personality and his sense of humor. Those times together were priceless for me."

The Mural

Many years after the Hopper family started singing, Claude and the other children began to recognize just how proud their father was of the group. On occasion he traveled great distances to hear the group perform.

"You know, he was proud and support-  ive of the entire family," Claude said. "Once, after we purchased a 1994 Eagle bus, I had a photograph taken of our childhood home— the old cabin. I hired a talented airbrush artist to paint a mural of the homeplace on the side of our bus. When the painting was complete, Mike took Dad to see it. When he first saw it, he broke down and cried. He said, 'Just think, that picture will be seen all over the country.'"

Being sentimental anyway, Archer was moved by the painting as it brought to mind a variety of precious memories that the fami-

Archer

ly enjoyed while living in that rustic five-room log cabin.

I'm Hungry

Archer was an active individual all of his life, even into his late 90s. Only in the last week of his life did he become sickly. He was taken to the hospital, although he didn't pass away until he came home from the hospital. He actually went home the day before he died.

"Several of us were in the kitchen small-talking that evening, while Dad was in his bed resting. At one point, he raised himself up from the bed and grumbled, 'Hey, kids! I'm hungry. I'm not dead yet!'"

The Hopper siblings scrambled to prepare a meal for their father. "We still chuckle about that episode," Claude said. "That was exactly how Dad was! He was a strong man with an incredible amount of willpower!"

Archer ate well and was in good spirits for the rest of the evening. He went home to be with the Lord on the following day. Archer passed away in December 1994, at the ripe old age of ninety-nine.

Chapter 37
Claude's Inspiration

Through thy precepts I get understanding: therefore I
hate every false way. Thy word is a lamp unto my feet,
and a light unto my path. I have sworn, and I will perform it, that I will keep thy righteous judgments.

— Psalm 119:104-106

The late Will Rogers once said he never met a man he didn't like.
Similarly, Claude says he never met a man he couldn't learn from. He
counts himself fortunate that he has been able to glean a great deal of
knowledge and insight from men and women across the country. His
unique perspective in business and in his personal life has been large-
ly shaped by his experiences on the road, and by the people he's met
over the last half-century.

It seems that Claude has spent the better part of his adulthood
studying human behavior and learning from others.

He is also an avid reader and especially enjoys reading motiva-
tional titles. "I have a lot of meaningful quotes that I've committed to
memory; but, for the life of me, I don't always know, or remember,
who really said them," he said, as he chuckled. "Most of the wise sayings or quotes have come from books I've read. Some quotations I
can't forget are the ones I heard as a child. For example, I remember
hearing Dad say, 'If you lie down with dogs, you'll get up with
fleas!'"

Another common saying was "The onliest thing you get from
straddlin' the fence is a sore backside." Claude recalls that it was Ben
Franklin who is credited with saying, "By failing to prepare, you are
preparing to fail."

Years ago, Dale Carnegie's writings inspired Claude through
one of his books, entitled, *How to Win Friends and Influence People.*
Many principles Carnegie offered in the volume have become
ingrained in Claude's thinking.

It was Reggie Brann, a friend, who gave Claude his first book by
Dale Carnegie. Carnegie, often called a pioneer on public speaking

and character development, is known for his pointers on everyday life, such as: don't criticize, condemn or complain; give honest, sincere appreciation; and become genuinely interested in other people. Carnegie also suggested, "Put enthusiasm into your work," and Claude has certainly taken that principle to heart.

Once when an aging Mark Twain was questioned about the reason for his own success, he replied: "I was born excited!" Perhaps Claude was born likewise. Throughout the years of the Hopper ministry, Claude has maintained an enthusiastic and passionate attitude toward the group and its future, and remains driven to succeed. As Thomas Carlyle, Scottish historian, critic and writer, stated: "The Man without a purpose is like a ship without a rudder—a waif, a nothing, a no man." Claude lives his life with purpose of ministry and mission.

Another title, *The Greatest Salesman in the World,* by Og Mandino, transformed Claude's life and philosophy at one time years ago. "Don't let the title deceive you," he said. "It's a small book about spiritual precepts and wisdom."

> I will live this day as if this is my last. And what shall I do with this last precious day, which remains in my keeping? I will seal up its container of life so that not a drop spills itself upon the sand. I will waste not a moment mourning yesterday's misfortunes, yesterday's defeats, yesterday's aches in the heart, for why should I throw good after bad. — **Og Mandino**

Claude says he truly values the blessings of traveling the world over with the Gospel message, but the longer he lives, the more he realizes the equal importance of having an impact at home. The founder of Temple University, Russell Conwell, in *Acres of Diamonds*, once said: "Any man can be great, but the best place to be great is at home. They can make their kind better; they can labor to help their neighbors and instruct and improve the minds of men, women and children around them; they can make holier their own locality; they can build up the schools and churches around them, and they can make their own homes bright and sweet. These are the elements of greatness, it is here greatness begins, and if a man is not great in his

177

own home or in his own school district he will never be great anywhere."

Family and civic responsibilities are of the utmost importance these days to the founder for the Hoppers, and he finds that his Christian walk affects all areas of life.

The Holy Bible

Above all, Claude says he's found that the habit of reading and studying Scripture has proved to be the single greatest source of personal satisfaction, providing lifelong fulfillment and life-changing power. It provides practical wisdom for everyday living. "It is alive. I have found over and over again, through my own personal experiences, that the Heavenly Father most often reveals Himself and His perfect will through His Word," Claude said. The Bible, the Word of Truth, is the ultimate guidebook for successful and abundant living in this world. It is the only roadmap to eternal life through Jesus Christ.

"Now that's something to ponder upon and rejoice in," Claude concluded.

Claude praying in the recording studio

Chapter 38
The Nuts And Bolts Of Ministry

What is the use of living if it be not to strive for noble
causes and to make this muddled world a better place
for those who will live in it after we are gone.

—Winston Churchill

Although it may not be discussed a great deal in public, Southern
Gospel groups, or even solo artists, must operate under a carefully
developed and tightly controlled budget in order to be successful.
Monthly expenditures and incoming revenues must be constantly
monitored, analyzed and anticipated.

"A group manager must consider the needs of the members and
the various operating costs involved when going into this type of
ministry," Claude said. The Hoppers continually tailor their fiscal
plan, being sensitive to budgetary restraints and the Lord's leading.
This is imperative if the singers expect to maintain a certain minimal
plane of living.

Claude knows what the ministry must earn each day to continue to be viable and meet everyday obligations. Even during a financial slump, bus payments, diesel-fuel expenses, payroll requirements,
hospitalization and retirement premiums and administrative costs
continue.

From the beginning of their full-time commitment, the Hoppers
were one of the few groups on the road with hospitalization insurance and a retirement program in place for members.

Claude stresses that a very delicate balance must be maintained
when merging business with Gospel singing. Anytime the business
aspects of a Gospel group supersede the focus on Christ-centered
ministry, there are problems.

"Being out of balance can be disastrous," Claude advised. "The
Lord will not bless a ministry that takes its eyes off Him. Perhaps a
ministry will even flourish financially, but that ministry will never
change lives, or speak to wounded hearts, if out of balance."

Joyce Hopper, Monroe's wife and longtime office manager for the Hoppers, first started with the organization in the mid-1980s. She is typically the first person someone speaks to when calling the Madison office.

Joyce explained how Claude places the emphasis of every concert on glorifying the Lord, and the rest seems to take care of itself. "For example, there have been many occasions when they sang at a function where few people attended and they didn't receive enough donations or product sales to meet the needs of the ministry," she said. "Then maybe a day or so later, things will turn around and a love offering will be above and beyond what any of them expected. So, really, it just seems to work out with the Lord; that's all I can tell you."

> But my God shall supply all your need according to
> His riches in glory by Christ Jesus.
>
> — Philippians 4:19

Joyce spends most of her office hours concerned with product fulfillment, filing reports, preparing correspondence, maintaining

Perhaps Claude doesn't believe in a clean desk

accounts payable and completing other managerial duties.

Another member of the office team, Tammy Nix, has worked, on and off, for the organization since 1999. "Tammy has helped compose letters and correspondence for Claude and Connie. She also assists in the office with mail-orders and running errands," Joyce said, "and is always a great help.

"Through the years we've had several individuals who have helped us in the office, including Donna, Paul Hopper's daughter," she added. "While she was here, she was a great help."

"Then there have been people through the years who *thought* they wanted to work here, until they arrived," she said, as she chuckled. "Once they start, they realize it's not so glamorous. It's a lot of hard work. It's not fun and games. I guess these folks thought that because this office concerns a Southern Gospel group it would be light and fun.

"If there is something I could say about Claude, it's that not many people really know him as I do. Most don't know his heart. When I first started here, I never dreamed I would be able to work for Claude for as long as I have. Yet, once I got to know and understand him, it made a big difference.

"I've witnessed him doing things—really nice things—for people who even talked negative about him in the past. I appreciate knowing that. He has a soft heart for people, even though he is dedicated to the business side of it all. I know his whole heart is in this ministry, and he wants to see it go on and on. He is also a forgiving and kind man, " Joyce said.

Reggie Brann, a Gospel promoter and a longtime friend of the Hoppers says Claude has gotten a certain amount of criticism, and sometimes a bad rap, for being such an aggressive businessman. He explained: "Claude wants to achieve certain goals, including the great things he wants to see the Lord accomplish through the North Carolina Gospel Music Hall of Honor and Museum, a pet project that takes much of his time and energy these days. It's not about money; it just takes resources to accomplish some of these objectives. Claude is a goal-oriented person who has a clear vision."

In Claude's way of thinking, business is not the secular side of the organization, as some artists maintain. Instead, he feels it is an intricate part of the balance of ministry, where stewardship and busi-

181

ness ethics are components of the overall service to the Lord.

"I've known the Hoppers since I was a teenager," Reggie added, "and I'm now fifty-two years old. I've booked them on many occasions. This family is of the highest integrity. I can also say they're in the ministry for all the right reasons. Business details do not get in the way of their passion for souls!"

Dennis Sparks, an associate of the Hoppers, added how he sees Claude as one of the great Southern Gospel visionaries. "This man has devoted most of his adult life to promoting and preserving Southern Gospel music, and furthering the Gospel message."

On a business level, Claude has been involved in a wide range of interests in the music industry. He has used his fortitude and any influence he might have to encourage the Gospel in song.

"By his example as a devoted Christian businessman, he's taught me to be a better steward of what God has entrusted me," Dennis added.

Les Butler said: "Through the years, even after I got involved in other realms of the industry, the Hoppers and I have worked on many promotions together. Their live video projects, *Jerusalem* and *Forever*, were Solid Gospel promotions.

"It was at that time we were shooting the video at the Renaissance Center, in Dickson, Tennessee, that I was standing backstage before one of their concerts. Claude walked up to me and said he genuinely appreciated everything I have done for the Hoppers throughout the years—including my help on the radio. He said that if it hadn't been for me, the Hoppers would not be! You know, he didn't need to say that, but he did. That's why fifty

Claude's greatest enjoyment is working around his farm

years later the Hoppers are where they are today.

"Claude is in a lofty position as a member of the board of directors for the National Quartet Convention, the North Carolina Gospel Music Hall of Honor and all his other involvements," Les added. "However, he still came over to me and thanked me. Wow! I was overwhelmed.

"Claude is deeply involved with the music business, as well as business outside the world of Gospel music. Through the years, he has diversified himself to where he can sustain them even through those low ebbs in the music industry."

Les commented that it's interesting to consider how much Claude has on his plate at any given time, with all his involvement in business; but then, in contrast, it's amazing how little Connie has to do with that side of the ministry at all.

"Connie's focal point is the spiritual side of their ministry. You need that combination: business and spirituality; and believe me, they handle both sides very well! It has helped them to be where they are today."

Connie and Claude at the farmhouse

Chapter 39
Dean And Kim

A good marriage is one which allows for change and
growth in the individuals and in the way they express
their love.

— Pearl S. Buck

Kim Greene, born on May 25, 1967, grew up in an atypical Christian
household with two ornery brothers, Tim and Tony Greene. She was
the only daughter of Carolyn and Everette Greene, and was raised in
Boone, located in the high country of North Carolina.

Her father and mother, both committed Christians, were musically inclined and participated in family-based Gospel groups in their
youth. Everette was also an accomplished pianist.

As you might imagine, the Greene home was full of music. It
was only natural that Kim and her brothers followed in their parents'
footsteps. With their guidance, Kim, Tim and Tony formed their own
little vocal group: the Singing Greenes, which was later renamed the
Greenes.

At the beginning Everette played piano for the trio and drove
the kids to and from various church services, revivals and homecomings in the area, while Carolyn sat quietly cheering them on from the
sidelines. The children quickly grew in ability and popularity and
eventually spent every weekend traveling from location to location.

For Kim singing was always a central part of her life. She was
determined to improve her own vocal abilities. Like a student cram-
ming for exams, she analyzed the styles of other artists, especially
one of her favorites, Reba Rambo, the daughter of legendary Dottie
Rambo.

During these homespun self-taught voice lessons, Kim isolated
herself inside her bedroom and listened closely to her tape player.
Over and over again she sang along with her favorite artists, imitating what she was hearing.

It was through listening to albums by various artists, ironically
including the Hopper Brothers and Connie, that Kim improved her

vocal abilities.

"Listening to Debra Talley sing with the Hoppers helped me more than anything," she said, as she remembered a time around the age of twelve or thirteen when her voice had begun to change—deepening in pitch—and she struggled to reach the high notes onstage.

While listening to Debra, she paid careful attention to how each note resonated. Although Debra had a naturally low speaking voice, she delivered on higher notes when necessary. By imitating Debra's tone and practicing harder than ever, Kim overcame her difficulties and continued to develop vocally. Before long she could not only hit the high notes again, she could sing notes in a broader range— higher and lower—than ever before. Kim says now that it was only through much prayer and practice that the quality of her voice improved.

The Greenes continued to improve and developed their own unique sound, and began to record and tour extensively.

Kim Greene Hopper

When Kim was a teenager the idea of dating while traveling full time seemed impossible. A rigorous touring schedule wasn't conducive to a teenager's social life. "Dating was almost nonexistent," Kim once said in a magazine interview. The only "dating," for the most part, consisted of talking to young fellows at Gospel concerts. Kim confessed that during high school she'd had her heart broken on several occasions by young guys who didn't understand or appreciate why she was always gone on weekends.

Kim enjoyed time on the road with her family; however, understandably, she struggled with the demands it placed on a teenage life. Later, as an adult, she said: "I really treasured what I was doing, and I loved to sing; but I grew up fast by being on the Greenes' bus. I missed out on many of the things that most children experience. So in certain ways it was difficult."

Kim remembers when she first met Dean Hopper. She was twelve. Her father, Everette, had called Claude and talked to him about his children and their trio. Claude said he'd love to hear them and suggested they come to a tabernacle in Spruce Pines where the Hoppers were scheduled to sing on the next weekend.

"When we got there, Claude asked us to do a few songs to open up. I don't remember seeing Dean before the concert, but I do remember being very nervous because they were such a professional group!" Kim said.

After the Greenes performed, the Hoppers got up to sing. It was then that Kim took note of Dean. She later confessed she was thinking, "Now this guy is cute!" She secretly developed a pre-teen crush.

"Dean was seventeen, and with our age difference, I knew I was too young for him to even be interested."

Yet within several years' time, as Kim matured, Dean found himself attracted to her.

"He never paid much attention to me until I was around nineteen or twenty. That's when he started calling me occasionally on the phone," Kim said, smiling. When, on occasion, the two families worked together, Kim and Dean would spend time together talking, too.

Although she thought he was a nice young man, Kim was cautious about getting too close, fearing it would constitute another disappointment and heartbreak.

Kim and Dean

Then in December of 1987, Dean called Kim and asked if she wanted to go out on a legitimate date during a ski retreat. She accepted his invitation.

While they shared a warm candlelight dinner, it seemed Dean couldn't take his eyes off Kim. For more than an hour they casually talked about their lives, careers and hopes for the future. They both laughed as they shared their most embarrassing moments and some of the funny things that have happened while on the road. Time seemed to slip by quickly as they enjoyed each other's company. At one point near the end of the evening, Dean leaned forward, smiled and whispered, "Kim, you look especially beautiful in this light."

She was speechless for several minutes as she sensed something unique about this young fellow sitting across the table from her. He wasn't anything like the boys she knew from high school. Dean was sensitive to her feelings

A great looking couple

and a perfect gentleman. He also had a sense of humor and loved to laugh. From the first date, Kim knew Dean was the one she wanted to spend her life with. They continued to see each other exclusively and their relationship blossomed. By March 1988 Dean and Kim were engaged and planning a wedding.

At first her parents, Everette and Carolyn, were pleased with the engagement because they knew Dean and the qualities he possessed. They knew his parents. And they knew Dean understood the challenges of a life on the road and the sacrifices that came along with it.

Kim and Dean married at First Baptist Church, in Boone, North Carolina, on November 10, 1988.

Afterwards, she moved from Boone to Madison to begin a home with her husband. For the next year she drove two and a half hours each week to get on the Greenes' bus, and was on the road three or four days a week. The initial plan was that Kim would continue with the Greenes, and Dean would sing with his family.

"Occasionally our families worked together or crossed paths, but most of the time Dean was on one bus in one part of the country, while I was on another bus in an opposite direction."

Dean and Kim talked many times about how they would handle their tour schedule before they married. However, the realities of the road were painful and stressful on the newlyweds, for they yearned to be together. Finding it much harder than either anticipated, they tried to adjust during the first months of marriage. All of their energies were used to adapt to the complications of being separated.

"We were together two days a week before heading back out to what was normal for us—touring. By the time we both got back home on Monday, we were strangers again. It was like starting all over."

As the months went by, they continued to travel separately and the intensity of the problems grew. Finally, they faced the fact that being divided wasn't going to work for them. With much prayer and distress over the situation, Dean finally took the initiative and decided he'd talk with Kim's parents about the problems.

"In desperation, Dean went to see Mom and Dad and explain the situation. He tried to gently explain to them that they needed to set a date for a replacement. I would, of course, help until a suitable replacement was found. He explained that because I was an emotional basket case, our marriage was suffering and this was what had to be done."

It was difficult for Carolyn and Everette to handle the news at first. In a strange way, it felt like Kim was betraying her family and the trio.

This was a major crisis in the career and lives of the Greene family, for the siblings had always been together in ministry. At the time of Kim's departure, Tony, Tim and Kim had been singing on the Gospel stage for over ten years, crisscrossing the country many times. Kim also arranged the vocal parts for her brothers. By leaving, there was going to be a hole left that would be hard to fill.

But as good parents who wanted the best for their daughter, Everette and Carolyn eventually concluded that if this is what would make Kim happy, then they would accept it.

Ironically, at the time, the Greenes had the number-one Southern Gospel song in the nation, "When I Knelt the Blood Fell."

Dean remembered what a difficult time it was for Kim to leave the Greenes. "There was a great deal of travail during that time period," he said. "Looking back, I see how God had this planned. If everything ended today, we would still believe God had a divine strategy in how he brought us all together."

"During this time the Hoppers found themselves in a difficult situation musically; they were without a soprano during a recording session for a new album," Claude said. "An exceptionally talented young man, Greg Bentley, had been singing with the Hoppers for several years. He had been hired as a fifth singing part. He had a unique tenor voice, but the group blend still needed that soprano voice, like we had with Debra Talley or Sharon Watts Meads. I'm not sure why we didn't just cancel the recording session, but in desperation, since Kim was in Madison, I asked if she would feel comfortable helping us out by singing some on this project."

Kim's departure from the Greenes was still relatively fresh in everybody's thinking. Claude never intended to put undue pressure on her, or hurt her family in the process. Yet, he was anxious because they were running out of time at the studio. He wasn't asking Kim to join the group. He just needed help.

Claude's original objective was to continue trying out other singers for the open position, but first things first: the recording had

to be completed.

"When we got into the studio, our first song was 'Here I Am,' and it was just magical," he remembered. "Connie and I openly wept, for the power of the Holy Spirit's anointing was so intense in that place. The vocal blend that resulted with Kim was incredible."

Several weeks afterwards, as he pondered the experience in the recording studio, Claude approached Kim about the opening for a soprano.

"Claude told me if I wanted the position, it was mine. Yet, if I wasn't interested, he was going to hire someone else. I immediately told him I wanted it, but I would like to take several weeks, at least, off the road to be with my husband."

As it turned out, Kim's time off the road was short. She was soon traveling with Dean and singing with the the same group she had admired as a child. At last, she felt she was where she was meant to be—with Dean.

As it turned out, that first song Kim recorded, "Here I Am," went to number one and was eventually named *Singing News* Song of the Year.

"In fact, the song was the Hoppers' first number one in their legendary career," Kim said. "So I took that as God's way of confirming for me that I was doing what He wanted me to do."

The powerful song, written by Sylvia Green, was released in February 1990. By May it reached the top position on the charts. It held solid in the position through August.

Kim joined the Hoppers in 1990, and Shannon Childress, of Madisonville, Tennessee, played piano for the group. Taylor Barnes, of Chattanooga, played bass guitar during many of their dates. Off and on again, during this era, Frank Mills also toured with the Hoppers as the bass player. Mike played drums and Claude, Connie and Dean sang.

"Kim's voice is just a God thing," Dean said. "She's amazing and I would like to believe we complement one another when we sing together. When she first joined the Hoppers, she had to change her vocal style, in that she had to sing consistently higher than she was accustomed. The experience broadened her range, and now she vocally has that indescribable power, where she can go from zero to ninety in about two seconds flat!"

Other chart toppers from the Hoppers during the 1990s included "One More Time," "From Disgrace To His Grace," "I Am," and "Pure Mercy."

By October 1990, "Lord, Don't Move That Mountain" was released. In August 1991, "Heavenly Sunrise" got radio airplay, followed by "That's Him" in early 1992. In October 1992, "Milk And Honey" was a popular recording. The song, "Mention My Name," was getting national exposure in spring 1993.

Through the 1990s, the Hoppers experienced a phenomenal boost in their recording career as the Lord continued to bless their efforts.

Meanwhile, the Greenes moved forward and continued to create inspiring hits and win industry accolades of their own.

Today, Tony Greene's wife, TaRanda, an impressive talent in her own right, sings soprano for the Greenes.

"TaRanda has been such a blessing for Tony, and she has been a real asset to the Greenes," Kim said. "She's an incredible talent and a lovely sister-in-law."

Besides having her music career, Kim, who always loved to cut

Kim makes sure every hair is in place for Bill Gaither

hair, earned a degree in cosmetology right after high school.

"My grandmother owned a hair salon, and I always wanted to be a hairdresser like her and a couple of my aunts," Kim said. "I remember even when I was a little girl, all my baby dolls were bald. I cut their hair as soon as I got them!"

After cosmetology school, Kim went to work in her grandmother's beauty shop until the family's touring schedule forced her to quit. She keeps her cosmetology license current by practicing her trade on the family's hair,

along with several celebrities, including Bill Gaither and many of the artists during the Gaither Homecoming tours.

"It keeps me practiced up," she said, noting that Bill is especially brave to trust her abilities.

Difficulties In Life

It's important to remember that the Hoppers are real people with real problems. In spite of the many blessings, they also experience their share of challenges and heartbreaks.

Mike met and began dating Denice Bradley during the 1990s when she was still in college. Denice, a native of Belle Vernon, Pennsylvania, was attending Belmont University, in Nashville, eventually earning a Bachelor's Degree in commercial music.

She and Mike married in 1996. In 1998, when a position came open after Shannon Childress retired from the group, she accepted duties as the pianist for the Hoppers.

Sadly the marriage didn't work out and Denice and Mike legally separated in 2005. A terribly heartbreaking event for the family, the situation remains a private and tragic matter where Mike finds solace in Christ, his family and music.

Chapter 40
Here I Am

So, I took [the song, "Here I Am"] as God's way of confirming for me that I was doing what He wanted me to do.

— Kim Hopper

In a letter written some time ago, talented artist and songwriter Sylvia Green described the circumstances surrounding the writing of the Hoppers' first number-one song, "Here I Am." As stated in the last chapter, this song was chosen as the *Singing News* Song of the Year.

In an excerpt from that letter, she stated:

> I actually wrote a verse and chorus of "Here I Am" and put it up for nearly a year. Then one day I was at my parent's home and started playing and singing the song at the piano. My dad walked into the room and asked who wrote it.
>
> When I told him, he said, "You need to finish that. It's a number one song!"
>
> So, trusting his wisdom, I finished the song. This also happened to be a time when I wasn't getting songs recorded and I began to question the musical calling I had always felt on my life.
>
> A friend, Reggie Brann (who is also a friend of the Hoppers), kept calling and encouraging me and telling me God wasn't through with me yet. Eventually, Reggie took the song directly to the Hoppers. It was then put in a drawer again.
>
> Eventually Connie Hopper remembered the song and brought it out during a recording project. They cut it, singled it, and the rest is history!
>
> There are so many testimonies with the song, but

I just have to tell you this one: There was an elderly gentlemen who had attended church all his life, but never really vocalized whether he had accepted the Lord as his Savior. His family was concerned about his salvation, as he was very ill.

Then the Hoppers came to town and his church took the senior saints on the church van to the concert (and the elderly gentleman attended). As the Hoppers began to sing "Here I am ... Here I am ... I'm the one the Shepherd left the fold to find...," all of a sudden a commotion broke out in the back of the church and the older gentlemen started running and shouting with tears streaming down his face, hollering, "I'm the one ... I'm the one!"

It was only a few days later that he passed away, but the family could now rejoice in knowing he had made it to Heaven!

Reggie later recalled the circumstances behind the song and said, "A lot went down behind the scenes with the making of 'Here I Am.' My wife, Sharon, and I personally delivered the tape of Sylvia's song to Claude and Connie at the farm, right after Dean and Kim's wedding. It was a long time after that that Connie called from a Nashville recording studio and wanted to locate Sylvia for permission to record, and to square away publishing rights. You know, I still have the single (the 45-rpm vinyl record) that I received in December 1989. It's the record from the radio station where I have a Gospel music program. Although it was first released in late 1989, the song was re-released on CD in early 1990, probably around February. I think the Hoppers remembered that song because I mentioned it so often to them. Sometimes, persistence pays off."

Chapter 41
Karlye Is Born

When I was born I was so surprised I didn't talk for a year and a half.

— Gracie Allen

"In October 1994, our grand-daughter, Karlye, was coming a little early," Connie recalled, "so Dean stayed home from the road and we got somebody to fill in temporarily. As I remember, we were singing at a revival in West Virginia. This fellow on our bus had a cell phone, but he couldn't get a signal in the Appalachian Mountains. We later found out that Dean had been trying to call all day."

Once they were able to call Dean from the church phone, they found out that the doctor

Grandma Hopper and Karlye

expected Kim to deliver that evening. That night the Hoppers sang for the first part of the program and then Claude and Connie left. They drove the pastor's car and headed back home. They arrived at the hospital around midnight, but Karlye Jade Hopper had been born two hours before they got there.

"When we saw that little newborn in the hospital, it was one of the greatest moments of our lives. Then, after spending time with Dean, Kim and our new granddaughter, we rushed back to the group because there was no one to take our place on the road."

Dean and Kim were the proudest of parents and considered themselves blessed to have such a beautiful, healthy baby girl. Within weeks, Kim and Dean hired a nanny, Denise Allman. With the babysitter's help, they brought Karlye on the road with them.

"Karlye didn't cry too much, and it was great to have her right with us," Connie said.

Poppy and Karlye

Karlye soon became an addition to the Hoppers' performances. During singing dates, Kim and Dean introduced the infant to audiences across the country. "We were bubbling over with excitement, and we wanted everyone to share in our blessing from God," Dean said.

Claude talked about his grand-daughter in an April 1995 *Singing News* interview: "It's truly an honor to travel week after week with my family. We now have three generations of Hoppers on the road, and it's a wonderful blessing."

Concerning the assistance of a nanny, Dean said that Denise is wonder-ful to travel with and a great help to them.

"Dad often jokes about it on stage, and says we have two more women on the bus [baby Karlye and Denise]," Dean said in 1995. "For years Mom was the only woman traveling, and now, all of a sud-den, the guys are beginning to be outnumbered."

By the time Karlye was four or five, she would sing on stage by herself. Now she sings with the family on several songs, including "We are America" [a powerful patriotic song from the Hoppers' *Great Day* project].

"I am amazed when I hear the amount of control in her voice, being that she's so young," Connie said.

As a toddler, Karlye's first word was "Poppy," which is still her pet name for Grandpa Claude. Claude affectionately calls her "Poppy," too. It's been said that the two are nearly inseparable, and Karlye especially enjoys playing at the farm. One of the "special toys" that Grandpa Claude allows her to enjoy around the property, with his supervision, of course, is his John Deere Gator, a small farm utili-ty vehicle he purchased for hauling supplies. She often drives it up and down the farm lane.

Dean and Kim are encouragers for Karlye—cheering her on in

whatever she wants to accomplish. Besides singing with the family, she currently studies tap, jazz and ballet dance, as well as the piano. "I want Karlye to have as normal a life as possible. If she someday chooses to sing fulltime, I definitely want it to be her choice," Kim said. "Karlye certainly has 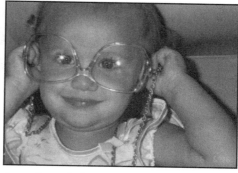 the ability, but I have stressed to her that if she wants to be a lawyer, teacher, doctor or even a ballplayer, I'll be thrilled. Whatever makes her happy is what Dean and I want for her, as long as she has grown in the faith and seeks God's will.

"I will say it would be a great blessing if someday I'm performing on stage with my husband, children and grandchildren. Yet, I will be blessed whether they sing or not, as long as they are looking to the Lord for a future," she said.

"As parents, we support them in whatever they want to do," Dean said. "We're here to give guidance in those directions."

Children always grow up too quickly

Chapter 42
Hoppers, Gaithers
And Homecoming Friends

Bill Gaither is a visionary, and he is one who is concerned about people.

— Claude Hopper

Before Kim joined the Hoppers, the group had already signed with Sonlite Records. The recording company, under the leadership of Chris White, was helpful to the Hoppers' career.

Chris remembered the very beginning of their business relationship: "I remember when I negotiated the first record contract with the Hoppers. I was new to this level of the business and barely had my feet wet when it concerned negotiating label contracts. I had heard rumors that Claude could sometimes be a hard-nosed businessman. I'll have to admit now [though I wouldn't then] that I was fairly intimidated by his reputation. My true moment of courage arrived on the day that Claude sat down in my office and we were negotiating the deal. It was just the two of us. [Today we wouldn't

Connie with Bill Gaither on stage

dream about doing that without a room-full of attorneys around us]. My moment of truth came when he looked at his road sales unit price in the contract. It seemed liked he stared at that number for hours—though it was probably less than a minute. I started to squirm in my chair thinking, 'Oh, man ... he ain't likening this. Maybe I should just lower the price before I make him mad.'

He finally looked up from the contract with a stern look on his face and said, "Son, is this the best you can do?" I saw the future of my entire career flash across my mind in a matter of a second. If I backed down, I would be backing down for a long time to come. I said to myself that I had a choice: crumble or stand my ground. I decided to prove to myself that I had the tenacity to stand for what I believed was right, for the sake of my company. So, I pulled back my chin, stuck out my chest and said, 'Yes, sir, it is.'

"I could hardly catch my breath to say the words. Claude looked back down at the contract for seemingly another hour before he finally raised his head and said, 'Add a nickel a unit to the price.' I responded, 'Excuse me?' He repeated, 'Add a nickel.'

"That day will be one of the memories in my career that I'll never forget, since Claude—displaying a total lack of greed—had chosen to allow us to make more profit than we were even asking for.

"From the beginning, there was a chord that struck me about the Hoppers: that Claude was determined to see the Hoppers reach the plateau that he thought they could experience. The Hoppers signed with me on the Sonlite label in 1989, and we had a great seven year run together.

"They garnered five number one songs in that period including

Song Of The Year honors," Chris added, "and numerous top tens. In that number was the Hoppers', as well as Sonlite's, first number one hit, 'Here I Am.'"

In those days no one knew much about Sonlite, and Chris explained that the Hoppers were a key element to Sonlite's success.

"We were with Chris at the time of our first number-one song, 'Here I Am.' We later were blessed to have several others," Connie said."

"We had some good songs and Chris had a knack for picking them," Connie explained. "I guess he saw something he could work with, and he really worked with us! It was a good relationship."

That was a pivotal time for radio airplay, Claude added, explaining how he personally became involved in promoting their music to radio. Then the Sonlight years eventually came to an end.

Bill Traylor, a well-known individual in the music industry, had a new label in conjunction with CBS at the time, called Riversong. That label eventually merged with Benson.

Traylor was named president of Benson and carried the Cathedrals along with him. Then Traylor left Benson and started his own label, Homeland Records.

"For business reasons, moving to Homeland Records proved to be an unsuccessful move for us," Claude recalled candidly, remembering that they seemed to get lost amidst the other artists with the organization.

The Hoppers began praying and looking for a recording label option near the time their contract was about to expire.

"We started negotiations and finally made a decision: Spring Hill had a great contract with the largest distributor in the business, and it would be a good organization to be associated with. They had signed the Martins, Jeff and Sheri Easter, Janet Paschal, Karen Peck and New River, and some other great talents. We eventually signed a contract, believing this was the right direction to go. The Lord has since blessed this business move. We have remained with Spring Hill ever since."

It was around August 1991 when Bill Gaither began work on what he thought might be his last big project. For a Gaither Vocal Band farewell recording, he invited many of the great Southern

Gospel music legends and artists who had personally inspired him to a recording session to help put the finishing touches on the recording. To document the occasion, he decided to have the moment video-taped.

The Speer Family, Glen Payne and George Younce of the Cathedrals, J.D. Sumner and the Stamps, Eva Mae Lefevre, James Blackwood, Howard and Vestal Goodman, Larry and Rudy Gatlin, Jake Hess and others were invited.

No one could have imagined that what has since become a global phenomenon originally started out as a spontaneous taping of a farewell project at a Nashville recording studio. The project became something more than a recording, for it was the first Southern Gospel reunion and the artists themselves were overwhelmed by the experience.

Not long afterwards, perhaps on the third or fourth video project, Claude and Connie were invited to Bill Gaither's recording studio.

Connie remembered: "It was late August. Our flight was a little late and when we got there, everyone had just started singing. When we initially walked into the studio I was absolutely overcome," Connie said. "All these people I had looked up to over the years were present in one room. It was such a moving experience for all of us. I doubt there was a dry eye in the room."

The Hoppers traveled to the National Quartet Convention, in Louisville, Kentucky, shortly after that videotaping. Connie and Claude shared the experience with many of their friends at Freedom Hall.

"At the convention, Bill Gaither came up to me and said, 'You are all over that video!'" she said. "I remember I was too scared to even speak to Bill at the time, because I was so in awe of him, so I guess I just gave him a puzzled look. I remember thinking, 'I know I didn't sing, so what in the world am I doing on this video?'"

He seemed to understand the confusion, and went on to explain: "Connie, you were so plugged in! That's exactly what we're looking for!"

Even now Connie remembers how the sweet Spirit filled the room with His presence on that first occasion.

As with the first videos, it was a gigantic hit with Gospel music

On stage with the Bill Gaither Homecoming Tour

fans across the country. Connie and Claude later went back and participated in another video. During the taping, Bill said there were people who were curious about their identity because they had never seen them before.

While they were at the second get-together, another overwhelming event occurred: Bill told the couple that there were two people that his wife, Gloria, wanted to personally meet—one was Connie Hopper.

"I was invited to sit with Gloria at the lunch break of the taping. I couldn't believe it! I was sitting with Gloria Gaither! I was a nervous wreck," Connie remembered.

"The sad—but now funny—part was that a day or two before we arrived, I'd accidentally smashed my thumbnail in a drawer on the bus and it was horribly black and blue. I was so ashamed of it. It was so noticeable!

"During the lunch, I kept trying to conceal my ugly thumb, when I happened to look over at Gloria—and lo and behold—she had one, too!" Connie recalled, laughing. "From that point forward, I calmed down and relaxed enough to enjoy the conversation. Today, I hold Gloria in highest regard. She is brilliantly creative, yet down-to-

Mike, Bill Gaither, Dean, Claude, Guy Penrod and David Phelps at the Hopper farm

earth and accessible. First and foremost she is a wife, mother and grandmother. She's also more open than I am. She's a unique and beautiful person".

Connie wrote Bill and Gloria a letter after that taping and told them both that even though she and Claude really didn't know them well, they had never been treated any nicer by anyone. "That was the beginning of a wonderful friendship," Connie said.

Shoutin' Time

"The Hoppers were invited to a Homecoming videotaping session in March of 1998. Ben Speer, who assists in talent and song selection for the Homecoming Friends, told Claude that Bill needed up-tempo songs, because he already had enough ballads," Connie said. "Claude told him we had a fast song we could sing. When our time came, we sang 'Shoutin' Time.' Then we encored it. The spirit and energy was so high in the room, we encored it again.

"As we were returning to our seats, Bill asked Claude if we could be at the Atlanta Dome taping in June. Claude explained that we were already booked at the annual *Singing in the Smokies* on that particular night, but since the videotaping started at 10:00 a.m., we

203

would be there, but would have to leave no later than 4:00 p.m. to make the date with our friends, the Inspirations. Bill said okay.

"The day before the taping we were booked at Natural Chimney, Virginia. We left there around midnight and finally worked our way through Atlanta traffic and arrived at the Dome around 9:00 a.m. We rushed to get in for the morning session. We had lunch and then started the afternoon taping session. As I listened to the groups, soloists and the choirs sing, I began to wonder if this audience would really like this old-time style song we were going to sing. I didn't have to wonder long—Bill announced our group and we started 'Shoutin' Time.' The hair began to rise up on my arms and I sensed the Holy Spirit moving during the musical interlude," Connie continued. "I turned to Claude and said, 'There is Someone here with us.' When I turned and saw 35,000 people standing, clapping and praising the Lord, I knew they also sensed the presence of the Holy Spirit. Kim Hopper outdid herself that day. I'm not sure if there were six or seven encores to 'Shoutin' Time' that day, but Bill used them all on the *Singing at the Dome* video."

Through the years, being included on the Homecoming videos, tours, and television shows has been been great for the Hoppers.

"It's really a rewarding experience for all who are involved," Dean commented. "It remains a thrill for us to be a part of the concert tour.

"To be the business mogul that he is, it's cool that Bill is still reachable," Dean said, "and he is a wealth of knowledge. He is just a very down-to-earth individual."

"Bill is a visionary, and he's one who is truly concerned about people," Claude said. "I don't care what one has done in his or her past; Bill has a way of overlooking and forgiving things. He is such an encourager! In Bill's viewpoint, if it's been placed under the Blood, it's time for everyone else to put it in the past, too!"

Bill is a master at coordinating mammoth projects. Claude doubts anyone else in Gospel music today could put together something as imaginative and powerful as the Homecoming video and concert series.

There have been breathtaking moments captured on film. "I remember one particular time when the Homecoming Friends were together and it was especially meaningful for me," Claude remembered. "I've never seen the power of God fall as it did on the night when Conrad Cook sang 'Take Your Shoes Off, Moses, You're On Holy Ground.' Now, because cameras were rolling, that precious moment in time lives on today!"

It wasn't Gaither or any other artist producing an effect or a pre-planned experience; it was the power of God working that day and it was glorious!

"That's one of Bill Gaither's great talents. He knows how to assemble large things, more so than anyone else I know. He knows what song will go into a particular place during a concert, too. But if he makes a mistake, you don't have to tell him. He'll tell you!

"I am pleased to call Bill my friend," Claude added.

The Hoppers have toured extensively with the Homecoming Friends. Claude reflects that during that time he once did an atten-dance analysis based upon one twelve month period, which includ-ed the National Quartet Convention, the Great Western Convention, Red Deere, Alberta concert, and the Homecoming dates. The Hoppers sang to a collective audience of one million people that year. Claude adds: "That was more people in one year than we sang to in the first two decades of our ministry. The Lord has surely blessed us mightily."

Vestal and Howard Remembered

The Hopper family has lost so many of their dearest friends over the years. And even today, it's difficult for them to sing on the Homecoming stage without thinking of dear friends like Howard and Vestal, Jake, Rex, J.D., Brock and the others who have since crossed over the chilly Jordan.

"We miss them sorely, and the Homecoming series now has a great legacy from all those who once participated and have since gone home to be with Jesus. We're so proud to be a part of it all," Connie said.

They grieved when they heard that Howard Goodman passed away on Saturday, November 30, 2002, at the age of eighty-one. Then, his beloved wife, Vestal, passed away a year later, on December 27, 2003, and the Southern Gospel community was devastated. The two losses deeply affected the Hopper family, as they recalled many of their fondest memories with the Goodman family.

In one of Connie's monthly columns in the *Singing News*, written shortly after Vestal's death, she chose to share a rather poignant meeting that happened many years ago.

In an excerpt from that article, Connie wrote:

> Our group first worked with the Happy Goodman Family in the early 1960s. I well remember how audiences thrilled to the great songs penned by Rusty Goodman and sung with excitement and power as only the Goodmans could.
>
> There are several remembrances that left an indelible mark on me personally. Claude and I had once invited the Goodman family to our home for a meal after a concert in our hometown of Madison, North Carolina. I left the concert as soon as our group had finished our last stand in order to get home and make final meal preparations. I was just finishing frying the last pan of chicken when everyone arrived. Other guests who joined us that evening were promoters J.G. Whitfield and W.B. Noulin.
>
> Vestal watched as I hurriedly put the food on the table and she asked, "Honey, do you do all this work yourself?"
>
> I answered that I did. She said, "Why don't you get some help?"
>
> My answer was, "Where would I find help?"
>
> Her response was very matter of fact, "Pray for it!"
>
> Without missing a beat, Vestal said, "I'm going to pray for you to get help with your work at home."
>
> That was in 1971. Dean was nine years old and Michael was two. Because she had been there, Vestal knew the toll of traveling three to five days a week, maintaining a home, family and office.
>
> Surely she prayed because in less than a month after that visit a young lady, Mary Chandler, came to our home to purchase music. It turned out that she was interested in changing employment and was very

interested in our ministry. She came to work with us.

I learned a lesson in prayer that I have never forgotten. The Prophet Daniel said, "And they that be wise shall shine as the brightness of the firmament; and they that turn many to righteousness as the stars for ever and ever." — (Dan. 3:12)

Daniel made up his mind early in life to do the right thing, even if it meant great personal sacrifice. His choice to serve God, though, put him in the category of those who will "shine like the brightness of the heavens." As I listened to the eulogies of praise that were appropriate for the farewell celebration of one who had affected so many lives, it seemed I could hear Vestal say in her matter-of-fact way, "Honey, would you like to be a star, one that continues to shine forever? Pursue a life that honors God and furthers His Kingdom. The discipline necessary for this achievement is rigorous, but this is the kind of life that gleams for all eternity."

Chapter 43
Tornadoes And Salvation

I truly believe, as I look back on everything today, that my sons have become stronger men of faith through these horrendous experiences.

— Claude Hopper

By August 1996, the Hoppers were seeing astonishing success, as reflected on the *Singing News* charts. For example, "Anchor To The Power Of the Cross" grabbed one of the top positions on the charts that month. Other popular releases during that time included "Giving All The Glory To The Lamb" and "Go Ask."

Around this same time, Dean had been dreaming of developing a recording studio. He felt this could be another avenue for expressing his musical creativity and helping others realize their own dreams.

He began to save his money and in 1997, he designed and built his first recording studio. This studio was much different than the one located inside a garage where the group first recorded—it included some of the most high-tech equipment of the time period.

The business was located above a coin-operated laundry in Stoneville, North Carolina, cattycornered from Debbie's Restaurant, a popular diner in town.

The studio business did well as Dean sharpened his skills. Besides working on Hopper projects, he recorded and assisted other groups as well.

Then, on a Friday afternoon, in mid-March 1998, a freak tornado slammed into the small town, killing two people and causing heavy damage to the town's central business district. The twister ripped through the recording studio, leaving the building and its contents in ruins.

It was heartbreaking for the Hopper family and for all the citizens of the region to see the devastation and loss of life in the small community of 3,000 residents.

"It was a great personal loss for Dean and other business people in town, too. I'm sure it was difficult for Dean to comprehend how his dream was transformed into a haphazard mound of rubble so quickly," Claude said.

Dean was able to thank God that no one was recording in the studio, or visiting the laundry downstairs, when the tornado hit.

Astonishingly, some time later, various pieces of paperwork from the studio were found as far away as Lynchburg, Virginia—over 100 miles away—where the high winds carried them.

Fortunately, the landlord of the building, Titus Sparks, required Dean to purchase insurance before starting the business due to the risk of fire from the clothes dryers downstairs. However, the insurance settlement was far less than the replacement value of the high tech equipment.

"It wasn't long after that adversity that I had a thought," Claude said. "I had a mid-sized barn on the farm I had already started remodeling, adding a restroom, bedroom and several other rooms. It was my original plan to turn half of the barn into private living quarters for visitors. But after thinking it over, I asked Dean and Mike to come over for a family discussion.

"When they arrived, I said, 'Boys, do you still want a recording studio? If that's what you want, you need to tell me. I'm fixin' to do it right now with the barn.'"

They both responded, "Yes! Sure we do!"

Through the Lord's provisions, the boys were able to establish a state-of-the-art digital recording studio. When all the remodeling was done and the equipment was installed, Claude announced, "Sons, make a business out of this. I plan to record right here from now on. In this way, when I'm ready to make a recording all I have to do is mosey across the yard and start singing."

Unbelievably, however, in January 2002, in an unfortunate turn of events, the new studio was also destroyed. The contractor who had originally remodeled the barn and built the studio came over one day to un-thaw water pipes. While using a blowtorch beneath the floor, he accidentally caught the barn on fire. Within a matter of minutes everything was engulfed in flames. The studio was a complete loss.

Although devastated at the time, fortunately, this time Dean and Mike had the necessary insurance coverage to rebuild and replace all the equipment.

Connie and Claude

"We now have another recording studio—our third. The current recording studio, located near the entrance to our farm, is appropriately called 'The Farm.' It's a fine facility. It is where all the Hopper studio albums are now recorded," Claude said. "Other groups have taken advantage of it, as well."

The particular building where the studio is located was originally built in the 1980s.

"A friend of ours from Pennsylvania, who always supplied us with fence posts and other needs, helped us," Dean said. "At the time the barn was being planned, Dad bought 8x8 locust posts for the structure. The posts were hard as a rock! The pastor of our home church helped me plant a lot of the posts. Then a construction worker from Virginia, who happened to be another friend, came down to help us complete the project. With his help, we built trusses right there at the barn site. We took a rope and pulley system and pulled those trusses eighteen feet into the air and placed them into position. It was a mammoth job and little did we know then that it would one day be our recording studio."

Mike added that in between the time of the tornado's destruction and the rebuilding of the second studio, he and Dean were back-up musicians for different studios around North Carolina, South

Carolina, Tennessee, Virginia and Georgia. Now that they have rebuilt their studio, they don't travel near as much as they once did.

"I guess it just made sense to have the studio in Madison, especially since it was sixteen hours round trip for our family to travel and record in Nashville," Mike said. "It's especially handy to have it just up the driveway from Mom and Dad's house, fifteen minutes from Dean and Kim's home, and two miles from my place."

Recording Nowadays

One of the things Claude enjoys while recording is that he can now gaze out a studio window and see the foliage surrounding the property, or watch his cattle grazing in the field.

Mike and Dean are normally involved in eight to ten recording projects for other groups and soloists within the course of a year, in addition to what they do for the Hoppers. "That is a lot, considering recording is such a lengthy, drawn-out process and we constantly tour."

There are smaller projects interspersed as well that may require them to provide one or two tracks for someone's existing recording, such as adding backup vocals or musicianship.

"It's a much easier process to record with today's computer software, such as Digidesign ProTools, although it still takes the same amount of time to complete a full project," Mike said. "With the new technology, we're all speaking the same digital language in the industry, which makes it easier to communicate among ourselves."

Reflecting upon the history behind the studios, Claude stated he is thankful that in each of the calamities, the Lord watched over the family and kept them from harm. "These tragedies were part of Dean and Mike's ongoing higher education," he said. "Through it all, they kept a positive attitude and haven't become discouraged."

In spite of temporary setbacks, the Heavenly Father has been forever faithful, continuing to work in their lives, subtly instructing them about the true meaning of life by showing how easily material things can disappear without warning. Only those things that are done for Christ, with the right motive, have eternal recompense. The brothers now seem much more appreciative of the Lord's blessings, and better equipped to minister to others who suffer personal loss.

"I truly believe, as I look back on everything, my sons are

stronger men of faith through these horrendous experiences," Claude said.

Salvation Experiences

Claude asked Christ into his heart when he was a young boy. After hearing the Gospel message preached, he stepped forward and walked down the aisle at an old-fashioned altar, at a small country church near his home.

"I remember it was a hot summer night, and three of my brothers were saved on that same night during revival services."

Connie accepted Christ at an early age, too, at a neighboring church in their community.

Both rededicated their lives to Christ while teenagers and were called into the ministry. They have continued to grow in the Lord ever since.

Dean remembered in great detail about his own salvation experience. "When you're brought up in church, and around Gospel music all the time, sometimes you feel like everything's right in your life when in reality everything isn't right at all. I would convince myself all was okay during the day; but, on many occasions, when it was late and I was lying quietly in my bunk on the bus, I'd pray, 'Lord, if I'm not saved, please, please, please save me.'"

At the age of fourteen Dean went forward at a youth revival at Ellisboro Baptist Church, in Madison. He walked down the aisle, prayed with the pastor, and even shook the preacher's hand. Yet after all that, he still felt like something was missing in his life.

A decade later, when he turned twenty-four, the group was singing in Dillon, South Carolina, at a Baptist church. This was during another youth revival.

"We were there to sing and there was a guest speaker that evening who had been in prison. This fellow's sermon and testimony was so compelling that he really had my attention. At the conclusion of his message, I recall he said these words: 'Even the demons of Hell tremble and know there is a God!'

"That statement hit me hard. I knew there was a God, too. However, I recognized that I didn't have the personal relationship that others often spoke about."

Through the speaker's words, the Holy Spirit touched Dean's

heart and he felt he had never really surrendered his life to Christ. During the altar call, Dean leaned over and whispered to his mother, and Connie walked to the altar with him. There they knelt and prayed.

"I think I was the only person who went forward that night. It must have looked odd to the congregation for one of the Gospel singers to go forward to get saved!" Dean said as he laughed.

"After that experience I got up with all my wants, desires and attitudes changed. I knew I didn't do that on my own. However, after that occurrence, for the next six months, Satan beat me up and told me repeatedly that I wasn't saved! Those kinds of doubts happened over and over again, and sometimes it had me discouraged."

There were many times when Dean questioned his salvation; but he clung to the Lord and continued to pray.

"After the night in Dillon, I spent more time at the altar; in time, the Lord gave me the assurance that I so desperately needed. Since then I have never doubted my salvation again," he said.

"We all have to go back to the Cross and ask His forgiveness; but it is so wonderful that we have our own Lawyer who sits beside God the Father. Jesus rises to the occasion when Satan tries to say things to us to make us doubt. He reminds the devil that His child's sins have been placed under Jesus' blood, and it is forever settled!"

Mike shared a similar testimony: "Recently we played at the little church where I once accepted Christ. It brought back a flood of memories for me. This church is located in a little town, Bilington, in Barbour County, West Virginia. Some years ago, we sang at a three-day revival there every year in October, along with evangelist Phil Hoskins, from Kingsport, Tennessee.

"It was on one night of that revival that Phil told a touching story about a young boy who went off to college. During the years he was away he got in with the wrong crowd. One Sunday morning, instead of going to church, he and his friends were going to ride bikes throughout the countryside. While they rode along they came upon a small rural church. Church members were ringing the bell for Sunday School as they peddled by. As the fellows rode by the church, the sound of the bell became fainter as they traveled on down the road. Finally, the one boy spoke up to his buddies and said, 'Guys, I'm going back. I'm going back to church while I can still hear the bell ringing.'

"That simple story really stood out in my mind, and I realized then that I needed to accept Christ while I could still hear His voice."

Mike went to his motel room after the service and tossed and turned in his bed. When he couldn't' stand it any longer, he went to Phil Hoskins' room at 2:00 a.m. in the morning and woke him up. "I need to get saved," Mike said.

Mike explained that even though he had been actively touring with the family for several years by that time, it was that particular evening in the Mountain State when he truly sensed the Lord's call on his life, and he surrendered.

"Looking back on that moment, I can't say I remember every word Phil said , but I do remember how, through his sermon, the Lord spoke directly to my heart. I've never regretted the moment when I gave my life to Christ," Mike said.

Possibly the most valuable lesson that can be gleaned from these two accounts of conversion is that each individual must make his or her personal decision to follow Jesus. Dean and Mike couldn't depend on Gospel music to save them, nor could they hold onto their parents' coattails. They—indeed all of humanity—must have their own personal relationship with the Lord Jesus Christ.

Dean added: "Every man and woman should take careful inventory of his or her life. Be sure you are counted in the faith. I am a prime example of someone who thought everything was fine—but my life really wasn't right. I recognized I didn't know Jesus intimately and needed that personal relationship."

Kim talked about her own conversion experience: "I was saved in 1975 when I was eight years old. It was a Sunday morning at my home church. We were always in church on Sunday mornings, Sunday nights and Wednesday nights, too. Of course, music was a big part of my life; but I also remember my Mom saying, 'You sit still and you listen!' We were on the front row, so we had to behave.

"I heard the Gospel message preached every week. For some reason, on a particular Sunday, something hit me and I remember how I just wanted to cry. I felt like there was a big gap in my life. When the pastor finished his message and gave the altar call, I was so young I didn't quite understand what I was feeling. I went up to my mama, who was already at the altar. I looked at her and I guess she somehow knew why I was there. She said 'Kim, do you want to be saved?' I said yes.

"She led me to the pastor and I remember at that point my life changed. When I got up from that altar there was a heaviness that lifted from me. It seemed like the sun shone brighter and, even at eight years old, I couldn't wait to tell everybody what happened.

"I was later baptized in the creek near our church.

"As a child I was a doubter. For a lot of years I questioned whether I was really saved. I struggled. It took me many, many years of searching the Scriptures and praying to find peace and assurance before I could rest in my faith."

Kim feels that she spent years making salvation too hard. She said, "I kept thinking that there was something else I had to do to be saved. It was really difficult for me to accept the idea that I didn't have to do anything but receive Jesus. That just seemed too easy.

"It was later during my first trip to Israel that things changed. The Holy Land tour made an indelible mark on me, and it was there I came to the point where I finally said, 'God, there is nothing else I can do! You have done it all! I have to trust in what You have done. If I die today, I'll die believing in You!'

"You know, from that day forward, I settled things and trusted Christ and His grace. There is nothing I can do, for He did everything necessary on Calvary!"

Chapter 44
Tammy Nix Tells All

What you see on stage is not stage talk. It's not stage presence. It's their life!

— Tammy Nix

Tammy Nix is an outgoing, energetic and charming young woman who works in the Hopper office. She described her role in the organization and shared a few of her own memories of the Hopper family.

Tammy knew a little about the Hoppers because she and her family listened to their records when she was a young girl. Then in April 1998, she went with church friends to a Bill Gaither Homecoming Concert, in Greensboro, North Carolina.

"When the Hoppers did 'Shoutin' Time' in Greensboro, I just went crazy! I turned to my pastor, who came along with our group, and said, 'We've got to get them at our church. He nodded and told me to handle it. So, that very next week I called the Hopper office to see if they had any dates available."

Joyce Hopper took down Tammy's information and said she would have Claude call her when the group returned from the West coast. A couple of weeks passed before Claude called and, as he does so often, asked, "Tammy, what do you do for a living?"

The two of them had a long conversation that day.

"Unfortunately, at that time, they didn't have any dates open," Tammy recalled. "However, before I got off the phone, I said to Claude that if he ever needed anybody to help out, I only worked three days a week at my job. So, I had extra time on my hands. That was eight years ago and here I am.

"I do a little bit of everything. I've traveled with them quite a bit and worked at their product table. I've helped in the office with Joyce, and worked with Claude and Connie with correspondence and emails. On occasions, I've handled the biggest part of their travel arrangements. I guess I just do whatever needs to be done."

Tammy described the first time she worked at their product table during a concert. The Hoppers were scheduled to sing at

216

Atlanta for a Gaither Homecoming.

"Little did I know when I volunteered that it would be a thirteen-hour day!" she laughed. "That was the time of the now-famous six encores of 'Shoutin' Time' you can see on the Gaither video. So it was a tremendous day all around.

"After their time on stage, they left to go back to North Carolina for another concert date. We stayed on at the product table," she said.

"That night when we were putting up the tables, videos, and CDs, a lady walked up to our table and wanted to know if she could meet Mr. Hopper. I told her I was sorry, but the family had already left for their next engagement. She asked me to give Claude a message. She proceeded to describe how much she appreciated the Hoppers' sincerity, because they had been at a concert at her church a few years before.

"At the time this woman had been trying to get her father, who was unsaved, to come to church. He finally gave in and attended the night the Hoppers were there. At the concert, she asked Claude if he'd talk to her father. Instead of brushing her off or walking away, Claude took time to speak to her father and he got saved that night! She told me she wanted to tell Claude how grateful she was for that, for her father passed away the next day unexpectedly.

"I stood there with major cold chills...but I also realized at that moment that the Hoppers are real people being used by the Lord. They are what they are on stage. What you see on stage is not stage talk. It's not stage presence. It's their life!"

Tammy said that over the years she has watched them closely while on the road after the singing stops. "They are truly committed, very generous and loving people," she said.

"They have become like a second family to me. Dean and Michael are like brothers! I actually come from a rather large family, but if I could pick another set of parents on this earth, it would be Claude and Connie Hopper."

Claude, The Matchmaker
"When I first started working with the Hoppers, regardless of where we went, Claude continuously tried to find me a husband," Tammy said and chuckled. "I told him I would really appreciate him not helping me so much. He's actually still trying, but he's not as

Having fun on stage

relentless as he once was, mainly because I threatened him ... and Connie threatened him, too!"

Tammy laughed as she told the story of how, on one occasion, Connie even tried to match her up with someone. They were riding down the highway on their way to Greensboro one day and Connie said, "Tammy, I've got somebody I'd like to introduce you to. He's a real nice fellow, although he is a little older. I think you both would enjoy having dinner. It would be a lot of fun!"

"If I remember now, I think she said this fellow was some relation to Claude. Connie continued, saying, 'Now, remember, he is a tad older, but he really doesn't look it! He's nice looking and a good guy.'"

Tammy started to get suspicious and finally asked: "Connie, exactly how old is this fellow?"

"Well...uh...he's sixty-five," Connie said, somewhat sheepishly.

"Sixty-five! My gosh, Con! I don't want to have dinner with someone I have to tuck in his napkin, wipe his drool, or help him with his Depends!" the young woman responded indignantly. A moment later she added, sarcastically, "But then again, I guess we could save money with his AARP membership, so maybe it's not so bad!

"The next day, we happened to be at a convention and a young lady walked up to our table. Connie was saying something to her about finding a boyfriend. I looked at the girl and interrupted, saying, 'Just a word of advice: if Connie Hopper says she has someone she wants you to meet, I have a suggestion for you: *RUN! JUST RUN!*"

Nowadays when the subject comes up with Claude or Connie, Tammy usually responds by saying something like: "That's okay, you just stick to what you do, and I'll stick to being single and happy.

"Claude has also had a lot of fun at my expense in other ways. He and Dr. Murray, another great friend of ours, have had quite a few knee-buckling belly laughs surrounding the fact that I supposedly talk a lot."

Tammy says she has learned a lot over the last few years by being around the Hoppers, especially about being a human being of character. "I've learned a lot more about what it really means to be a true Christian, and how important it is to forgive and reach out to others.

"I started out, really, with the intent of being a blessing to them; but, eight years later, I can honestly say I have been the one who has been blessed by working with their ministry," Tammy concluded.

Chapter 45
Jerusalem

You'd think after years of singing in almost every place imaginable, it would grow old for them! But that day I saw the passion of a young convert as he relayed his belief that God had ordained that song for this time and that place: Jerusalem.

— Charles Brady, *Caraway Media Group*

There are certain occasions that have made indelible marks on the Hoppers, such as the days at Watermelon Park or performing at the Presidential Inauguration Ball. Likewise, one of the most inspirational and exciting events in their lives was a special trip to the Holy Land, in August 2004.

It has been said the Tower of David is one of the most picturesque and historically significant locations in the Middle East. The Tower of David's Citadel Museum, at Jaffa Gate, with its extensive collection of artifacts, architectural highlights, exquisite courtyards and lush archaeological gardens, is one of the focal points of Israel's ancient capital city.

It was at this especially appropriate location in Israel that the Hoppers performed their hit, "Jerusalem," while being captured on film for the Gaither Homecoming video project in the Holy City. Bill Gaither and the Gaither Vocal Band, Ernie Haase and Signature Sound, Russ Taff and many of their dearest friends were in attendance for the occasion.

"We had a rehearsal the night before the actual taping. When we started singing 'Jerusalem,' the Spirit started moving. As we tried to sing, we were so blessed—because we felt God's awesome presence—that it became too difficult for us to even finish the song," Connie recalled. "It was incredible, something I really cannot describe adequately."

By the time they performed the song for the actual videotaping the next evening, the Lord gave them a tremendous blessing again, but they managed to get through the song without stopping.

Connie explained that it was overwhelming, inspiring and touching to be able to sing that particular song in ancient Jerusalem, at the location that was once part of Herod's palace.

In all the years the Hoppers have been traveling and singing, this experience stands out as one of the most unforgettable. They stood and sang near where Christ once appeared before Herod. Later the Hoppers traveled with other Homecoming friends to several landmarks

Charles Brady

throughout the Holy Land, including Mount Calvary and the Empty Tomb. They sang traditional hymns and Gospel classics.

"Words cannot begin to describe the feeling you get as you walk the streets of the Holy City," Mike added. "The entire experience was overpowering and inspiring to all of us."

Claude said that when the Hoppers first recorded "Jerusalem," they never dreamed they would one day sing it in the city of Jerusalem. "It's incredible how God works—miracle after miracle. The Lord's timing is perfect and precise, and it was as if this moment was predestined," Claude said. "This was a wonderful moment for the Hopper family, and for me personally."

Charles Brady of Caraway Media Group spoke with the Hoppers shortly after they returned home from the Holy Land, then commented:

> I was backstage with the Hoppers in Wilkesboro, North Carolina, right after they returned from Jerusalem. To have Claude Hopper share with me what it was like to sing "Jerusalem" in the Holy City, with tears in his eyes and passion and excitement in his voice, was almost overwhelming for me personally. You'd think, after all the years of singing in almost every place imaginable, it would grow old for them! But that day I saw the passion of a young convert as he relayed his belief that God had ordained that song for this time and that place—Jerusalem. That was a conversation I will always remember and hold with great fondness for the rest of my life!

Chapter 46
Dennis Sparks
And Health Issues

Blessed is the man who makes the Lord his trust.

— Psalm 40:4

Dennis Sparks, the booking agent for the Hoppers, has proved to be invaluable to Claude and to the Hopper organization.

Dennis described how he started with the Hoppers:

> I have now known of the Hoppers for about thirty years. In the mid 1980s, God was dealing with me and I began to play my saxophone at local churches. I had formerly played in orchestras and bands, but I was being led to play for the Lord. During that period, I had done recordings, but they weren't really professional.
>
> I had gone to see the Hoppers several times in concert, and since I lived close to Madison, I eventually met with Claude and Dean one day and asked them if they could help me produce a professional recording of my music.
>
> It was from that time our friendship grew. We did recordings, which we finished in 1987 and 1988.
>
> I think we immediately had a lot in common, in that they were a family organization and I was involved in a business with my own family. Because of this, I knew the types of things families in business sometimes deal with. I could look at it from Dean and Mike's perspective, and I could also see it from Claude's side as well.
>
> I originally started doing a bit of troubleshooting for Claude when the group needed assistance with contracts, insurance plans and other business deal-

ings. However, it wasn't until a tornado wiped out my little town and left me homeless, car-less, and jobless that my involvement with the Hoppers increased. During the cleanup from the tornado, we reassessed what we had and eventually put back what we could to make a livelihood. That's also when I began more like a full-time situation with the Hoppers.

I've got two college degrees and twenty-six years of entrepreneurship under my belt—but honestly, I have learned more from Claude Hopper than from all of that.

Claude meshes Christian theology with good business unlike anyone else I have ever met. His philosophy of trying to help people help themselves and to help his organization at the same time is really unique, and it has helped me in my own outlook and businesses.

"I see Dennis as a great businessman," Connie said, explaining that he is the part of the Hoppers' organization that most people never see. "He advises us in a lot of areas, and Claude and Dennis spend a great deal of time together discussing schedules, concert dates and future business decisions. Of course, Claude then makes the final decision."

Connie explained that what Dennis Sparks does for Claude is such a blessing, especially now, and apparently it was meant to be from the start.

"It's got to be God! Dennis is a great guy and is now such an important component in the Hopper ministry. He coordinates all of our bookings and is involved in a variety of business concerns for the group."

Dennis added:

Just like every other business, there are cash flow issues; there are profitability issues that we have to deal with, but we always prevent it from being the overall motive for the ministry.

Through the years, it has been a blessing to see this ministry grow by leaps and bounds.

For example, I remember the time when the Hoppers did their first Gaither Homecoming Tour. Even though the Hoppers had been on the Gaither videos for several years, they had never traveled with the live tour.

The way this all came about was really unusual. We were with Bill Gaither and others at the Southern Gospel Music Hall of Fame banquet at Pigeon Forge. That night I coaxed Dean into asking Bill if the Hoppers could sing at their Greensboro concert the next year.

The reason I urged him to ask was because there had just been a giant Greensboro Homecoming concert. I went to the event and thought, "Wow, the Hoppers really need to be here, too!"

Bill Gaither was gracious to Dean and said, "Call my office next week and we'll see what we can do to set it up for next year."

We did exactly that. We called Mr. Gaither's office and the concert was scheduled for the group. Then we waited a whole year. Finally, when the Greensboro concert came up, the group went on stage and sang "Shoutin' Time." The whole place exploded with excitement!

Incidentally, the Hoppers were scheduled to be in Tulsa, Oklahoma, the following night. So they left me at Greensboro with the product tables and boarded their bus to head out of town in order to beat the traffic. Mr. Gaither came up to the Hopper table and asked, "Dennis, where's Claude? Where's Claude?"

At that moment we could actually see the top of the bus pulling out of the Coliseum parking lot, and Bill said, "Stop them! Stop them!"

I whipped out my cell phone and called the bus and asked them to stop for a few minutes. Gaither then went down to their bus and said, "Claude, we've got to get together! We really need to talk."

He had been thrilled with the audience reaction to the Hoppers that night. So from that point, the Hoppers became actively involved with the Gaither Homecoming tour. That's how it all came about.

Besides performing all his duties for the Hoppers, Dennis operates a catering business and runs Debbie's Restaurant in downtown Stoneville, North Carolina. Both businesses have boomed in the last few years. Dennis also has several other business interests as well.

He has been an intricate member of the *Axis Talent Agency*, a firm Claude organized and implemented in the mid-1990s along with Charlie Smith, of Atlanta, Georgia. It eventually evolved into the in-house booking agency for the Hoppers.

Dennis ties up a lot of the loose ends of the business, dealing with certain aspects that Claude no longer needs to oversee, taking much of the pressure off his shoulders.

"Dennis has been a life-saver for Claude," Connie said, "especially since Claude had his first mini-stroke, or TIA, in July 2001."

Dennis Sparks

This first transient ischemic attack (TIA) happened while Claude was in Canada. A TIA is described as a temporary interruption of blood flow to part of the brain. These episodes can cause a person to have vision problems, slurred speech or other debilitating effects, but the symptoms usually end after the first ten to fifteen minutes.

They say even though the symptoms pass, every TIA should be treated as an emergency, since there is no distinct way of knowing whether the symptoms are from a full-fledged stroke. A mini-stroke itself is a strong warning signal that a stroke may ensue.

Claude, Dean and Mike had traveled to Canada for the Canadian Quartet Convention. Connie and Kim hadn't arrived yet.

The men had gone on ahead, and the women were planning to travel there the next day.

"The fellows were all staying at a friend's house. They were in the basement shooting pool and then, out of nowhere, Claude had this peculiar attack! For several minutes he couldn't walk or move his foot.

"Then he kind of pulled out of it," Connie explained. "It bothered him, but he refused to say much about it. He later told me he would go to the doctor when he got home.

"The next time that it happened it was in February 2002. Claude was attending a board meeting of the National Quartet Convention, in Louisville, Kentucky. I think the mini-stroke was so bad that time that he lost use of his hand, and it caused him to spill his food. When he came home, he had trouble buttoning and unbuttoning his shirt since he still didn't have full use of his hand," Connie said, adding that this remains a topic that Claude finds uncomfortable discussing.

His doctor set up a series of tests, including a CT scan, which showed that Claude had a blocked carotid artery. The physician wanted to perform surgery—a carotid endarterectomy.

Anyone who knows Claude knows he is the type who is always upbeat, forever displaying a cheery, positive attitude about life, choosing to look at the "glass half-full." Yet, at this time, Claude had come face to face with the unknown, and fear began to creep into his world. The word "surgery" caught him unaware, and he was understandably troubled.

Besides having to face his own mortality, he was also concerned about his family and several important upcoming commitments and business concerns.

As it so happened, the date was approaching when the Hoppers were scheduled to sing for the first time at Carnegie Hall along with the Homecoming Friends. Because Claude really wanted to be at this historic event, he asked his doctor if the surgery could be performed as soon as possible so he could mend in time to attend the show.

As with all surgeries, this procedure has a certain element of risk attached to it. Claude and Connie realized the potential complications, what with the blockage being actually removed from the carotid artery. The family immediately started calling friends from churches everywhere in order to form a circle of prayer.

While he waited for the scheduled operation date to come, he undoubtedly had to deal with feelings of uncertainty and anxiety. He and Connie spent much of this period of time seeking God's face and studying His Word. They found comfort as the Lord reminded them through the Scriptures that He was sufficient for every situation, including this complicated medical procedure.

He pondered special verses, such as, "I sought the Lord, and He heard me, and delivered me from all my fears" (Psalm 34:4), and was reminded of what he already knew: a Christian can turn to God for comfort at such difficult times and find confidence and assurance. The Lord already had everything in control, regardless of the outcome of the surgery, and as the song says, if you're His child, you're a winner either way.

Connie said they were all somewhat anxious about the operation, but it was scheduled right away just as Claude had requested. While everyone was praying in the family waiting room, Claude came through the surgical procedure wonderfully and the doctor later released him in time to sing at Carnegie Hall.

"Although I still think he started back on the road too quickly, he has been going strong ever since!" Connie said.

God once again answered the prayers of His people and blessed the family by bringing Claude through the operation with flying colors.

Since the mini-strokes, the only remaining effect Connie has noticed are some minor changes in Claude's ability to remember.

"I think it may have slightly affected his short-term memory, or it may just be a side effect of the medication," Connie said. "The situation is relatively minor in scope. Most of the time he walks up to folks he knows and calls them directly by name; then there are other occasions when he can't put a name with a face."

"It's pretty embarrassing for me when I'm talking to someone I have known and talked with many, many times, but for the life of me, I can't remember his or her name," Claude added. "But besides these fleeting minor lapses in memory, I am doing just great!"

Connie agrees, adding that he never stops!

"He always knows what he wants to get done and pushes himself to get it completed." She chuckled as she added: "You just can't slow my husband down!"

227

Claude is confident he survived the surgery for a reason. He knows the reason he has made a complete recovery is because God is not finished with him yet. So, as long as he is able, his strategy is to continue to move forward, promoting Jesus Christ through Southern Gospel music wherever and whenever he can. His passion is to personally share with others the Good News of salvation that is found only in the cleansing blood of the Savior.

He speaks with contagious excitement and bold determination, saying that as Christians, we have the ultimate answer to all of life's problems and are charged to let our light shine in a dark, sin-filled world: "We should share Jesus with others everywhere we go, whether we are on the concert stage, at the work place or on the golf course."

Chapters 47
An Interview With Danny Jones

I suspect Connie, Dean, Mike and Kim have literally wanted to kill [Claude] on certain occasions, because when he has an idea he won't let up! Nothing detains him from accomplishing the goal.

— Danny Jones, *Singing News Magazine*

Danny Jones

Danny Jones, editor of *Singing News Magazine*, first saw the Hopper Brothers and Connie in the early 1980s when the lineup included Roger and Debra Talley, Claude, Connie, Will and Dean.

"It was at that time, in the 1980s, that they really started making a big name for themselves," Danny said. "I guess I first saw them just before Will Hopper and the Talleys left the group.

"The Hoppers came along in the industry at a tough time. The Goodmans were riding on such a high, as well as the Hinsons," he said. "Both of those groups had a powerful driving style. The Hopper Brothers and Connie were a bit more laid-back musically, and I suspect it was hard for them to fit into those kinds of markets. But once the Hoppers got their foot in the door, people listened and started realizing that they liked their style as well.

"I think that the Hoppers can be credited for opening the door for many other artists who had good songs and smooth singing. Their songs seem to stand out over and above the average, and have always been consistently high quality."

He also noted that the group tends to use arrangements that are often unpredictable, believing that they use unique hooks musically and vocally which are not typical of mixed groups.

"In Southern Gospel music, it all begins with a song. The Hoppers have been really good at finding some very good songs and unique tunes, such as 'Citizen Of Two Worlds,' which is certainly not your typical Southern Gospel song. Yet, they made it work for them."

Danny also described the personalities in the group, saying that

Connie, especially, is "one of the most genuine Christians you'll ever meet." Because of the blending of qualities and temperaments, along with each member's full commitment to ministry and family, the group has been especially balanced and successful.

"With Connie, what you see is what you get! She is very down-to-earth, personable and humble and you can't help but like her. She is everybody's friend; everyone likes her. And she will pray with someone at the drop of a hat.

"She can also be a zany nut, too! She loves to laugh, and she has a genuine heart for being a servant. She is a wonderful example of a ballad singer, and she handles those ballads beautifully.

"If the whole world was made up of Connie Hoppers, we would have no problems and everything would be ideal!"

"And then there's Claude!" Danny said, dropping his head and laughing. "He works very hard and he's very, very driven! Once he sets his mind on something he wants to accomplish, he will see it through—regardless of the obstacles. I suspect Connie, Dean, Mike and Kim have literally wanted to strangle him on certain occasions, because when he has an idea he won't let up! Nothing detains him from accomplishing the goal.

"Because he is on the board of the National Quartet Convention, wherever he is on any given night, regardless of whether the Hoppers are the only performing group or they are one of twelve groups singing at a church, stadium or concert hall, Claude can be found handing out NQC brochures at a side door before the concert. He does everything he can do to get the word out about the NQC, and Southern Gospel music in general, and other projects, too. He is very motivated!

"He is also one who wants to see his family do well, in all areas of life—not just monetarily or in the industry—and he seems determined to leave something for his family, his children and grandchildren for that day when he and Connie can no longer be around.

"Claude loves his time on stage, too. He enjoys being with and talking with people," he added. "It seems obvious when he's singing—he is having the time of his life!"

Danny then explained that he sees that same type of work ethic in Claude's sons, Mike and Dean. In his opinion, Mike is the one who keeps the Hoppers together in a sense.

For a concert, Mike pulls all the music together and controls the various tracks on stage. From a technical standpoint, he takes care of many duties, including the group website. He went on to say that the Hoppers were the first group to incorporate video footage on their Internet site—which is because of Mike, who stays up-to-date on technology and is extremely gifted in that area.

"Mike was also the first and only drummer so far to win the *Singing News* Favorite Musician Award. I think he is destined to be a leader in the Southern Gospel music industry," Danny continued.

"Of course, Kim has earned her accolades as a vocalist. She is a key player for the Hoppers. By her presence, she has made everyone else better, too.

"Dean does very well and has certainly improved over the years and has one of the most consistent voices in the industry."

Danny believes that besides having a powerful voice, Dean demonstrates his technical and musical skills and creativity in the recording studio and through promoting the group, often through personal phone calls to radio stations and newspapers.

"The Hoppers are master marketers, where they have nearly always had to rely on promoting themselves," Danny said. "They have also made sure they have a variety of products coming out all the time—songbooks, cassettes, compact discs or videos.

"They make sure that they are constantly in the forefront. They have set the standards in the industry in many ways. Many groups today imitate the Hoppers, musically and through their marketing strategies, and have found their own successes.

"I am especially pleased to call them friends."

Chapters 48
In The New Century

Be on guard; stand firm in the faith; be men of courage, be strong.

— 1 Corinthians 16:13

A lot has taken place since the new millennium for the Rockingham County Southern Gospel group. They now march boldly, yet humbly, into the 21st century as a professional, award-winning family group. After nearly a half-century on the road, they happen to be well-respected members of the Southern Gospel music community.

To see them on stage it's apparent that they are full of contagious enthusiasm as they sing about the vital message of redemption and hope.

"We have been extremely blessed, and God continues to astound us as He touches men, women and children with His message of hope," Connie said.

The Hoppers' classic, "Stepping On The Clouds," was released in 2000; "Occupy Till I Come" followed that chart topper. Then, in February 2001 the song, "Yes I Am" took a position on the charts and remained there through June. Then "Marriage Supper Of The Lamb" was offered in the fall of 2001. "Here They Come," "She Cries," "But For The Blood," and "I'm Saved" did especially well, too.

In June 2004, the Hoppers were invited to perform for the Texas State Republican Convention, at San Antonio, Texas. Over 15,000 delegates attended this event, which has been called the largest political gathering in the world. The family sang the patriotic "We Are America" at the program, sharing the stage with such notables as Congressman Sam Johnson, Sgt. Eric Alva and David & Cheryl Barton, of Wallbuilders.

Simultaneously, their single "God Is Good" had already peaked by March and was still on the charts in June. Then "Jerusalem," written by Paula Stefanovich, was released. Besides hitting the top position on the charts just prior to the Hoppers trip to the Holy Land, its success also coincided with the 2004 National Quartet Convention, in

Louisville, Kentucky.

During the convention, it was performed at Freedom Hall on center stage after it had been officially announced as the number one song in the nation. Songwriter Paula Stefanovich came on stage to direct an accompanying mass church choir from Lexington, Kentucky. The choir, dressed formally in black, marched toward the stage from the four corners of the coliseum, with victory banners raised high, as Mike Hopper began the powerful drum intro.

The Hoppers victoriously "brought down the house" as over 21,000 people rose to their feet to worship a risen Christ and celebrate the New Jerusalem. It was an awesome, unforgettable moment for everyone who attended the historic evening.

"Second to our performance in Israel, in August of the same year, it was one of the highlights of our career," Connie recalled.

"Afterwards we had a 'Number-One Party' at our booth for the public, where we served cake and refreshments. We thought it important to somehow thank everyone who supported us and made the achievement possible. It was a great, exciting evening!"

In the same year, the Baptist Associations of the states of Georgia and Virginia selected the Hoppers to perform for the delegates at their annual conventions. On November 9th, they performed at the Roanoke Civic Center in Roanoke, Virginia, singing for the Virginia State Baptist Association. On November 14th the Hoppers sang at the 183rd Session Kick-off Celebration for the Georgia State Baptist Convention at the International Trade Center in Atlanta, Georgia.

Each year, beginning in November 2004, the original Hopper Brothers reunite as they celebrate their anniversary in ministry with a concert on Thanksgiving weekend in Eden, North Carolina.

Claude described last fall's concert:

"My brothers and I still love to sing together. I'm proud of each of them," Claude said. "From the moment we walked on stage at Eden, it seemed so familiar. For a moment, it was as if time somehow rolled back to the 1950s. The Lord blessed us musically and reminded us of the wonderful life we've shared together. My only disappointment is that my brother Paul was not there to enjoy the night with us, for He's now with the Lord."

Hopper Heritage Tour

It was in 2005 that the Hoppers began their long awaited *Hopper Heritage Tour*. The tour, offered only at select locations due to its scope and production necessities, includes a full audio/visual program, where the Hoppers perform songs from their beginnings, as well as favorites by other artists and groups who have inspired them. The concert series became an instant success.

"The tour continues through 2007 in recognition of our fiftieth year," Mike said.

At each concert large screens are suspended from the stage, which displayed scenes from a special collection of rare film and still photographs from the past.

"Mike is a genius with a computer," Joyce Hopper stated. "He has been responsible for setting up the multi-media program for the special tour," and the end result has been described as a musical tapestry that isn't particularly typical of a usual Hoppers' family concert.

According to Claude: "This is the project of a lifetime for our family and an opportunity for us to lay emphasis on our American Christian heritage and thank our many ministry friends for years of support."

A portion of the proceeds derived from this ongoing tour are applied directly toward the North Carolina Gospel Music Hall of Honor.

In the truest sense of the word, the *Hopper Heritage Tour* has marked the beginning of a new era for the Hoppers. By continuing their exhaustive touring schedule, over 220 days on the road annually, they consider themselves "about their Father's business," which is, for them, singing Christ-centered songs that speak to the human heart and testifying of God's love, grace and forgiveness.

"We pray persistently for God's anointing. Our ministry and time spent on the road would be meaningless and empty without Christ," Connie said. "We are willing to go and sing, for He is everything! He is worthy of all praise.

"Perhaps all of this is really about a simple North Carolina family—we're really nothing special—that has been given a wonderful privilege to share the message of Christ and see lives turn toward Jesus!

"We recognize, from our own experiences, that God has the

answers to life's darkest problems. He is sufficient for every situation and need. Only He can set the captive free!"

Southern Baptist Convention

Recently, the Hoppers were honored to sing at the Southern Baptist Convention on June 14th, 2006, in Greensboro, North Carolina.

The group was well received by thousands of Southern Baptists in attendance. Afterwards, the keynote speaker, Secretary of State Dr. Condoleezza Rice, spoke to the audience about faith and country.

"The moving of the Holy Spirit was both powerful and stirring that morning," Claude said. "I find myself amazed and speechless at the new doors the Lord opens for this ministry."

Regrets From A Life On The Road

Among the uncountable blessings of the years of ministry, there have been heartaches, challenges and maybe a few regrets, as well.

"We have always been proud of our two sons," Connie said. "However, looking back on everything today, perhaps one of the greatest regrets is that Claude and I left the boys so much when they were young."

Dean talked about early childhood memories: "In the early days when I was extremely young, before we moved to the farm, we lived near my mom's parents. Dad parked the bus at the Sardis Primitive Baptist Church, which we laughingly called the 'Sardis Terminal.'

"Once Dad brought the bus over to our house to pick up something. When he got out of the bus and went in the house, I snuck out and hid in the bus, in my uncle's bunk. For a while, they couldn't find me. I really wanted to go with them, even if it meant secretly stowing away. They eventually discovered me in the bunk, and I went back inside the house and stayed with Grandma and Grandpa. It was often difficult for me to watch Mom and Dad drive off.

"Even when Mom and Dad were home, it seemed like Dad, who has always been a workaholic, stayed up late in his little office making phone calls in order to secure singing dates for the group in the future. By the time the Hopper Brothers and Connie went full time, they had to invest even more time in the group and on the road, because it was now everyone's sole livelihood.

235

"Although there was some loneliness and sadness along the way, for the most part I had a wonderful childhood with fond memories of my grandparents. I'm grateful."

The group sang part-time when Dean was a small boy; when they went full time, there was a difficult transition period he had to go through. On the other hand, the family's full-time ministry was all Mike had ever known.

"At the time, I was convinced the boys would be happier at home with a babysitter," Connie reminisced. "When the boys were home, they had their own bedrooms, toys, bicycles and later, even minibikes and motorcycles. I thought it was best that they had continuity and stability by being on the farm and around extended family.

"One evening Dean came to me in 1978," Connie remembered tearfully, "just as he was starting his sophomore year and said, 'Mama, I've always tried to do everything you've ever asked me to do. Now, I have a request: if it's at all possible, I would like to join you and Dad on the road full-time. If I go on the road and it doesn't work out, I'll go back to public school.'

"I didn't have another argument. Dean has been on the road with us ever since. Perhaps if I could go back and do it all over again, I would bring the boys on the bus from the start. I now think it would have been a better situation. Leaving every week was difficult for them—and for us."

Don't Rob Me Of A Blessing

Sometimes it feels like family is put on the back burner when a hectic touring schedule is underway. For a typical week, the group members are only home for two or maybe three days before returning to the road. The schedule is grueling. A particular circumstance brought thoughts of family to Claude's mind, and he chose to act upon his feelings.

"Some time ago a close friend of ours passed away," Claude said. "The loss greatly affected Connie and me, and I became reflective afterwards."

After her funeral Claude sat down and wrote heartfelt letters to each individual in his family. He wrote his sons and each of his siblings. He described each of their strong points and qualities, expressing how much he cherished each one.

"Everything I wrote was positive and complimentary, since it came from the very seat of my emotions. I shouted and wept as I scribbled out the letters. The experience was intensely personal for me.

"Because of the personal nature of the letters, in each case for the closing line, I wrote: If you ever acknowledge receiving this letter, you will rob me of my blessing!"

Claude also enclosed in each letter a modest monetary gift as his gesture of love, believing it to be a blessing to share a portion of what he had received with those he loved so dearly.

"And, as requested, nobody acknowledged the letters ... that is, except for my youngest son, Mike," Claude said, as he laughed.

One day, not long after the letters were delivered, Mike walked into the farmhouse. He noticed his father was busy working at his desk. He stared at Claude with a puzzled look on his face. Mike grinned and raised his eyebrows in anticipation as he asked in an ornery, joking manner, "So, Dad, am I gettin' another one of your ... uh ... letters?"

Claude couldn't help but laugh out loud at his son's remark.

Touched By An Angel

In 2001 Mike had the once-in-a-lifetime opportunity to be a special guest on the popular television show *Touched By An Angel*. It was on episode #724, "Shallow Water, Part 1," that aired on May 13, 2001, and episode #725, "Shallow Water, Part 2," which aired on May 20, 2001.

The cast on the two episodes included Rue McClanahan, Nell Carter, John Schneider, Randy Travis, David Canary, Keb' Mo', Delta Burke, and Faye Dunaway.

The heart-touching story revolved around the fictitious Winslow family and included a Southern Gospel group, The Winslow Family Singers, portrayed by Bill Gaither, Mark Lowry, Guy Penrod, David Phelps and Gloria Gaither. There was also a special appearance by the Gaither Homecoming Singers and band.

"I was sitting at a small diner in Madison, called Bob's, having a cheeseburger. I got a call on my cell phone. The person on the other end of the phone said, 'Hi, my name is Marcie Gold. I am with the television show *Touched By An Angel*. We'd like you to come out and be a part of it.'"

Mike chuckled and sarcastically said, "Yeah, right," supposing it was a prank call. However, as Marcie described what his role would be, he realized she was serious and he answered, "Well, yes! I'd love to come!"

Mike said that this all happened because of Bill Gaither. The casting person for the television program wanted Bill and the Gaither Vocal Band to do two episodes (a two-hour story) with Randy Travis, and Bill needed a band.

It so happened that at the same time the show was being shot, the Hoppers were singing at the West Coast Quartet Convention, held in California. Mike left the convention a day early to be at the television shoot at Salt Lake City, where the episode was being taped.

Mike smiled as he recalled that day: "If anyone from the audio world thinks recording is a long and drawn-out process, they need to shoot television! It's just standing around forever! Technicians spend hours getting the lighting and the cameras set up, and then you may get a chance to shoot a minute's worth of actual film. Then you wait another two or three hours while the lighting and cameras are moved. Then they shoot the same scene from a different angle.

"I will never forget the bus wreck scene. It was taking forever to get the shot! We shot a minute's worth of film and then everyone in the bus was asked to step out for several hours. We all waited for our next call to step back on the wrecked bus for another minute of film. During one of the breaks I was standing by Randy Travis' tour bus, talking to his driver. As we talked I happened to notice Bill Gaither pacing back and forth on the set while talking on his mobile phone. Every once in a while as he paced, he'd walk near me and say, 'Uh, uh, uh ... this is not for me!'

"Bill Gaither's attention span is nonexistent! He is naturally hyper! So the whole filming process was complete torture for him," Mike said laughing. "The entire experience was fascinating. We finally finished the episode, and Bill survived the ordeal. It was a real honor to be asked on the show."

Chapters 49
The Hoppers Today

Yet there is one thing that has never changed since 1957: we still love singing.

— Connie Hopper

Over the years the Hoppers have not only grown in fame, but have carried the Gospel message in song to nearly every state and to several foreign lands, including England, Ireland, Israel, Canada and the Bahamas.

A lot has changed with the Hoppers since they first sang in tobacco warehouses or community social events. For example, the Hoppers no longer practice every Friday night as they once did in the early days, mainly due to a lack of time.

"We hardly get to practice any more, due to limited time. It's actually a little peculiar how we do things now. We rehearse in our living room once a new album comes out," Connie said, "or we might take recorded copies of our specific parts from the songs on the bus with us, so we can review and practice.

"We also use the convenience of split-tracks nowadays, where we sing with the background musicians that originally performed on the album soundtrack."

It's exciting in that with split tracks, the Hoppers can eliminate certain instruments digitally such as the drum part from the recording so Mike can play his drums live at the concert, or Dean may occasionally play the bass guitar part by eliminating the bass track.

The split-track system makes the concert sound much more consistent with a Hopper album, but it still gives the group the flexibility to have live musicians and spontaneity. It would be cost-prohibitive to tour with a stage-full of musicians, including string and brass sections.

Today the Hopper sound is much more progressive and polished than it was in the earlier days of the group.

"I guess we were more straightforward at the beginning, with simpler arrangements and fewer musicians. With our most recent projects, Dean, Mike and Kim are able to create and pick up new elaborate arrangements quickly, and it comes naturally for them. It takes a bit more work for Claude and me," Connie said as she grinned.

The group is now considered one of the most innovative mixed groups in the industry. They are one of the few remaining Southern Gospel groups that have continuously toured for nearly fifty years. Yet, their music and arrangements continue to be fresh, relevant and creative.

Home Sweet Home

These days, when the bus rolls into the outskirts of Madison after a week's worth of travels, the Hopper family looks forward to the opportunity of just being home, now more than ever! Regardless of where they perform, a piece of Rockingham County remains with them and in them. Coming home after a heavy schedule is especially sweet at this juncture of their lives.

"For me a wonderful day is just being around the house. I enjoy cooking and reading," Connie explained. Connie also enjoys writing a monthly column for *Singing News Magazine* during her time off. "Through the years we have never allowed ourselves a great deal of time on the farm, because we have always been on the road. So, time at home is especially dear.

"There are times I wish we could retire, or at least slow down. Sometimes my allergies are so bad that it's hard on my voice—I stay hoarse a lot. Although I am grateful for all the Lord has allowed me to be a part of, I would really like a chance to spend more time on the farm," she admitted hesitantly.

"However, I doubt I could ever quit completely. Perhaps I could do speaking engagements at some point in the future and pursue my writing. Whatever God has got for me, I'm willing to do—even if it is to continue touring for the rest of my life."

Connie said that so far she has never felt led to ask her husband to come off the road, even though she's aware that he has the same desire on occasion. Connie also wonders if the farm would be enough for Claude after being on the road for so long.

"He has such a love for people. Yet, I know there is coming a time when he will consider retiring, or at least slowing down on some level. Perhaps God is putting the same thing in our hearts at the same time. Regardless, the Hoppers would go on, even if Claude and I retire.

"But, before the rumors start, we both sense we are still needed on the road at this time. Even though we get tired more easily nowadays due to our age, we still love the fans and the chance to minister," Connie said.

It was in 2005 Connie wrote an article for *Singing News*, expressing what it was like being on the road night after night. Here is an excerpt from that column:

> John Adams, the second president of the United States, lived to be 90 years old. One morning as the elderly Adams took his daily "constitutional," another walker greeted him by saying, "And how is Mr. Adams today?" Adams is said to have replied, "This old tenement I live in may be falling down, but John Adams, sir, is quite well indeed." Those words reveal a keen sense that life is much more than the condition of our mortal bodies.
>
> Twenty years ago, I wouldn't have given much thought to that narrative. Having just returned from a ten-day tour with concerts in different cities every night, facing a mountain of laundry, the cleaners, and correspondence, paying bills, visiting my brother in a nursing home ... and getting it all done in time to catch the bus at midnight Wednesday night for the next tour, I find that I can relate to the story. The person within me wants to accomplish everything and prepare good home-cooked meals for Claude and the family. The physical body I live in says, "Hey, what about that gift certificate to the steak house, or how about Madison's famous "Fuzzy's Barbecue?" Paul the Apostle wrote, "Though our outer nature is wasting away, our inner nature is being renewed day by day." (2 Cor. 4:16)
>
> The offer of life made in Jesus Christ does not depend on the age or mileage of our physical bodies. Christ does not offer merely a refurbishing job on the

same old tenement—new paint and wallpaper and a general sprucing up.

He offers life that springs from a different source—the eternal, invulnerable life of God. It is not biological life; it is divine life that defies biology. It outlasts the pains and wounds of this life and is offered to us in the midst of them. When life seems gone, Christ offers life. This is not rational hope based on what we can do, on whatever energy we can summon up. It is hope based in the radical, irrepressible, undying life of Christ being lived out in us. When we feel overwhelmed by grief or sadness or weariness or depression, the cross of Christ is our promise that suffering and even physical death do not have the last word. The Psalmist named the source of hope: "You, O Lord, are my hope." —Psalm 71:5

"We are committed to Christ's ministry. I personally hope to continue for as long as the Lord can use me," Claude added. "Connie and I are especially appreciative of the moments at home, too. So many sentimental memories are here at the farm for us, and so much of our future, too. We find ourselves becoming more reflective these days."

The Farm Today

Claude talked about living on the farm today: "I am blessed to live on a beautiful, productive farm. It takes a great deal of hard work and commitment to keep everything moving along smoothly." Visitors to the farm are likely to first notice Claude's huge, black prize bull—interestingly named "Shoutin' Time"—standing guard over the lush green pasture. There are several head of cattle, and at various times, other livestock, too, including unpredictable and often cantankerous goats.

Not long ago, Poppy Claude surprised granddaughter Karlye with a new four-legged friend: a registered palomino quarter horse.

Also, in 2006 Claude purchased several unusual donkeys, often called "Christian donkeys," for they have a strip of dark hair that runs down their backs and shoulders. These distinct markings are in the shape of a cross.

Their is a legend behind this breed that the cross markings appeared on the donkeys after Jesus triumphantly rode one into Jerusalem. Of course, there's no actual evidence that this is true, but the donkeys on the Hopper farm remind Claude of the importance of a fulfilled prophecy (written 500 years before Christ) which confirmed that Jesus was, indeed, the Messiah.

"Being home is important, for it's a beautiful place where I find true relaxation. I love the livestock and the smell of the country air and the memories from the past. But for me, each day is a treasure, regardless of what we're doing or where we are. As long as we're together as a family, everything is going well for me!" Claude said. He joked, "As long as I'm on this side of the ground, it's a good day!"

Currently, Claude is deeply involved in the development of his pet project, the North Carolina Gospel Music Hall of Honor. Along with Dean, Mike, Dennis Sparks and several others, Claude has spearheaded this non-profit enterprise and hopes to take an even stronger role in its development during the coming years. In order to recognize and award the state's Gospel music artists and industry pioneers and innovators, a state-of-the-art museum and a magnificent performance hall are being planned. The completed venture will make it possible for fans and tourists to enjoy the musical heritage of North Carolina at a facility located in Mayodan, which formerly housed Washington Mills.

The family heritage continues through this venture, for, as stated earlier, Claude's mother worked at Washington Mills during the Great Depression. So now, coming full circle, the mammoth structure will commemorate all forms of Gospel music and the musical legacy of North Carolina.

During his limited time off the highway, in addition to working on his farm, Claude also oversees the Hopper Heritage Foundation, Hopperworx, Hopper Direct, Hopper Brothers and Connie Publishing Company, and several other business enterprises.

"I recall it was Branch Richey, a baseball executive, that once said, 'It is not the honor that you take with you, but the heritage you leave behind.' It's with this thought that the Hopper Heritage Foundation was organized," Claude said, "so that the Hopper ministry can still minister to others after we're long gone." Keith Key is the COO of the foundation and, with the assistance of a board and advisory council, the non-profit entity plans to support, encourage and assist Gospel artists and the industry for many years to come.

Hopperworx markets a custom line of road cases and sound reinforcement products for traveling artists. Hopper Direct is a new online discount music store. Of course, Claude is heavily involved in publishing music and songbooks. He also remains a part owner and is on the Board of the National Quartet Convention and the Southern Gospel Music Association.

And in his spare time, if he has any, Claude enjoys his favorite hobby: golf.

Dean, Kim, Karlye And Lexus Jazz

On the subject of time off from the road, Kim said that a "normal day for me revolves around the health and happiness of my family.

"I feel God-called to share His message. There seems to be an excitement in the audience when we are singing. But I'm aware there are also people there who have needs—hurting people who are suffering. They come for encouragement and to find answers to their troubling questions. This is what we are there for, to support Christians and direct the lost to Christ. But with all that said, I also appreciate the occasional breaks from a hectic tour schedule."

During these times Kim is every bit the full-time mom, who gets enthusiastically involved in everyday "normal" duties, such as washing dishes, housekeeping, laundry, paying utility bills and running various errands. Time at their home for Kim includes interior decorating and "tinkering with landscaping." She also enjoys reading.

In a 2003 *Singing News* interview, she commented: "I think because of the stage and spotlight, people think we aren't normal people with normal lives." Kim explained that some people seem to think that the Hoppers are exempt from the typical daily happenings of life. Fans sometimes wrongly assume that the members of the family are immune to personal problems and the mundane practices of an ordinary life.

That's certainly not true.

She mentioned several examples, including how her brother Tim Greene has been sick for a long time with a life-threatening allergy to aspergillus mold, and her younger brother, Tony, at the time of this writing, is a candidate for a kidney transplant.

The Passing Of Everette Greene

Kim's father, Everette Greene, passed away in November 2004. On the night of his passing, Karlye was having trouble sleeping, so Kim and Dean had allowed her to come into their bedroom and sleep with them. Kim was expecting Lexi at the time.

It was one of those rare nights when they were home from the road. Around midnight the phone rang. Dean answered the call. Kim could tell by what Dean was saying that something was wrong. After hanging up the phone, Dean said, "Kim, we need to pack some things and drive over to Boone tonight."

Kim blurted out, "It's Daddy—isn't it?" as she burst into tears.

Ten-year-old Karlye was awakened by the commotion. Immediately the lyrics from the song "Jerusalem" came to Karlye's mind, and she said: "Mama, just think, Papaw is no longer in a wheelchair! He's walking golden streets where the angels have trod, in that City of God. So, Mama, don't be sad for Papaw. Let's get up and pack our bags so we can go be with Nana!"

Kim has since shared that testimony before audiences, explaining how the Lord used the words of that song to minister to her at such a time of heartbreak—spoken from the lips of her own child.

"We are just real people with everyday problems and heartaches, as well as triumphs," she said. "From what we've experienced through periods of brokenness, we can better minister to others who are also hurting. I know it to be true that the Lord offers His peace in the midst of the storm."

Mom with Lexus Jazz Hopper

Then on January 3rd, 2005, almost eight weeks earlier than expected, Kim started having contractions. She called the doctor's office and the nurse said she should head for the hospital and be checked. They wouldn't let her leave.

During the time Kim was being checked out at the hospital, her

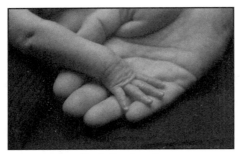

Such tiny hands

brother, Tony, and sister-in-law, TaRanda, started calling and e-mailing pastors and ministry friends for prayer. Claude and Connie phoned friends and began praying for their daughter-in-law and granddaughter as well.

People across the country responded by praying earnestly for Kim, Dean and the baby.

"By the time we were at the hospital, Kim was going into full-blown labor, and the medicine the doctors gave her couldn't stop it," Dean said.

The next few hours were extremely critical and stressful as the hospital team evaluated Kim's condition and the health of the baby. Minutes seemed like hours as the family prayed and waited for someone from the surgical staff to come to the waiting room and give an update.

Finally, by 12:39 a.m. on Tuesday, January 4th, Lexus Jazz Hopper arrived, weighing only four pounds, fifteen-and-a-half

Sisters, Karlye and Lexi

ounces, and eighteen inches long. Both baby and mother were pronounced healthy, miraculously.

By the evening of January 4th, Kim and Dean were able to gently wrap their arms around their tiny bundle. Dean added, "I feel very blessed, not only for the good progress that my wife and new baby daughter are making, but also in the fact that all our family was able to be here and not on the road. The Lord is so good! We all so appreciated everyone's prayers and kindnesses."

Lexi

"This is a good time in our lives," Kim said, as she smiled.

Since she was premature, their baby had to remain hospitalized for seven weeks, until doctors were sure she was fully developed and eating properly. During that period, Kim took time off the road to be with her. It wasn't long before Lexus was released and able to go home with her parents.

Within a few months, nanny Denise Allman, Karlye and Lexi joined the rest of the family back on the road.

The Family And Church

Claude, Connie, Dean, Kim, and Mike are longtime members of Ellisboro Baptist Church. Several others in the family go there as well, including Will and Peggy and Monroe and Joyce.

"We all go to the same church," Joyce said. "The family is very committed to their local church.

"Early in 2005 we had an interim pastor, Rev. Dan Jones, because our regular pastor was serving in Iraq. The acting pastor knew of the Hoppers, but had never seen them in concert. He wanted to go to their annual reunion concert, held in Eden, North Carolina, but unfortunately there was a death and he couldn't attend. So he was later talking to Will and asked, 'Do you think I will ever be able to hear the Hoppers while I am here?' Will immediately began working out all the details in just a matter of days."

A date was set for the Hopper Brothers and Connie to sing at their own church, with the original members—Will, Monroe, Steve, Claude and Connie.

"The church couldn't hold everyone who came," Joyce said. "I'm telling you that from the time they started singing the Spirit was so strong. It was one of the best concerts I've ever attended. That was a concert I wish everyone could have seen."

According to the local newspaper, *The Messenger*, it had been over 40 years since the group sang at their home church. News editor Steve Lawson wrote that after singing in churches, coliseums and stadiums across the U.S. and around the world, Claude was actually nervous about a concert a stone's throw from his childhood home.

"I figured we'd have a good time getting together with thirty or forty people from our home church," Claude said. "The turnout was just incredible."

"This was truly an historic event," Claude's brother, Steve, said shortly after the church service.

The Future

Although it's been said there is no place like home, and they cherish their moments at Madison, the Hoppers are fully committed to full-time ministry for Christ.

"We still have loads of fun on the road, too," Connie said, smiling. "It's something we're all accustomed to and now that our immediate family travels together, it's especially rewarding in many ways."

Kim chuckled and said: "You learn to be content to live in a little cubicle on a bus. I'm very secure in my little cubicle. A lot of days when we're preparing to leave and I'm running around our house, I think if I can just get into my little room and put all my stuff away, I'll be able to rest. I can get in my bunk, which is about 4' x 5' or so, and read or hang out with my kids, or do whatever needs to be done. There's comfort in that for me—that's home to me. I'm actually on the bus more than I am at our real house."

"In many ways, I have never been more energized than I am right now," Claude stated. "As we celebrate a half-century of min-

Will, Steve, Claude and Monroe Hopper — They still have it!

istry, our family's enthusiasm continues to grow.

"The Hoppers keep a vigorous touring schedule, and if the Lord tarries, we hope to be around for a long, long time," Claude said. "It was Dr. Charles Stanley who once explained it best that Christians can be tired, weary and emotionally distraught, but after spending time alone with God, He injects our bodies with energy, power and strength. That is exactly what seems to happen to us."

"When I look at the Hoppers today," Dean said, "I see how Mom's got such heart, besides her ability as a singer and songwriter. She has the ability to reach out to others from the stage with words that minister and encourage. Dad remains a stable force as our bass singer, an outstanding emcee and a Southern Gospel music states-man. Mike keeps the rhythm section going and even sings more these days.

"Kim has this wonderful gift through her exceptional voice. And as for me, I just try to fill in the gaps and perhaps step out every once in a while. It all seems to work together as a tight-knit team. Only by God's design could this even be possible. It's all about Him."

From meager beginnings in a log cabin on a rural tobacco farm to appearing at churches, civic centers and coliseums across the country, the years have been colorful and fulfilling for the Hopper family.

"I guess we have spent the equivalent of years inside a narrow tour bus. Living in tight quarters is now commonplace to all of us. Rather than seeing beautiful sights along the way, most of the time we travel at night. It's easy to become mesmerized by the endless lines on the highway. Perhaps it's a lesson in life, too; sometimes it seems as if life is a series of endless potholes and detours, or a dreary and endless passing of white lines," Claude said and smiled. "Yet just like our time on the tour bus, the Lord goes with us through it all and strengthens us. There are wonderful blessings awaiting us at our destination."

When it is all said and done, perhaps one of the keys to the Hoppers' successful ministry over the years relates directly to their perseverance and faithfulness to the Lord's call and purpose. As President Lincoln once said, "Having chosen our course, without guile and with pure purpose, let us renew our trust in God, and go forward without fear and with manly hearts."

Likewise, the Hopper family has chosen a course and moved forward with perseverance. They have a pure purpose and have placed their confidence in Christ to complete the journey.

"We are just a normal family. We live on fast-food, sugary snacks and covered dishes from generous friends," Claude said. "God doesn't always show us exactly what He is doing through this ministry. There are even times when we stay exhausted and burdened down due to a hectic touring schedule or unusual family or business concern.

"There are other moments when we are all incredibly energized and encouraged by the Spirit of the Lord. Regardless of the circumstances—good or bad—one thing remains constant: it is always a joyous occasion to see the Lord work in the life of others and to see souls miraculously saved.

"We really count it all joy to be in His service. For the Hopper family, we have come to a point where we feel it's necessary to reflect on how Christ has actively worked in our ministry and individual lives. We now focus ourselves on the Southern Gospel music industry and how it continues to inspire and share the Good News to others.

"For any success that we have

"We know the Lord has a plan for each of our lives. With this, we concentrate on finding His will for each one of us personally, and for the Hoppers as a group. We delight ourselves in Him and He directs our paths."

After all these years, with an eye on the future, it seems certain that the Lord will continue to unveil his wonderful plan through the Hoppers.

After All These Years

—*From The One Foundation Project*
(Solo by Claude)
By Geron Davis

I started walking with Jesus a long time ago,
But nothing but trust in my Lord to show me the road.

Though there's been times when He had to
dispel all my fears,
I'd do it all over again, after all of these years.

CHORUS:

The road hasn't always been easy,
But He said he'd not leave me alone.
I've had to walk through some valleys,
But He's always given a song.

There've been some sad times
Even more glad times,
We've shared both the laughter and tears,
Yes, it's been worth every mile,
after all of these years.

Mom had us walk three country miles
to church every week,
And she helped fill our six-room log
house each day with God's peace.
But looking back through all my memories,
one thing is clear:
He's still the best thing I have after all of these years.

RECITATION:

Oh, I've had many long trips; and yes, and lots of fast food.
Well, I've even dressed in Sunday School rooms.
And I've often wondered, does everyone's home smell like
diesel fumes?
But the memories all add up to joy that's so very dear,
And I'm glad to still be serving Him after all of these years.

CHORUS:

The Road hasn't always been easy,
But He said he'd not leave me alone.
I've had to walk through some valleys,
But He's always given a song.

There have been some sad times
Even more glad times,
We've shared both the laughter and tears,
Yes, it's been worth every mile,
after all of these years.

Yes, He's still the best thing I've found after all of these years.
Yes, I'd do it all over again after all of these years.

The End

Afterword

Friends And Colleagues
Discuss The Hoppers

The more we have visited North Carolina, the more wonderful people we have encountered. One of the dear Carolinian families we have been fortunate to meet during our travels is the Hopper family. Connie and Claude have opened up their home to us on many occasions, and what a treat! Fried chicken, ham and green beans cooked like green beans are meant to be cooked – those are all things we can count on when Connie is hosting. But it's not just the food we have appreciated; it's the warmth that can only be compared to being at home. When you travel as much as we do, it is a luxury to feel so close to home so many miles from Indiana!

The Hoppers have worked very hard and have traveled the world singing the Good News of Jesus; and no matter how many miles they put on their bus, or how many albums they have sold or awards they have won, they have never wavered from their traditional Southern roots. I think that says a great deal about who they are and why they keep singing. It's not only a gift for music they possess; it's a calling.

— Bill and Gloria Gaither

The Hoppers are very special to me. They have kept a good name and walked after the ways of God. I always enjoy being with them, and Connie is one beautiful lady — inside and out!

—— Dottie Rambo

The Hoppers are a gospel institution. I remember hearing them when I was a kid and they were called "The Hopper Brothers and Connie." Connie had her hair piled on her head in a Pentecostal style at that time. Not a high rise like Vestal's, but a loose second story that would sway back and forth to the music as she sang. I can remember it vividly. But I was looking through the eyes of a twelve year old, so who knows? Everything is bigger when you're twelve.

And, in the last few years I've had the privilege of getting to know Connie and all of the Hoppers while traveling with the Homecoming Tours. They are such nice people. Claude's a great businessman. And Connie can cook! I've eaten in their home; I know.

When they sing you see their hearts. They love Gospel music and The One they're singing about.

— Mark Lowry

I have known the Hoppers for years and years. What I especially like about them is that they are the same off-stage and off-camera, as they are in front of crowds and people. They are good people, and I like being around good people. I also like how they get after it when a song starts!

— Guy Penrod, *Gaither Vocal Band*

I have a lot of love and respect for Claude and Connie and all of the Hoppers. They have not only been a wonderful Gospel music group for eons, but it is my humble opinion that they represent all that is right about America. Family. Faith. Values. Sacrifice. Dedication. Leadership. Love. And Longevity.

On top of all that

… they have chosen to share their lives by ministering to all of us. May they keep on singing until the Lord comes!

—— Joe Bonsall, *Oak Ridge Boys*

The Hopper Brothers and Connie are a part of Gospel music history. I remember the all day singings with dinner on the ground in North Carolina. In those days, it actually was the brothers with Connie. They have always been a class act in my book. I am so happy that Claude and Connie have continued the family tradition. I am also very honored to call them my friends. Occasionally, when they are recording in Nashville, I go by their session just to see how they are doing. I believe they are recording some of their best work musically right now. It always makes me happy to know that they have been so successful. May God continue to bless them.

— Duane Allen, *Oak Ridge Boys*

The Hoppers have always been loved and respected in Gospel Music. Having grown up in North Carolina, I know every kid wanted to sing with their group. I'm thankful for the heritage they've handed down in quality and integrity.

— Ivan Parker

The Hoppers are some of the finest people I have ever known. I have known them and worked with them for over 40 years and have enjoyed their friendship.

— Les Beasley, *the Florida Boys*

I remember my Dad taking our family to see the Hoppers at a little church in our hometown of Dahlonega, GA, at Cavender's Creek Baptist Church. I was probably about 8 or 9 years old. That was my first experience of the then Hopper Brothers and Connie. This family has made its mark in Gospel Music as one of THE best family groups to ever grace a stage, whether it's in a church or in a concert. The Hoppers have set a fine example for others to follow. We are honored to call them our friends.

— Libbi Perry Stuffle, *the Perrys*

I attended a concert when I was 16 years old at my high school, featuring the Hoppers. I'll never forget how blessed I was by their music. That night, I rededicated my life to the Lord. The Hoppers will always be special to me.

— Karen Peck Gooch, *Karen Peck and New River*

It has been such a wonderful privilege to tour with the Hoppers. As we have both been on the same Homecoming stage with Bill and Gloria Gaither across the country, I am just excited about all that God has done and is doing in the lives of Claude, Connie, Kim, Mike and Dean.

I've always appreciated their gifts and abilities that God had given to them as they have communicated night after night in song and sometimes in testimony of their love for our Lord. But as we began to have devotions weekend after weekend on the tour, I came to know Claude, Connie, Kim, Dean and Mike in even more intimate ways. They have such a great love for our Lord and for His people. I firmly believe that they are not just singing to sing; but they are singing because Jesus has given them an internal song which just seems to bubble over with great joy as they grace the stage. I am so happy for them as they celebrate their anniversary of ministry. I love them very much and I want nothing but God's very best for them. Connie is one of the Godliest women I know, not just in music but across the board. I have the utmost respect for her.

— Lynda Randle

I first met the Hoppers back in 1962 when they were known as the Hopper Brothers and Connie. I was playing piano with the Tennesseans Quartet. We worked with a promoter, C.R. McClain, in the Statesville, North Carolina, area. The Hoppers were always friendly and helpful to a young person just getting started in Gospel music. My congratulations to them for their many years of service.

— Eddie Crook, *founder and president of The Eddie Crook Company, Inc.*

I participated in a Lithuanian Campus Crusade for Christ event overseas in 1995. I returned there on a missionary crusade in 1996 and

1997. One thing I realized during my first visits to the country of Lithuania was that Lithuanian have a great love for music. So, approximately three months before my second departure, I wrote the Gaither Homecoming Friends and asked if they would consider offering music cassettes or anything of inspirational value for this crusade.

Artists responded and donated items for the crusade. In particular, I remember that Gloria Gaither sent fifteen videos to show and distribute overseas. Then I received an especially huge shipment from the Hoppers! They were more than generous in helping with this 1996 missionary effort! The Hoppers also committed themselves to weekly prayer for the people of Lithuania.

Over five hundred citizens made decisions for Christ during the 1996 crusade. Most were precious older people in there '60s, '70s and '80s, who heard the Gospel for the first time. I returned again in 1997 and the Hoppers again made product donations for the people.

The Hoppers are great folks who have a heart for souls. They definitely have fans overseas.

— Rev. Al Oliver, *missionary*

We have been friends of the Hoppers for many years and fans for even more. The classic stories Claude and Connie can share in a history of the family and the group are limitless and downright exciting to anticipate. I'm looking forward to this book finally getting into my hands and on my shelf, as I know you are. If the book is even one half as powerful as they are on stage, it's going to be a page-turner.

To Claude, Connie, Dean, Kim, and Mike—we all know "what time it is:" "It's Hopper time!"

— Don Reid, *the Statler Brothers*

The biography of the Hoppers, that sounds like a great story to me. We'll hear about Connie's old boy friends; okay, I know Connie had boyfriends and not all of them were old. We'll find out that Dean is not a nice guy, it's just an act. We'll find out that Kim can't sing; it's just lip-synched. We'll find out that Claude is ... I mean Claude was ... I should have said Claude could have been cleared of all those charges if he hadn't jumped bail that last time. Mike tells all about that in the book. It's all in there, except times, dates and Claude's real name.

It's a great book!

— Harold Reid, *the Statler Brothers*

This letter is written concerning the Hoppers, Gospel music's premier Gospel singing family. I heard them sing first at one of the Gaither Homecoming video tapings. They were one of many guests that were invited to perform, and they had me from the first note that came out of their mouths, and they still have me ... I am a fan and am glad to be associated with them.

— Jessy Dixon

I never remember learning who the Hoppers were. Growing up in North Carolina, the singing family felt a part of the landscape: our cherished "bragging rights" in the burgeoning genre of Gospel music. They were known as people of integrity, sincerity, and humility. They wore matching clothes and traveled in a tour bus. It just didn't get better than that.

I am one of the very fortunate ones who have shared their stage and watched their performances from the wings. I have heard the soft whispers of encouragement and quick prayers between verses. I have seen tears of joy and hope and gratitude absorbed into a white lace handkerchief. I have watched packed arenas come to a quiet standstill as Connie shared her rich, homespun perspective.

All these years later some things have, thankfully, remained unchanged. The Hoppers continue to record extraordinary songs with dynamic arrangements; they continue to make good business decisions, and they still love the people in the seats. They've kept our bragging rights intact.

Fifty years later, it still doesn't get better than that.

— Janet Paschal

I have known the Hoppers for most of their singing career and I am privileged to call them friends. They have a reputation of sincerity and Godliness, and that has made them successful both as a singing group and as a family. Congratulations Claude, Connie and family on your upcoming anniversary. May God grant you many more years of ministry.

— Jimmy Blackwood

For me to realize how someone has impacted my life, first I must realize what it would be like had I never met that person. When I think of Claude and Connie, I think of two people that have impacted my life in a great way. I love so many things about them ... their consistency, their continuing strive to excellence, their determination, their obvious love for each other, and last yet first ... their love for Jesus. Thank you Claude and Connie for showing me an example of what I have to be if I am to bless hearts with this music as you have for all these years.

— Rodney Griffin, *Greater Vision*

I have the greatest appreciation and respect for the Hoppers, and I love their music. They are people with great integrity, and they have greatly influenced me and my own ministry. I congratulate them on a half-century of faithful ministry.

—Gerald Wolfe, *Greater Vision*

I have known the Hoppers for over 40 years ... and have always found them to be "real" people who love the God they've sung about for so long. They always seem to stay current with their music. I appreciate that they have remained the same genuine people I first met when I was a teenager. It's my pleasure to consider them real friends who have encouraged my life.

— Ann Downing

I first encountered the Hoppers many years ago in April 1982, when my daughter, Dawn Michelle Barker, was only ten years old. My family first met them at our church, and I guess we really hit it off from the moment we met. Claude and Connie immediately took an interest in my daughter, who sang.

If the Hoppers were within one thousand miles, my family and I went to see them! Three months after we first met them, we went to Watermelon Park for the first time. There were five professional groups participating that year. After the second group sang, Claude motioned to me to come up on the hillside, where the stage was located. He told me he wanted to put my ten-year-old daughter on stage to sing. She did a wonderful job. From that point on, she sang with them on many occasions.

Because of Claude and Connie's encouragement and help, within six months my daughter recorded an album entitled, Sincerely Yours. Connie wrote some gracious comments for the back of cover. Producers for the project were Ron Pauley, Roger Talley and Claude Hopper. Musicians included Roger Fortner, Roger Talley, Craig Ham and Steve "Rabbit" Easter.

I have seen the Hoppers pray with strangers and the sick. I have seen them feed the hungry, encourage new Gospel artists and give the plan of salvation to the lost. The Hopper family has always had a way of touching people, publicly and privately. They are wonderful people.

— Bob Barker, *accountant, Logan, WV*

I met the Hoppers many years ago, and they are one of the funnest groups I ever hung out with. They are so much fun on the road. I love these guys!

— Russ Taff

If the whole world was made up of Connie Hoppers, we would have no problems and everything would be ideal.

— Danny Jones, *Singing News Magazine*

I started playing piano for the Hoppers in 1974. I just thought I had an education until I started traveling with this group. We traveled all over the country, and up until then, I had never been out of east Tennessee. I owe my whole Gospel music education to Claude and Connie Hopper. They will never know what they mean to my family and me. Actually, we love them and consider them our family.

— Roger Talley, *The Talley Trio*

The Hoppers' website calls them "America's Favorite Family Of Gospel Music." It's not an idle boast. The Hoppers have been in the forefront of what we call Southern Gospel music for nearly half a century. And with good reason: God has blessed them abundantly. But those blessings have flowed because the Hoppers have given back their time, their diligent efforts and their gifts, even sacrificially, to spread the Gospel through their music. You won't find anyone more devoted to the growth of Southern Gospel music, its history and, most importantly, its ministry than the Hoppers. You will find their story fascinating and inspiring reading.

— Paul Heil, *host of the nationally syndicated radio program "The Gospel Greats"*

As a family group ourselves, we have always related to the Hoppers and have admired them for sticking together as a family group for so long. They have always put out quality music and songs that lifted up the name of Jesus. They have evolved through the years only to become the best of the best in Gospel music. We pray that our Heavenly Father will bless them with many more years of singing for Him!

—The Ruppes

The Hoppers have meant a great deal to me and my family. They are superb examples of integrity and honor in the industry.

—Mike Collins, *author*

I first met the Hoppers in October of 1982 at a church in Roanoke Rapids, North Carolina, which is not far from where I grew up. I was so excited to go see and hear them live, to hear their "young" son, Michael, on the drums and Dean on the bass. That night, when I spoke to Claude, I encountered his first joke to me, although I didn't know at the time that he was joking. Years later, we still laugh at what he was joking to me about that night. That began the first of many jokes that Claude would tell me! What I never could have imagined at that time was that eight years later, I would be given the privilege and opportunity to play with the Hoppers as their bass player. During my six years as the bass player for the Hoppers, I learned so much as a musician because I was in the midst of such fine talent. But far beyond all the musical knowledge I gained being with them, years later I would realize all the wisdom I gained being with Claude and Connie and how it has helped me in so many areas of my life. My association with the Hoppers was so much more than being their bass player. I always felt like family and I still do today. Claude and Connie have been such positive influences in my life and to this day, I talk to them weekly, getting advice on everything from cutting lawns to matters of the heart and soul. Since my time with the Hoppers, I have played with many different artists as a freelance bass player. But no matter where I am or whom I am playing with, I will always consider myself a Hopper.

— Frank Mills, *Ocean Isle Beach, NC*

The Hoppers have been steadfast in the faith, using their God-given talents to bring joy to many. Claude and Connie are favored in Heaven, feared in Hell—they are no strangers to the throne of Grace!

— Tony Greene, *the Greenes*

I have been afforded the unique privilege to spend time back-stage and see firsthand the Hoppers and their interaction with pro-moters, other artists, media representatives and of course thousands of fans onstage and off. Southern Gospel has been given a special gift by God in allowing us the honor to partake in the incredible talent and graciousness of the Hoppers.

Claude, Connie, Mike, Dean & Kim are some of the sweetest people I have personally ever met. To see the passion that this family has to share the Gospel in song night after night is inspiring. To expe-rience their graciousness and the warmth of their friendship and love of people is just incredible. The Hoppers embody everything good and worthwhile in Gospel Music, and their talent is unmatched in any genre of music. After forty-seven years of faithfulness to the call of God on their lives, the Hoppers have never sounded better. It is as if the Hoppers have fulfilled right before our eyes the Scripture when the governor of a wedding feast looked at a young groom and com-plimented him for "saving the good wine until now."

— Charles Brady, *Caraway Media Group*

Many years ago, Dwight L. Moody said, "If I take care of my charac-ter, my reputation will take care of me." During the last fifty years, the Hoppers have built a tremendous reputation. They are recognized as "America's Favorite Family of Gospel Music." They have received many industry awards, fan awards and individual awards. They have built their reputation because they have taken care of their character. The Hoppers have remained faithful to their calling.

— Keith Key, *CFM, Merrill Lynch; COO, Hopper Heritage Foundation*

Claude Hopper, an astute business man, made his most important deal at a stoplight in Madison, NC, where young Connie Shelton was waiting for the light to change. Before the light turned green Claude talked Connie into playing piano for his group the Hopper Brothers. Connie's first thought was to say "no" but those of us in Gospel Music are glad she said "yes." In 1961, Connie again said "yes" to Claude's marriage proposal. Their union produced two sons, Dean and Mike, two key ingredients for the outstanding success of the Hoppers we know today. The hard-working nature of Claude and the gentle nature of Connie have proven to be a match made in Heaven. The friendship they shared with me and my late husband, Rex Nelon, would comfort me through the hard times after his sudden death in England, just hours before the taping of the London Homecoming. Claude stood beside Rex as he left this shore for Heaven and Connie held me and brought comfort as I was faced with this loss and sadness beyond belief. Their love and friendship did not end there. When in Nashville they continue to bring so much fun and joy into my home by stopping by for dinner or a good night's sleep. The world loves the Hoppers on the stage. I do, too. But my favorite place is with my friends in my home.

—Judy Spencer Nelon

I was introduced to Gospel music in 1976 when I was only eleven years old. From that very first concert, I was hooked. Over the next few years I would begin to follow the Gospel artists' concert circuit, sing with local groups, and purchase every album I could get my hands on. When I was only fifteen years old, I tried my hand at something new. I promoted a concert at my local church in the coalfields of West Virginia. It was there I would meet this wonderful group of people, known as the Hoppers, who would sow seed into my life that would create a harvest from which I would reap for years to come.

I'm not even sure how it all happened, but somehow amidst collecting all of their albums—both old and new (which I still have)—and attending every concert within driving distance of my home, I began selling Hopper albums in my community, sometimes door to door, and to friends and family.

I remember calling Rhonda at the Hoppers' office, and with Claude's permission, she would send me a shipment of product and trust me to return a check once the product sold, which I always did only to request more to sell. I loved selling Hopper music.

I have come to realize that we are all given two options with the gifts and talents with which we've been blessed: to sow them as seed, which blesses both the sower and the reaper continually, or to hoard them up for ourselves and live in constant fear of the day our supply evaporates. I am grateful that the Hoppers have chosen to use their gifts and talents as seed; they have sown well into the lives of countless thousands of people over the years.

Every member of the Hopper family seemed to share a unique kindness and genuine love of people. They were the same whether singing in our little church, which seated only 200 people, or singing to huge crowds such as those who attended their own Watermelon Park annual singing.

At age fifteen, when promoting that first concert, I had no idea we should plan a meal, or at the least a snack, for the group. Shortly after the Hoppers' arrival in Maybeury, West Virginia, I remember Will Hopper asking me if there was a place to get a bite to eat. I took him, along with Claude, to the best place in town: my mom's kitchen—unannounced, of course! My mom was a phenomenal cook but on this particular day, with no time to prepare, sandwiches were the best she could do. Still to this day, I don't know if I felt more honor or embarrassment as Claude and Will Hopper sat at our kitchen table eating bologna sandwiches and promising us that bologna was as good as steak when they were growing up on a North

Carolina farm.

That gracious spirit would become the example I could always depend on with the Hoppers. I remember attending my first Watermelon Park sing. I was so excited about having new artists, one in particular. I enthusiastically approached the kind-faced individual only to find that my enthusiasm was not reciprocated. As a teenager who loved Gospel music and the artists who carried the message, this was a huge disappointment for me. Looking for answers, I remember consulting with Connie Hopper. She allowed me to pour out my heart and quickly made everything better with her Christ-like response: "That individual has simply probably had a rigorous tour schedule before arriving here. She's probably just fatigued. I know her to be a very pleasant and kind person; don't let it bother you." Connie's words of compassion and understanding would refill my ears and heart for years to come in various relationships. Even at my young age, I was conscious of the delicate way in which Connie preserved and protected all the parties involved in this scenario. I am certain the kingdom of God would explode exponentially both in number and maturity if more would heed this great example.

More recently, when a colleague in ministry fell victim to the enemy's attack, I wasn't at all surprised to find the Hoppers among the first on the list who called to offer encouragement to the one who was hurting, bruised and feeling alone. I remember thinking, "Well, of course, I expected nothing less. That's who the Hoppers are, everyone's cheerleader, a support system to all who have need." They have been more than just Gospel music singers; they have been and still are mentors for untold numbers of singers, ministers, teachers, pastors, and Christians everywhere.

I have watched them pour their hearts out night after night through Anointed singing, heartfelt testimonies and explosive laughter and then close the service with the altar full of people getting their needs met by the Master.

I have never left a Hoppers' concert without wanting more. The entire family possesses rare qualities of wisdom and tenderness. Whether on the stage, on the bus, in the office, over the phone, or in person at their kitchen table or yours, they are always the same,

"Givers of life, messengers of peace and power."

— Joseph Mark Copolo, *Roanoke, Virginia*

It has been one of the greatest honors of my life to be able to work on this project. Connie and Claude graciously opened their home and lives up to this author, my wife, Cheryl, and daughter, Josie.

They are genuinely good people, and it's been a privilege to get to know them. Plus, Connie Hopper makes the best tomato sandwiches in the world!

— F. Keith Davis, *Chapmanville, WV*

I could tell a lot of stories about my time with the Hoppers, but I will just say that some of my best memories have come from that relationship. I do have a real funny story about one night when Connie was going to spend the night at my house with me and my wife after a recording session. You see it goes like this .... okay, Connie, I won't tell it. We had a lot of fun times together and when that happens, you appreciate them. I still have a lot of Hopper awards on my wall in my present office. It's been gratifying to see the growth of the Hoppers over the years, knowing I had the opportunity to see their rocket lift off the ground. Every element of their group has played such an important role in their overall success. What needs to be said about the vocal and performance ability of Kim and Dean? Michael has long been one of the industry's leading percussionists—and a very good young businessman in his own right. Claude's ability to be the leadership foundation for the group has been admired by many, and that's all we'll say about Claude's talents! But to me, when you say the word "Hoppers," the first person that comes to my mind is Connie. Not that everyone else has not played an intricate role in the group's success over the years, but for me Connie has been that consistent component that people have admired and even counted on, *including me.*

Claude has been blessed to have had such a talented and dedicated family around him to help him realize the dreams he had many years ago, of having a ministry that would be built on the Rock. "Here I Am" was the song that helped start them on the way, and I believe that "Here I Am" has been the Hoppers' cry unto the Lord.

Truly they have been used for the building of the Kingdom, and I cherish the time that I was blessed be a part of that wonderful experience.

— Chris White, *co-executive officer of Crossroads Entertainment & Marketing; president of Sonlite Records*

THANK YOUS

Author's final note: As we were putting the finishing touches on this manuscript just before sending it off to the printer, Claude was very concerned that there were so many people who have helped them in their ministry through the years, or inspired them along the way, that he couldn't possibly name them all, so he wanted to add a sincere word of appreciation to those unnamed friends:

"There are literally hundreds of people who may not be mentioned in this account, but whom we wish to thank for their help and support in Gospel music: our peers in the industry, as well as those outside the industry—the hardworking pastors, Sunday school teachers and our faithful fans—who come from all types of backgrounds and circumstances and who have prayed for us, encouraged us, and supported this ministry in many ways over the years. From the bottom of our hearts, we would like you to know that we love and appreciate you; and we know that we would not be where we are today without you. And of course, first and foremost, all praise, glory, and honor belong to our awesome Lord and Savior, Jesus Christ—our reason for singing. God bless you, my friends." — *Claude Hopper*

Author's Special Recognition

I am grateful, and the Hoppers are appreciative, to Scarlett McClendon for assisting with research for this project. She provided select interview materials that have been utilized throughout this book. Her advice was also invaluable for the development and completion of this volume.

I greatly appreciate and thank the management and staff of *Singing News* for graciously allowing me to root around in their archive room. Through their kindness and generosity, they have permitted me to use valuable information that made certain portions of this book possible. This magazine is truly *The Printed Voice Of Southern Gospel Music*.

Photo Credits: I wish to thank Charles Brady, (www.thesoutherngospel.com) of the Caraway Media Group, for graciously allowing me to use select certain photos from his personal collection. He has been a great friend to the Hoppers and to me. Thanks so much, Charles.

Also, Mary Hamilton, an excellent photographer, offered a variety of wonderful photographs of the Hoppers on stage. You have seen many of her snapshots inside this volume. Mary, thank you for your permission and extreme generosity.

A special thank you to all of the Hopper family for allowing me to use many personal photos.

A special thank you to: Dr. John Hagee, Dr. Charles F. Stanley, Bill and Gloria Gaither, Mark Lowry, Guy Penrod, Cheryl R. Davis, Josie Boytek, Chip Tinder, Tim Fortune, Dottie Rambo, Larry Ferguson, Les Butler, Maurice Templeton, Libbi Perry Stuffle, Jerry Kirksey, Danny Jones, Les Beasley, Janet Paschal, Ivan Parker, Duane Allen, Joe Bonsall, Eddie Crook, Dennis W. Sparks, Russ Taff, Rev. Al Oliver, Jessy Dixon, Dr. Jerry Stock, Charles T. Murphy, Paul Heil, Bob Barker, Sylvia Green, Roger Talley, Debra Talley, Kirk Talley, Karen Peck Gooch, Libbi Perry Stuffle, Reggie Brann, Tony Greene, Lynda Randle, Charles Brady, the Ruppes, Jimmy Blackwood, Gerald Wolfe, Rodney Griffin, Joseph M. Copolo, Ann Downing, Mike Collins, Geron Dais, The Southern Gospel Music Association, James Goff, Jr., Mary Hamilton, Frank Mills, Don Reid, Harold Reid, Keith Key, Chris White, Judy Spencer Nelon, the North Carolina Gospel Music Hall of Honor and, of course, the entire Hopper and Shelton families.

For this project, the Hoppers held a Biography Title Contest, and fans were encouraged to submit their ideas via the Hoppers' website. Angel Dorsett, of Mt. Airy, NC, will now receive a cruise for her winning title suggestion, "After All These Years." Ms. Dorsett's entry was chosen at random from a group of submissions with the same title. The Hoppers want to thank Angel and all their friends and fans who entered this contest.

Bibliography

Close Harmony: A History of Southern Gospel, by James R. Goff. Copyright © 2002 by the University of North Carolina Press. Used by permission of the publisher.

Hold On: The Authorized Biography of The Greenes, by Mike Collins. Copyright ©2004, the Greenes and Mike Collins. Used by permission of the publisher.

The Peace That Passeth Understanding, by Connie Hopper; 1979 Brings Illness, Copyright © 1980, The Hopper Brothers And Connie Publishing. Used by permission of the publisher.

Singing News Magazine, News and Photo Archives. Used by permission of the publisher.

If you enjoyed this book, please tell a friend about it.
WOODLAND PRESS, LLC
118 Woodland Dr., Suite 1102
Chapmanville, WV 25508
Romans 8:28